TWELVE MILLION MURDERS

Horrors, such as occurred at
Auschwitz, at Dachau, and at Belsen,
seem almost beyond belief. Yet, as this
book shows, the extermination of
millions of men, women, and children
was a calculated plan to destroy whole
nations and races.

On the lowest computation, twelve
million people were put to death by the
Nazis—not in battle, but murdered:
mass production genocide.

THE SCOURGE OF THE
SWASTIKA has not been published
with any thought of sensationalism: it
is absolute, irrevocable fact—based on
eye-witness accounts, captured
German documents, and records of the
Nuremburg war trials.

Lord Russell of Liverpool
C.B.E., M.C.

The
Scourge of the Swastika

CORGI BOOKS
A DIVISION OF TRANSWORLD PUBLISHERS LTD

TO MY WIFE
to whose advice and co-operation
at all its stages this book owes
so much.

THE SCOURGE OF THE SWASTIKA
A CORGI BOOK 0 552 10300 4

Originally published in Great Britain by
Cassell and Co. Ltd.

PRINTING HISTORY
Cassell edition published 1954
Corgi edition published 1956
Corgi edition reprinted 1957
Corgi edition reprinted 1958 (twice)
Corgi edition reprinted 1959 (twice)
Corgi edition reissued 1960
Corgi edition reprinted 1962
Corgi edition reissued 1964
Corgi edition reprinted 1964
Corgi edition reissued 1966
Corgi edition reprinted 1967
Corgi edition reissued 1970
Corgi edition reprinted 1972
Corgi edition reprinted 1973
Corgi edition reissued 1976
Corgi edition reprinted 1977
Corgi edition reprinted 1979

This book is set in 9/10pt Times

Corgi Books are published by Transworld Publishers Ltd.,
Century House, 61–63 Uxbridge Road,
Ealing, London W5 5SA.
Made and printed in Great Britain by
Hunt Barnard Printing Ltd., Aylesbury, Bucks.

CONTENTS

ILLUSTRATIONS
Between pages 112 - 113

PREFACE

In his opening speech at the trial in Nuremberg of the major German war criminals, Sir Hartley Shawcross, Chief Prosecutor for Great Britain and Northern Ireland, said this:

Apologists for defeated nations are sometimes able to play upon the sympathy and magnanimity of their victors, so that the true facts, never authoritatively recorded, become obscured and forgotten. One has only to recall the circumstances following upon the last World War to see the dangers to which, in the absence of any authoritative judicial pronouncement, a tolerant or a credulous people is exposed. With the passage of time the former tend to discount, perhaps because of their very horror, the stories of aggression and atrocity that may be handed down; and the latter, the credulous, misled by perhaps fanatical and perhaps dishonest propagandists, come to believe that it was not they but their opponents who were guilty of that which they would themselves condemn. And so we believe that this Tribunal, acting, as we know it will act notwithstanding its appointment by the victorious Powers, with complete and judicial objectivity, will provide a contemporary touchstone and an authoritative and impartial record to which future historians may turn for truth and future politicians for warning.

As everyone knows, the 'authoritative judicial pronouncement' of which Sir Hartley spoke has been given. There have been numerous other war crime trials[1] the proceedings of which have been published and are there for all to read. But many have no time to do so, and many would not wish to if they had.

This book is intended to provide the ordinary reader with a truthful and accurate account of many of these German war

[1] In the British Zone of Occupation in Germany alone, 356 war crime trials were held involving more than 1,000 war criminals. The Judge Advocate General of the Forces, Sir Henry MacGeagh, GCVO, KCB, KBE, QC, who was head of the United Kingdom National Office of the United Nations War Crimes Commission, was responsible for the trial of all enemy war criminals brought before British Military Courts.

crimes. It has been compiled from the evidence given and the documents produced at various war-crime trials, and from statements made by eye-witnesses of war crimes to competent war-crime investigation commissions in the countries where they were committed.

For their kind offices in obtaining access for me to sources of official information in their respective countries, my grateful thanks are due to His Excellency Monsieur René Massigli, GCVO, KBE, the French Ambassador; His Excellency Monsieur le Marquis du Parc Locmaria, CVO, the Belgian Ambassador; and Doctor D. V. Stikker, Ambassador for the Netherlands.

I am also greatly indebted to Major Peter Forest, formerly Chief Interpreter in the War Crimes Group, British Army of the Rhine, for editing the footnotes regarding German terms, ranks, and titles; and last but not least to Mr Anthony Somerhough, OBE, QC, formerly Head of the British War Crimes Group in Germany, for the loan of certain photographs and many helpful suggestions.

PROLOGUE

BEFORE 1939 there had been regrettable incidents in modern wars between civilized nations amounting to war crimes. In Belgium and France in the early stages of the First World War many excesses were committed by German troops during their rapid advance towards Paris.[1] Towns and villages were looted and set on fire, women were raped, and innocent people murdered. Although these crimes were more than mere sporadic outbursts of 'frightfulness' on the part of isolated units or single divisions, they were not part of an organized campaign of terrorism planned before the outbreak of hostilities and faithfully carried out in obedience to orders.

During the Second World War, however, war crimes were committed by the Germans on an unprecedented scale. They were part and parcel of the Nazi conception of total war and were carried out in pursuance of a preconceived and preconcerted plan to terrorize and exploit the inhabitants of invaded and occupied territories and to exterminate those elements among them who might be found most inimical to German conquest and Nazi domination.

Before the war, the Nazis had created in their own country under the 'Führerprinzip' a tyranny almost without equal in history. They encouraged and fostered racial hatred by the principle of the 'master race' with its ultimate and inevitable objective of world hegemony. They set brother against brother, children against parents, Gentile against Jew. They endeavoured to debauch a whole nation and those who refused to be debauched they terrorized and finally threw into concentration camps.

It is only when one recalls what was done in Germany between 1933 and 1939 that once can see in their true perspective the crimes committed during the war in occupied territories.

The suppression of free speech including freedom of the Press,

[1] See Appendix II, page 221.

9

the control of the judiciary, the confiscation of property, the restrictions on the right of peaceful assembly, the censorship of letters and telegrams, the monitoring of telephone conversations, the regimentation of labour, the denial of religious freedom: these are the bonds with which a tyrant binds his subjects. If Hitler thought so little of the 'master race', is it surprising that he should have regarded as less than vermin the peoples of the countries which his Armies invaded?

That the German people did not all yield easily, or willingly accept the Nazi doctrine and programme, is not disputed. Had they done so there would have been no SS,[1] no SD,[2] and no Gestapo. It was only by fear, torture, starvation and death that the Nazis eliminated at home the opponents of their régime, and it was in this way that these organizations of oppression gained the experience and the training, later put into practice abroad with such thoroughness and brutality, that made them the nightmare and the scourge of Occupied Europe.

The crimes which are described in this book were not haphazard; that must be self-evident from their very magnitude. The enslavement of millions and their deportation to Germany, the murder and ill-treatment of prisoners of war, the mass executions of civilians, the shooting of hostages and reprisal prisoners, and the 'final solution' of the Jewish question were all the result of long-term planning. This had been proved beyond doubt and the Germans themselves have provided unchallengeable evidence in the records, returns, inventories, orders, and other documents, all carefully preserved, which fell into Allied hands after the surrender of the German forces in Europe.

For when they employed prisoners of war on prohibited work the Germans rendered returns to the appropriate army formation; when they looted they made immaculate inventories of their booty; when they gassed Jews and others they sent detailed reports to RSHA[3]; when they shot hostages they posted up lists on public buildings 'pour encourager les autres'; when they conducted painful and disgusting experiments on unwilling inmates in their concentration camps they made careful case-notes. As fast as they committed these crimes so, with characteristic thoroughness, they collected and tabulated documentary evidence of them.

---

[1] Schutzstaffeln—Nazi Party troops.
[2] Sicherheitsdienst—security service.
[3] Reichssicherheitshauptamt—Reich Security Head Office.

10

In *Mein Kampf* Hitler had written years before, 'A stronger race will drive out the weaker ones, for the vital urge in its ultimate form will break down the absurd barriers of the so-called humanity of individuals to make way for the humanity of Nature which destroys the weak to give their place to the strong.' That is the law of the jungle: little wonder that it brought in its train so much misery, agony, destruction, and death.

And how were these criminal plans put into execution? The German High Command and the General Staff cannot escape all responsibility.

When old Marshal von Hindenburg so suddenly and unexpectedly called Hitler to power in 1933 many of these men doubtless looked down their noses at him. But it was not long before most of them became his accomplices; and those who did not, like von Fritsch, were got rid of in characteristically shameless fashion. Thenceforth the full weight of the pyramid of the German Officer Corps, with that military yes-man Keitel at its summit, was right behind Hitler. These men aided and abetted him in planning and waging aggressive war, and in committing war crimes and crimes against humanity without number. Only when the tide of Nazi success was clearly ebbing did critical whisperings first begin to echo through the corridors of the German War Ministry.

The International Military Tribunal for the trial at Nuremberg of the major German war criminals declined to declare the General Staff and High Command a criminal organization. Nevertheless, in their judgment they said of these men:

> They have been responsible in large measure for the miseries and suffering that have fallen on millions of men, women, and children. They have been a disgrace to the honourable profession of arms. Without their military guidance the aggressive ambitions of Hitler and his fellow Nazis would have been academic and sterile . . . they were a ruthless and military caste. . . . Many of these men have made a mockery of the soldier's oath of obedience to military orders. When it suits their defence, they say they had to obey; when confronted with Hitler's brutal crimes which are shown to have been within their general knowledge, they say they disobeyed. The truth is that they actively participated in all these crimes, or sat silent and acquiescent, witnessing the commission of crimes on a scale larger and more shocking than the world has ever had the misfortune to know.

But it was the Leadership Corps, the Gestapo, the SD, and the SS, who were the principal instruments of tyranny which Hitler used.

They were the organizations that carried out these dreadful crimes; the mass murders of the concentration camps; the murder and ill-treatment of prisoners of war; the impressment of foreign workers for slave labour; the inquisitorial interrogations; the tortures; the experiments on human guinea-pigs.

These dreaded 'black-coats', with Heinrich Himmler at their head, hung over Occupied Europe for five long years like a black thundercloud pregnant with sudden death.

The opening chapter of this book describes the origin, establishment, and organization of these bodies and the sadistic cruelty which was their stock-in-trade.

CHAPTER I

HITLER'S INSTRUMENTS OF TYRANNY

FROM the very moment Hitler came to power he and the Nazi Party began to put into execution the common plan or conspiracy whose aims had already been set out in *Mein Kampf* and which included the commission of crimes against peace, war crimes, and other crimes against humanity.

The framework of this conspiracy was the Nazi Party; the Leadership Corps was the chain of civil command by which the master plan was activated. Every member was sworn in annually. 'I pledge eternal allegiance to Adolf Hitler. I pledge unconditional obedience to him and to the Führer appointed by him.'

From the Führer at the fountain source, through Gauleiter, Kreisleiter, Ortsgruppenleiter, Zellenleiter, and Blockwart the stream of Nazi doctrine flowed into every home. The Gauleiter for the district, the Kreisleiter for the county, down to the Blockleiter who was responsible for some fifty households.

Each of those functionaries, at his own level, had a staff which dealt with every aspect of a citizen's life; education, propaganda, journalism, finance, justice.

Immediately below Hitler were the Reichsleiters; Rosenberg, von Schirach, Frick, Bormann, Frank, Ley, Goebbels and Himmler. Each was responsible directly to the Führer for a definite facet of Nazi policy. They carried out their Leader's directives. Their supreme task was stated to be the preservation of the Party 'as a well-sharpened sword for the Führer'. They were concerned with general policies and not detailed administration.

Next in importance were the administrators, once described as 'a hierarchy of descending Caesars'.

Germany had been divided into a number of large administrative regions, each of which was called a Gau. Each had a political leader, a Gauleiter, who was directly responsible to the Führer for his own area.

The Gau was further sub-divided into counties, urban and rural districts, cells and blocks. The Nazi official thus touched life at every turn, but it was the smallest Caesar—the Blockwart—who was the biggest tyrant of them all.

It was he who spied on every household; it was he who had a stool pigeon in every family; it was at his level that the impact of Nazi propaganda was brought to bear full-square upon the individual.

According to the Party manual, it was the duty of the Blockwart to find people disseminating damaging rumours and to report them to his superiors. 'He must not only be a preacher and defender of the National Socialist ideology towards the members of the Nation and the Party entrusted to his political care, but he must strive to achieve the practical collaboration of the Party members within his block zone. . . . He must keep a dossier about each household.'

It was in the presence of the Blockwart that every little German came face to face with his Führer, and there were half a million of them. Thus did Hitler hold the whole Reich in the hollow of his hand.

As it was in peace; so it was in war. There was a Gauleiter in Holland and a Gauleiter in Alsace; Poland, the Baltic States, the Eastern Territories, each had its Gauleiter, and the lessons learnt in the early days of Nazism at home were put into practice abroad. The same system which had bent all Germans to the Führer's will was to be used to enthral the peoples of the territories which his armies had invaded and which were now under German occupation.

There were doubtless many Germans who were never ardent Nazis and who regarded Hitler as a vulgar upstart and his cronies as unpleasant toughs. None of these, however, were in the SS, which was the hard core of Nazism. Its members were all blind disciples of the Führer and had no other loyalty to God or man.

During the early stages of the trial of major German war criminals at Nuremberg there appeared in the columns of a local newspaper an account of a visit made by some journalist to a camp in which SS prisoners were interned. All had asked him but one question: 'What have we done except our normal duty?' If aiding and abetting the commission of several million murders can be described as normal duty then they had done little else.

In this book are chapters dealing with the extermination of the Jews, the enslavement and deportation of workers from the occupied territories, the shooting of hostages and mass executions of

14

civilians, and the murder and ill-treatment of Allied prisoners of war. In all these crimes the SS, SD and Gestapo played a leading part.

In peace these organizations had been entrusted by the Nazi leaders with the responsibility of 'rendering harmless'[1] all opposition. In war they were to break down all resistance to the German occupation.

The similarity of the methods used to accomplish these objectives ensured that the normal duties of these bodies in peace constituted their training for war. By persecution, by terror, by torture and the ever-present threat of the concentration camp they had made Germany safe for Hitler. When war should come, by these same means, now well tested and perfected, they would keep in subjection the inhabitants of those countries which German troops might invade and occupy.

It was in 1929, four years before Hitler came to power, that Heinrich Himmler was appointed Reichsführer SS and assumed control of the Schutzstaffeln which then had only 280 members. He proceeded to build this force into a private army and police force, enlisting only those who were reliable and fanatical followers of the Führer. By the time Hitler became Reichschancellor the SS had reached a strength of 52,000. Their mission was stated to be the protection of the Führer and the internal security of the Reich, and Reichsführer Himmler left no one in doubt of the methods by which it was to be accomplished.

We shall unremittingly fulfil our task to guarantee the security of Germany from within, just as the Wehrmacht guarantees the safety of the honour, the greatness and the peace of the Reich from without. We shall take care that never again in Germany, the heart of Europe, will the Jewish-Bolshevistic revolution of subhumans be kindled from the interior or through emissaries from outside. Without pity we shall be a merciless sword of justice to all those forces of whose existence and activities we know, on the day the slightest attempt is made be it today, after a decade, or a century hence.

A merciless sword they undoubtedly were; but without honour and without justice.

For such a task a highly organized force was necessary and the Suprme Command of the SS was set up—consisting of twelve

[1] A Nazi euphemism for murder.

15

departments. The main body of SS, the Allgemeine, was the trunk from which all the branches grew. It was organized on military lines and divided into districts, sub-districts, regiments and other lower formations down to platoons. At the outbreak of war it numbered 240,000 scoundrels of the deepest dye.

It was composed, for the most part, of those SS men who were not specialists. They were, to borrow a phrase from the Services, the general duty men of the Schutzstaffeln. One of their grim duties was staffing the concentration camps, and nearly all the guards at such camps were provided by the Allgemeine.

Next in importance was the Security Service, or Sicherheitsdienst, known later throughout Occupied Europe, as well as in the Reich itself, by the dreaded initials SD. Originally merely the intelligence service of the SS, it became more important after Hitler was made Reichschancellor and by 1939 it was one of the main departments of RSHA.

By then, Reinhard Heydrich, its chief, had expanded it into a vast system of espionage which watched with beady eyes, like some great vulture, the private life of every German citizen and became the sole intelligence and counter-intelligence agency for the Nazi Party.

Three years after Hitler's accession to power Himmler was appointed, in addition to being Reichsführer SS, Chief of the German police in the Ministry of the Interior, and the reorganization of the German police forces with two distinct branches began. There were the uniformed police or ORPO,[1] and the security police or SIPO,[2] which in 1939 became amalgamated with the SD under RSHA.

The Geheime Staatspolizei, or Gestapo as it was universally known, was a State organization and was first set up in Prussia by Göring in 1933.

This was a political police force. Unlike the ordinary police, it was not concerned with the prevention and detection of crime, but with the suppression of all independent political thought and of individual political convictions, and the elimination of all opposition to the Hitler régime.

The network of oppression was at last complete, and within this spider's web sat Himmler, his SS all around him, and behind, the shadow of the concentration camp.

Thus was Germany 'entirely and completely possessed by

---

[1] Ordnungspolizei—uniformed police.
[2] Sicherheitspolizei—security police.

National Socialism', as Hitler put it when speaking in the Reichstag in 1938. Thus was the nation mobilized. And for what purpose? For aggression, for conquest, for world domination, for total war. And war came; invasion, success, until two-thirds of Europe lay under the German heel with the SS, SD and Gestapo ready to keep it so. This machinery of Nazi tyranny was in good running order. Designed and manufactured years before with skill and care, it had been tuned up and tested in peace time. This was to be its finest hour!

As the German armies advanced into enemy territory, specially formed operational units of the SIPO and SD accompanied them. These Einsatzgruppen, as they were termed, were officered by staff of the Gestapo and KRIPO,[1] who were given SS commissions.

The rank and file were Waffen-SS and ORPO. These groups were attached to Army Groups or Armies and operated usually in the Army Rear Area. Whilst they were under tactical command of the Army Commander, their own special tasks were given them by RSHA to whom they were directly responsible.

After these special tasks had been performed and as the fighting moved on, the occupation administration was organized on a more permanent footing. These Einsatz Groups then became the stationary headquarters of the SIPO and SD and were allotted areas of jurisdiction. They had their own chain of command under the Military Commander of the occupied territory, but independent of it, with direct approach to the Chief of the Security Police and SD.

In the countries under German military occupation, executive action was usually taken by the Gestapo, which was a much larger organization than the SD or KRIPO. From 1943 to 1945 the Gestapo had a membership of about fifty thousand, whereas the KRIPO and the SD numbered only fifteen thousand and three thousand respectively.[2] The initials SD were commonly used in the German Intelligence and Police services officially and unofficially to denote SIPO and SD, and are so used in the following chapters of this book. In the occupied countries, except when they worked in plain clothes, the Gestapo usually wore the SS 'black coat' with SD insignia.

From the beginning of the war until its conclusion the SS were

[1] Kriminalpolizei—C.I.D.
[2] The SIPO and SD consisted of the Gestapo, KRIPO and SD. Although the total strength of the SD proper was, between 1943 and 1945, only about 3,000, the initials SD were generally used as an abbreviation for the term SIPO and SD, and in the occupied territories members of the Gestapo frequently wore uniforms with the SD insignia.

specialists in 'Schweinerei',[1] and it was no coincidence that the prologue to the invasion of Poland was entrusted to them.

The stage was set for aggression. On 22nd August 1939 Hitler made a speech at Obersalzberg to his Commanders-in-Chief.

> The destruction of Poland is in the foreground (he said), the aim is the elimination of living forces, not the arrival at a certain line. I shall give a propagandist cause for starting the war, never mind if it is plausible or not. The victor will not be asked later on whether he told the truth or not. . . . I am only afraid that at the last minute some 'Schweinehund' will make a proposal for mediation. . . . The way is open for the soldier *after I have made the political preparations*.

Frontier incidents were, therefore, brought about by the Nazis with the help of the SS. One such incident was the attack on the radio station at Gleiwitz near the Polish border. The object of this exercise, known as 'Operation Himmler', was to make it appear that a raid had been made on this station by the Poles. Reinhard Heydrich when briefing the SD official who was to carry it out said, 'Actual proof of these attacks by the Poles is needed for the foreign Press as well as for German propaganda purposes.'

The radio station was to be attacked by five or six SD men and held long enough to allow a Polish-speaking German, who would accompany the raiding party, to broadcast a speech in Polish. The effect of the speech was to be that the time had now come for a conflict between Germany and Poland and that all Poles should unite and strike down any German from whom they met resistance.

After receiving this briefing, the leader of the raid then went to Gleiwitz, where he was to receive the code word from Heydrich. While waiting there he visited Heinrich Müller,[2] Chief of the Gestapo, who was in the district. Müller discussed plans for another border incident which would make it appear that Polish soldiers were making attacks on German troops. A number of condemned criminals would be supplied by Gestapo for this operation. They would be dressed in Polish uniforms and be left dead at the scene of action, having been given fatal injections and then gunshot wounds. These dead 'Poles' would give the impression that they had been killed whilst attacking the German troops. One of these dummies would be supplied for the Gleiwitz

---

[1] Filthiness.
[2] Obergruppenführer Müller. Chief of Amt IV of RSHA.

operation. They were referred to in all correspondence by the code name 'Canned goods'.

The incident at Gleiwitz took place on the evening preceding the German invasion of Poland and was thus described by the SS leader of the raiding party:

> At noon on 31st August 1939 I received by telephone from Heydrich the code word for the attack which was to take place at 8 p.m. that evening. Heydrich said that I was to report to Müller for 'canned goods'. I did this and Müller had the body delivered at the radio station. I had him placed on the ground at the entrance to the building. He was alive but completely unconscious. We seized the radio station as ordered, broadcast a speech of three or four minutes over an emergency transmitter, fired some pistol shots and left.

Just as the SS had rung up the curtain on the invasion of Poland, so were they to have let it fall at the end of the performance. In April 1945 plans had been drawn up by Obergruppenführer Kaltenbrunner for the destruction of the concentration camps and the liquidation of all their inmates. Thus was all evidence of the extermination programme to be destroyed. These plans, which were known by the code word 'Cloud A-1' and 'Cloud Fire', were never carried out. The drama ended before the curtain could drop.

The SD and Gestapo were jointly responsible for the mass murder of hundreds of thousands of innocent civilians in occupied territories and the torture and ill-treatment of thousands of others. 'Nacht und Nebel' prisoners, hostages and reprisal prisoners, Allied soldiers, sailors, and airmen who had taken part in commando operations, all of these were handed over to the SD for 'special treatment'.[1] They were also responsible, through the Einsatzgruppe, for the massacre of myriads of Jews as part of the 'final solution' programme.[2]

In another chapter of this book will be found an account of massacres committed by these groups under Obergruppenführer Ohlendorf in the Ukraine and Crimea, to whose evidence at the Nuremberg trial this reference was made by one of the Counsel for the United States of America:

Mankind will not soon forget this sickening story of the evil

---

[1] See Chapter II.
[2] The 'final solution' of the Jewish question meant the extermination of the Jews and was a definite part of the Nazi policy.

killers whose very stomachs turned at the awful sight when they unlocked the doors of these death cars at the graveside.[1] These were the men who sat at the edge of anti-tank ditches, cigarettes in mouth, callously shooting their naked victims in the back of the neck with automatics. These were the men who, according to their own corpse accountants, murdered some two million men, women, and children. These were the men of the SD.

Their methods were sometimes more than even a Gauleiter could stomach. After the SD had been let loose in Lithuania, the Gauleiter of Riga wrote to Rosenberg, then Reich Minister for Eastern Territories, pointing out rather apologetically that the SD's behaviour 'almost bordered on sadism'. From the details contained in the report it would appear that this phrase was something of an understatement.

'To have buried alive seriously wounded people,' he wrote, 'who then worked their way out of their graves again is such extreme beastliness that it should be reported to the Führer and the Reichsmarschall. The civil administration of White Ruthenia makes every effort to win the population over to Germany in accordance with the instructions of the Führer. These efforts cannot be brought into harmony with the methods I have described.'

Special teams of SD and Gestapo were stationed in prisoner-of-war camps to screen prisoners and weed out those who were considered radically or politically undesirable. Such prisoners were then transferred to concentration camps for 'special treatment', which in the SS dictionary of death meant killing.

The SD were also responsible, together with the Gestapo, for administering the 'Bullet Decree'.[2] This directed that all escaped officers and NCOs, other than British or American prisoners of war, should on recapture be handed over to the SD. They would then be taken to Mauthausen Concentration Camp and executed by being shot in the back of the neck.

These organizations were also used by Reichsminister Fritz Sauckel to impress foreign workers for his slave labour programme. They helped to administer the scheme in the occupied territories, and when the wretches whom they had shanghaied arrived in Germany the Gestapo had them under surveillance

---

[1] Thousands of civilians were killed by these Einsatzkommandos in specially constructed gas vans.
[2] The 'Kugelerlass' of 4th March 1944.

and were responsible for apprehending those who managed to escape from the labour camps in which they were confined whilst still physically capable of work.

In August 1942 Keitel issued an order to the effect that immediate counter-measures would be taken by the SD and Gestapo against single parachutists who were dropped in occupied territory or in Germany to carry out special missions. 'In so far as single parachutists are captured by members of the Armed Forces, they are to be delivered the same day, after a report has been sent to the competent Abwehr office, to the nearest agency of the Chief of the Security Police and SD.'

Many 'lone hands' were dropped in France during the occupation to liaise and co-operate with the French Resistance Movement. It was the business of the SD and Gestapo to track such persons down and deal with them, and if they were captured by the Wehrmacht they were at once handed over to the SD. After interrogation they were sent to a concentration camp from which but few returned. A number of young women who were flown from England and parachuted into France under the auspices of the French Section of the War Office met their death in this way.[1]

In October 1942 Hitler personally issued the 'Commando Order', which provided that all Allied servicemen who took part in commando raids and were captured by the Germans would be put to death. This order stated that if individual members of commandos working as agents or saboteurs fell into the hands of the Wehrmacht or the cvil police in any of the countries occupied by the Germans they were to be handed over to the SD immediately. These men, who wore uniform and landed in enemy country openly, were entitled to be treated as prisoners of war.

In pursuance of this Führerbefehl, however, large numbers were handed over to the SD by the German troops who captured them. Most of them were then executed within twenty-four hours but a few were transferred to concentration camps.

The SD and Gestapo were also given power in some occupied countries to execute, or to send to concentration camps on their own initiative, persons who had themselves committed no offences but were related to others who were alleged offenders.

This characteristic example of Nazi injustice was given the

[1] See *Odette* by Jerrard Tickell (Chapman and Hall, 1949) and *The Natzweiler Trial* (William Hodge and Co.).

high-sounding title of 'collective responsibility of members of families of assassins and saboteurs'.[1] In fact it was a typically Teutonic method of wreaking vengenance upon the innocent relatives of members of the Resistance Forces who had so far eluded capture.

Such powers were given to the Gestapo in Poland in the middle of 1944 because the internal security situation had recently worsened and the 'harshest measures' had to be applied to 'alien assassins and saboteurs'.

The Reichsführer SS, in agreement with the Governor General (Hans Frank), therefore ordered that in all cases where Germans had been assassinated or attempts had been made, or where saboteurs had destroyed vital installations, not only was the culprit to be shot but all his kinsmen were to be executed and his female relatives above the age of sixteen sent to concentration camps.

The Gestapo also conducted third-degree interrogations of prisoners of war. The methods used included 'bread and water diet; hard bunk; dark cell; deprivation of sleep; exhaustive drilling; and flogging'. The removal of finger nails and toe nails was also used to induce unco-operative prisoners to talk.

Throughout the length and breadth of Occupied Europe and Germany itself there were few war crimes committed against the civilian population in which the SS, the Gestapo, and the SD did not play a leading part.

They murdered hundreds of thousands of men, women, and children; they shot recaptured prisoners of war on the pretext that they were attempting another escape; they established, staffed, and administered the concentration and forced-labour camps; they cleared and burned ghettos and sent their occupants to extermination camps; they impressed many hundreds of thousands of foreign workers to be deported to Germany as slave labour; they executed captured commandos and paratroopers and they protected German civilians who lynched Allied airmen.

Speaking of them on German Police Day, their Chief, Reinhard Heydrich, said: 'Secret State Police, Criminal Police, and SD are still surrounded with the furtive and whispered secrecy of a political detective story. Brutality, inhumanity bordering on the sadistic, and ruthlessness are attributed abroad to the men of this profession.'

The third and last branch of the Schutzstaffeln was the Waffen-

[1] Sippenhalft.

SS, a fighting force specially trained for aggressive war. Its origin was thus described in an official Nazi publication, *Organization Book of the Nazi Party* (1943):

The armed SS originated from the idea of creating for the Führer a special long-service force for the fulfilment of special missions. This should make it possible for members of the Allgemeine SS, as well as volunteers who fulfil the special requirements of the SS, to fight in the battle for realization of the National Socialist idea, weapon in hand and in their own units within the framework of the Army.

It was not, however, until the outbreak of war that this force became known as the Waffen-SS Totenkopf Verbände, or Death's Head units, later formed into SS Totenkopf divisions which as early in the war as May 1940 earned undying infamy at Paradis in the Pas de Calais.[1]

The Waffen-SS was 'Himmler's Own'. Though under the tactical command of the Wehrmacht higher formations, it was equipped and supplied through the administrative departments of the SS and under their disciplinary control. That it should fight with chivalry was not Himmler's intention and it was essential, he said once when addressing a conference of SS commanding officers, that the necessity of the SS standing firm and carrying on the racial struggle without mercy should be so thoroughly instilled into every recruit that he became saturated with it.

In recent years in Germany there has been a host of apologists for the Waffen-SS, and indignant speeches in its defence have been made at Stahlhelm[2] reunions by German generals convicted of war crimes but since released an an act of clemency.

The men of the Waffen-SS, these generals say, were simple, upright soldiers who fought with chivalry for their Fatherland and Führer, and to stigmatize as criminal the force in which they had the honour to serve is an insult to the living and the dead.

Such was not the considered opinion of the International Military Tribunal at Nuremberg, who in their judgment said:

There is evidence that the shooting of unarmed prisoners of war was the general practice in some Waffen-SS Divisions . . .

[1] See Chapter II.
[2] The Stahlhelm (Steel Helmet), purporting to be an old comrades' association was, first formed about 1920. However, it soon became an extreme Nationalist body and supported Hitler from his early days, very shortly becoming affiliated to the NSDAP. Many members of the NSDAP were, like Göring, members of both organizations. As the NSDAP became more powerful the Stahlhelm lost its importance and later became absorbed in the SA (the Sturmabteilung, Hitler's Brownshirts).

units of the Waffen-SS were also involved in the widespread murder and ill-treatment of the civilian population of the occupied territories. Waffen-SS Divisions were also responsible for many massacres and atrocities in occupied countries such as the massacre at Oradour-sur-Glâne and Lidice ... the actions of a soldier in the Waffen-SS who in September 1939, acting entirely on his own initiative, killed fifty Jewish labourers in Poland whom he had been guarding were excused by the statement that as an SS man he was 'particularly sensitive to the sight of Jews' and had acted 'quite thoughtlessly in a spirit of adventure', and a sentence of three years' imprisonment imposed on him was dropped under an amnesty.

All that is true; but this much may be said of the Waffen-SS. To this extent the Waffen-SS differed from the SS proper. They were mere amateurs in crime. Their profession was soldiering, it was their business to fight, and affairs like Oradour-sur-Glâne were in the nature of a side-show.

The professional criminals were the Allgemeine SS, the Gestapo, and the SD. Although the simile sounds singularly inappropriate and not a little distasteful, it would be correct to say that the Waffen-SS were the Gentlemen and the others were the Players.

No account of these criminal organizations would be comlete without some mention of the Hitler Jugend,[1] which was the forcing house for future SS men.

This body of adolescent fanatics was raised by Baldur von Schirach in the early days of the Nazi movement. They were subjected to an intensive programme of Nazi propaganda, stuffed full of the iniquity of the Versailles Treaty, the need for Lebensraum, the theory of the Master Race, the Führer principle, and much other indigestible Nazi doctrine, and were imbued with what the Nuremberg Tribunal described in its judgment as 'the noble destiny of German Youth—to die for Hitler'. von Schirach 'planted into the young generation the great tradition of death for a holy cause, knowing that with their blood they will lead the way towards the freedom of their dreams'.[2]

von Schirach travelled all over Germany, during the years before 1933 when the Nazi Party was at its nadir and the wearing of its uniform illegal, calling on German youth to join the HJ.

[1] The Hitler Youth, often designated by the initials HJ.
[2] These words are from a speech by Admiral Raeder on German Hero's Day, 1939. The freedom referred to was stated in another part of the speech to be the 'freedom to rearm'.

'It was at this time,' he said, 'that the HJ gained its best human material. Whoever came to us during this illegal period risked everything . . . with pistols in our pockets we drove through the Ruhr districts while stones came flying after us.'

In those days there were still many who saw in Adolf Hitler only the upstart Schickelgruber.[1] Among the older Germans who remembered and missed the traditions of Hohenzollern Germany there would remain many who, even if they did not actively oppose it, would not enthusiastically collaborate with the new régime. It was therefore most desirable that there should rise up a new generation who had known no Germany but Hitler's.

But the HJ was not merely used to train the young in the aims, ideology and objectives of the Nazi Party *pari passu* with their scholastic education; it was organized in 1938 so as to form a natural recruiting ground for the SS. This was begun by the creation of the Streifendienst[2], which was in effect the organization's own police force.

In a document entitled 'Organization of the Streifendienst' which was drawn up by Himmler and von Schirach, it was agreed that as the Streifendienst in the HJ was to perform tasks similar to those carried out by the SS, it would be organized as a special unit for the purpose of securing recruits for the Allgemeine SS. Furthermore, the document provided that recruits for the Death's Head units of the Waffen-SS and for officer cadet schools should also be obtained from the Streifendienst.

From then onwards the militarization of the HJ proceeded apace. It was organized on military lines with uniforms and quasi-military ranks, and by August 1939 Keitel noted that 'thirty thousand HJ leaders are already being trained annually in field service. An agreement with the Wehrmacht will make it possible to double the number.'

The object of this training was, in the words of von Schirach's deputy, to ensure 'that a gun feels just as natural in the hands of a German boy as a pen'.

During the war which followed quickly on the heels of this agreement, thousands of former Hitler Youth members, now in the Waffen-SS, committed war crimes throughout the occupied territories, such as the massacres at Oradour-sur-Glâne and

---

[1] This was not really Hitler's name. His father, however, was the illegitimate son of a servant-girl, Anna Maria Schickelgruber. This girl subsequently married Herr Hiedler, alias Hitler, who later acknowledged Hitler's father as his son and thereby legitimized him.

[2] Patrol Service.

Paradis. Many thousands more blood-thirsty young ruffians were waiting impatiently to take the places of those who fell.

Such were Hitler's instruments of tyranny. Throughout this book their names and their misdeeds will appear and reappear. They were the threads in the vast tapestry of Nazi war crimes. They were at the bottom of every beastliness, behind every brutality. Himmler had good reason to be proud of them and Europe to fear them.

CHAPTER II

ILL-TREATMENT AND MURDER OF PRISONERS OF WAR

IN the Dark Ages prisoners of war were either butchered or enslaved. In the Middle Ages they were imprisoned, exchanged or liberated for ransom. It was during the seventeenth century that they were first regarded as captives of the State, and not the personal property of their captors, but even then they were often treated with great cruelty, enduring grievous privations and being subjected to many indignities.

It was not until the eighteenth century, however, that it became generally recognized that the object of captivity, unlike ordinary imprisonment, was merely to prevent prisoners of war from rejoining their own forces and again taking up arms.

The basis of International Law in relation to the treatment of prisoners of war as it stood at the outbreak of war in 1939 was the Prisoner-of-War Convention of 1929. This was signed at Geneva on the 27th of July, and subseuqently ratified by all the belligerents save Russia.

The Preamble of the Convention stated that the signatories desired to mitigate the inevitable rigours of war, as far as possible, and to alleviate the condition of prisoners of war.

Nevertheless, during the Second World War, the Convention's provisions were repeatedly disregarded by Germany. Prisoners were subjected to brutality and ill-treatment, employed on prohibited and dangerous work, handed over to the SD for 'special treatment', lynched by German civilians, sent to concentration camps, shot on recapture after escaping, and even massacred after they had laid down their arms and surrendered.

On 26th May 1940, sixteen days after Hitler had launched his great offensive against the West, the British Expeditionary Force was in general retreat. Some of the British troops were still in the Pas de Calais covering the Channel Ports.

By nightfall the 1st Battalion of the 2nd SS Totenkopf Regiment of the SS Totenkopf Division had crossed the La Bassée Canal and taken up a position near Mont Bernechon. The following morning they attacked through Le Cornet-Malo and before noon had reached the hamlet of de Paradis where remnants of the 2nd Battalion The Norfolk Regiment were still holding out, including Battalion Headquarters.

At 11.30 a.m., the senior surviving officer, Major Ryder, who was then commanding the battalion, received a message from Brigade Headquarters. This told him that the Norfolks were cut off and could thereafter expect no assistance or communication from Brigade. By noon, ammunition had run out and further resistance became impossible so Major Ryder called his outlying troops in and decided that an attempt to surrender would be made.

A first attempt was unsuccessful. It had been made by three Norfolks walking out into the open without firearms and holding a white towel. These men, however, were at once shot down by the Germans. A second attempt was then made. This was successful and the surrender was accepted.

From the churchyard and surrounding houses about a hundred survivors were collected and made prisoners by the Germans. A number of seriously wounded were left in the cellars of Battalion Headquarters in the care of the medical officer and the remainder were paraded on the Rue Paradis and marched away in a westerly direction.

After going but a short distance the prisoners were halted and searched. During the search they were subjected to various indig-nities and severe ill-treatment. Many were hit on the head with the rifle butts of the SS soldiers whose officers were present but did not interfere.

Before giving themselves up, the Norfolks had destroyed all their weapons and when searched had only a few scanty personal possessions. These and their equipment were removed from them.

After a considerable interval had elapsed they were marched back along the road and, all unsuspecting, into a small field near a farmhouse. It was here that the massacre was to take place.

Inside the field two machine-guns, belonging to No. 4 Company of the Totenkopf Battalion had been mounted and the Company Commander, Fritz Knocklein, was standing with a group of officers and NCOs on the roadway by the entrance to the field. On his order the prisoners were marched into the field with their hands behind their heads.

An order to fire was then given by Knocklein and repeated by the Feldwebel[1] in command of the section of machine-guns.

[1] Sergeant.

Both machine-guns opened fire simultaneously, traversing from right to left along the British column, which by then was marching right across the line of fire.

The prisoners were mown down, some of them falling into a small depression in the ground and this apparently saved the lives of the only two survivors, Privates Pooley and O'Callaghan, though both were wounded. When the guns ceased firing the German troops, fixing bayonets, jumped amongst the fallen bodies and finished off all those who showed any signs of life. Officers and NCOs also fired their revolvers and rifles.

The owner of the farm, who had evacuated it during the fighting, returned the following day and found over two hundred empty cartridge cases on the site where the machine-guns had been mounted.

The two survivors lay still until nightfall, when they crawled out from under the heap of bodies. They lay hidden in a burnt-out farm building for three days, where they were found by a French woman who succoured them so far as she was able, despite the great risk to herself, and brought them food from time to time. Collected eventually by a French ambulance, they were taken to the hospital at Bailleul, where they came once again under German control and were later taken to Germany as prisoners of war.

Private Pooley, owing to the seriousness of his wounds, was repatriated to England in 1943, in accordance with the provisions of the Geneva Prisoners-of-War Convention, and when on his return he first told his story to the British military authorities no one would believe him.

Knocklein's company did not even bother to bury the corpses and spent the night in drunken celebration within a stone's throw of the scene of the crime.

The bodies, which were later buried, were exhumed by the French authorities in 1942 and removed to de Paradis churchyard. On exhumation, about fifty bodies were identified; the remainder are buried in unknown graves. It was also established, when the bodies were examined, that a number of the prisoners who had been shot down had already been slightly wounded in the battle, for many still bore traces of bandages on hands, arms, and legs.

At the time of the massacre[1] the Totenkopf Division, to which

[1] This crime is generally known as the 'Paradis Massacre'. Knochlein was tried by a British Military Court in 1948 and sentenced to death.

Knochlein's unit belonged, was in the XVIth Army Corps commanded by a Wehrmacht general. The incident was reported by someone to Corps Headquarters and the Divisional Commander was ordered to make a report. His explanation being unsatisfactory, a questionnaire had been sent to him and an immediate reply demanded.

When the Totenkopf Division left the Corps Area no reply to the questionnaire had been received. A full report was thereupon made by the Corps Commander to higher authority but no further action was ever taken, although this document was eventually forwarded to Berlin.

That nothing was done was doubtless due to the personal intervention of no less a person than the Head of the Waffen-SS himself, Reichsführer Heinrich Himmler, for it was surely more than a coincidence that the Totenkopf Division whilst in billets in Bailleul was, on the 29th May, visited by him.

But the shooting of the Norfolks at de Paradis was not the only occasion when Allied prisoners of war were killed unarmed after surrender.

One hundred and twenty-nine American prisoners of war were murdered in a field at Beignes in Belgium on 17th December 1944 during von Rundstedt's forlorn hope, the Ardennes offensive.

During the offensive a column of American vehicles was moving along a road near St Vith when it came under heavy artillery and machine-gun fire. The column was forced to halt and the soldiers in the vehicles crouched in the ditch at the side of the road to take cover from the bombardment.

After the shelling had continued for a quarter of an hour, two German tanks and a few armoured cars appeared from the direction of Weismes, and after reaching the crossroads turned south in the direction of St Vith. The ditch in which the American soldiers were taking cover then came under enfilade fire from the German tanks and armoured cars and after suffering very heavy casualties the survivors dropped their weapons and came out of the ditch, with hands raised above their heads, to surrender. They were then marched back along the road as far as the crossing, being relieved of their personal belongings *en route*, and collected in a field just off the St Vith road.

An account of the shameful massacre which then took place is contained in an official American report on the incident, extracts from which appear below:

Other German soldiers in tanks and armoured cars halted at the crossroads and searched some of the captured Americans and took valuables from them . . . at about this same time a German light tank attempted to manoeuvre itself into position on the road so that its cannon could be directed at the group of prisoners in the field . . . some of these tanks stopped when they came opposite the field in which the unarmed American prisoners were standing in a group with their hands raised or clasped behind their heads. A German soldier, either an officer or a non-commissioned officer in one of these vehicles stood up, drew his revolver, took deliberate aim and fired into the group. One of the Americans fell. This was repeated a second time and another American soldier fell to the ground.

At about the same time, from two of the vehicles on the road, machine-gun fire was opened on the group of American prisoners in the field. All or most of them dropped to the ground and stayed there whilst the firing continued for two or three minutes. Most of the soldiers in the field were hit by this fire. The German vehicles then moved off towards the south and were followed by more which also came from the direction of Weismes. As they came opposite the field in which the American soldiers were lying, they also fired with small arms from the moving vehicles at the prostrate bodies in the field . . . some German soldiers, evidently from the party who were on guard at the crossroads, then walked to the group of wounded American soldiers who were still lying in the field . . . and shot with pistol or rifle, or clubbed with a rifle butt or another heavy object any American who still showed any sign of life.

In some instances the victims were shot at point-blank range, for when the corpses were later removed it was found that many had been shot between the eyes, in the temple, or the back of the head.

The massacres of Paradis and St Vith were both inexcusable contraventions of the laws and usages of war in relation to prisoners.

During 1941 and 1942 a number of successful raids on shipping and installations in Norway were made by British Commandos, resulting in effective damage to the German war effort. Perturbed by these operations, Hitler decided that they should be discouraged and to that end on 18th October 1942 issued an order regarding the treatment of certain categories of prisoners of war. This is generally known as the Commando Order.[1]

Its provisions were as follows:

Paragraph I.

For some time our enemies have been using in their warfare methods which are outside the International Geneva Convention. Especially brutal and treacherous is the behaviour of the so-called Commandos who, as is established, are partially recuited from freed criminals in enemy countries. Their captured orders divulge that they are directed not only to shackle prisoners but also to kill defenceless prisoners on the spot, the moment they believe that the latter represent a burden in further pursuance of their purpose or can otherwise be a hindrance. Finally, orders have been found in which the killing of prisoners had been demanded on principle.

Paragraph II.

For this reason it has already been announced in an addendum to the Armed Forces Report of 7th October 1942 that in future Germany in the face of these sabotage troops of the British and their accomplices will resort to the same procedure, i.e. that they will be ruthlessly mowed down by the German troops in combat wherever they may appear.

Paragraph III.

I therefore order that from now on all opponents brought to battle by German troops in so-called commando operations in Europe or Africa, even when it is outwardly a matter of soldiers in uniform or demolition parties with or without weapons, are to be exterminated to the last man in battle or while in flight. In these cases it is immaterial whether they are landed for their operations by ship or aeroplane or descend by parachute. Even should these individuals, on their being discovered, make as if to surrender, *all quarter is to be denied on principle*. A detailed report is to be sent to the OKW[2] on each separate case, for publication in the Wehrmacht communiqué.

Paragraph IV.

If individual members of such commandos working as agents, saboteurs, etc., fall into the hands of the Wehrmacht by other means, such as through the police in any of the countries occupied by us, they are to be handed over to the SD immediately.

[1] Known in Germany as the Kommandobefehl.
[2] Oberkommando der Wehrmacht, Supreme Headquarters of the Armed Forces.

It is strictly forbidden to hold them in military custody or in a prisoner of war camp, even as a temporary measure.

Paragraph V.

This order does not apply to the treatment of any enemy soldiers who in the course of normal hostilities (large-scale offensive actions, landing operations, and airborne operations) are captured in open battle or give themselves up. Nor does it apply to enemy soldiers falling into our hands after battles at sea or trying to save their lives by parachute after an air battle.

Paragraph VI.

In the case of non-compliance with this order, I shall bring to trial before a court-martial any commander or other officer who has either failed to carry out his duty in instructing the troops about this order or who has acted contrary to it.

Signed: Adolf Hitler.

The Kommandobefehl was in complete violation of the laws and customs of war as then applicable to all the belligerents concerned, and Hitler appears to have entertained some misgivings about the welcome it might receive from those to whom it was addressed[1] for on the same day that it was issued he sent out a covering letter explaining why he had felt it necessary to issue an order so repugnant to the rules of warfare in relations to prisoners of war.

He stated that, as in no previous war, there had developed a new tactical method of disrupting lines-of-communication, intimidating those sections of the population who were working for Germany and destroying industrial plant and installations in occupied territory used by the Germans for their war economy.

In the East these methods took the form of partisan warfare which was already costing the Germans dearly in manpower, transport and materials. England and America were pursuing a similar kind of warfare though under another name and were using air transport to drop troops, food and equipment and landing sabotage parties from submarines or rubber dinghies.

The effects of this activity, Hitler explained, were extremely grave. The destruction of a single electric power station, for example, could cost the aircraft industry many thousand tons of aluminium, thereby preventing the building of numerous aircraft.

---

[1] The recipients of the order were the High Command of the three services, C-in-C Norway, C-in-C South-East, High Command West, High Command South, High Command Twentieth Mountain Army, Panzer Army Africa, Reichsführer SS and Chief of SIPO.

This type of warfare, Hitler maintained, was without danger to the enemy. For since he landed his sabotage troops in uniform, and in addition provided civilian clothing, they could appear, as required, either as soldiers or civilians.

The letter continued:

> If the German war effort is not to suffer the most severe damage as a result of such action, it must be made clear to the enemy that every sabotage party will be exterminated without exception to the last man . . . it must not be permitted *in any circumstances* for demolition, sabotage or terrorist groups simply to surrender and be taken prisoner in order to receive treatment in accordance with the provisions of the 'Geneva Convention for the Treatment of Prisoners-of-War'. . . . I therefore expect not only the Commanders-in-Chief, and the armies they command, but the individual commanding officers, not only to grasp the necessity for such action but to apply themselves with all energy to carrying out this order . . . *should it prove advisable to spare one or two men in the first instance for interrogation reasons, they are to be shot immediately afterwards.*

The writer of that letter need have had no apprehensions that his order would not be obeyed. It was almost universally carried out to the letter, and in many theatres of war British commandos and members of the Special Air Service Regiment, all of whom were entitled to be treated on capture as prisoners of war, were illegally executed in pursuance of it.[1]

At the date of its issue the Commander-in-Chief of the German forces in Norway was General von Falkenhorst and in due course he received copy No. 4 together with Hitler's explanatory letter.

Not only did General von Falkenhorst pass on both these documents to his subordinate commanders but a few months later he found it necessary to remind them of its provisions. Accordingly he issued a second order marked 'Top Secret' and addressed to 'Officers Only' on the subject of 'Treatment of Prisoners of War'. In it he referred to the Führerbefehl[2] of 18th October 1942 and wrote:

> I am under the impression that the wording of the above order, which had to be destroyed, is no longer clearly in mind and I therefore again bring to particular notice paragraph 3. Failure

---

[1] Save in North Africa where Rommel burned it.
[2] A direct order from Hitler.

to comply with the order is subject to severe punishment. (Paragraph 3 was then quoted.)[1] If a man is saved for interrogation he must not survive his comrades for more than 24 hours.

Naturally all civilians, Norwegian police, and unwanted members of the Wehrmacht must at all costs be kept away. PW movements are to be avoided. The strictest secrecy is the express duty of all commanders concerned. . . . If, in exceptional cases, saboteurs are brought to bay in the presence of Norwegians or with their assistance (e.g. guides, police), they are not to be shot on the spot but are to be taken prisoner and handed over to the SD as soon as possible.

Thus did von Falkenhorst not only repeat the Führerbefehl himself; he added to it.[2]

In September 1942 a raid was made by two officers and ten other ranks on the town of Glomfjord in Norway. It was known to the Chief Military Planner at Combined Operations Headquarters[3] as 'Musketoon'. Its object was the destruction of a hydro-electric power station. On completion of their mission the party was to make their way to Sweden whence, it was expected, they would be repatriated.

The party left England in a Free French submarine on 11th September, landed in Norway four days later, and on 20th September attacked the power station causing considerable damage. All ranks were in uniform.

On their journey into Sweden after the successful completion of the raid, the part were attacked and all but four captured by a German patrol. One member of the party was wounded and later died of his wounds; the remainder, including the two officers, were taken to Gestapo Headquarters in Oslo and thence to Germany.

What happened to them then was not precisely known for some time, although information was received that the officers had been sent to Offlag IV(A), known amongst the British prisoners of war as the 'naughty boys' camp', from which they disappeared after a

[1] See page 32 above.

[2] Falkenhorst was tried at Brunswick in 1946 by a British Military Court, sitting with a judge advocate, for his participation in carrying out the Commando Order and was found guilty of eight charges alleging that he incited the forces under his command not to give quarter to Allied soldiers, sailors, and airmen taking part in Commando operations and to kill them after capture and with being concerned in the killing of a large number of Allied prisoners of war by handing them over to the Security Service (SD) for execution. He was sentenced to death by the Court but this sentence was commuted to one of life imprisonment by the Commander-in-Chief, British Zone of Germany, then Marshal of the RAF Sir Sholto Douglas.

[3] Brigadier Antony Head, CBE, MC, now Secretary of State for War.

stay of one day. The parents of one of these officers, who made inquiries through the Red Cross, were told through information given by the Commandant of Offlag IV(A) that their son had escaped. This was untrue and the reason for this story being given was only learnt subsequently. The officer had been recognized in the camp by other prisoners and it was not therefore possible for the Germans to say that he had been shot in battle. It is now known from a captured German document that both these officers were shot by the SD 'for taking part in a sabotage operation'.

A similar fate befell the members of an operation called 'Freshman' which left for Norway in November 1942 in two gliders to attack a hydro-electric power station at Vemork in Southern Norway. The raiding party consisted of two officers and twenty-seven other ranks all in uniform. None of these men ever returned to this country and a German communiqué issued at the time stated that 'the sabotage troops were engaged and annihilated'. They had not, however, been annihilated in battle. Owing to bad weather the two gliders became separated and one came down near Egersund. About eleven of the occupants survived the crash and these were captured by the Wehrmacht, taken to a camp, and afterwards shot. The second glider crashed near Stavanger, and although a number of men survived these were all captured and eventually shot, after an argument between the Wehrmacht and the Gestapo, as saboteurs.

Another Commando raid in the spring of 1943 was launched against shipping in Norwegian harbours and coastal waters. Known as 'Operation Checkmate' the force consisted of one officer and six other ranks, all in uniform. The whole party were captured three or four weeks after they left British shores and taken to a prison at Grini. Where these men spent the next two years has never been discovered, but in 1945 five of them were shot in Sachsenhausen Concentration Camp and one at Belsen, only a few weeks before the German capitulation. The fate of the seventh is unknown as he has never been heard of since his capture.

Not all these raids on the Norwegian coast were made by British troops. In 1943 a raid was made by a party of Norwegian naval ratings and a British telegraphist. All wore uniform, naval hats, and khaki battledress. The Norwegians had their red anchor sewn on the left sleeve and the telegraphist wore a Royal Navy flash. What happened to these men has been told in a statement made by a former Obersturmführer of the SIPO, Hans Blomberg, who was later tried as a war criminal and sentenced to death for being concerned in their murder.

In July 1943 Blomberg was head of the SIPO in Bergen and was informed by the German Admiral von Schrader that a Norwegian MTB had been captured by German naval forces near Bergen and that some of the crew had been made prisoners, including a few wounded. Schrader said that these sailors were 'pirates and not soldiers' and were to be shot by the SIPO in accordance with the Commander-in-Chief's order. Blomberg set the wheels in motion and the execution was carried out the following day after the prisoners had been interrogated.

Blomberg's statement ended as follows: 'The firing squad took the dead bodies to Calmarhus garage in a lorry and guarded them there. During the following night, they were placed in coffins and taken on board a boat. The mate of the boat was Oberwachtmeister[1] der Wasserschutzpolizei[2] Tiedman from Hamburg. Explosives were fastened to all the coffins which were then blown up under water in accordance with general practice.'

All these sailors and soldiers were bona fide members of the Allied forces, dressed in uniform, taking part in legitimate warfare, and as such were entitled to the protection of the Prisoner-of-War Convention of 1929, which was binding on all the belligerents concerned.

In September 1944 parties of paratroopers from the Special Air Service Regiment[3] were being dropped in the Vosges Mountains whence they operated to disrupt enemy rail communications in Eastern France. One such party, which consisted of an officer and ten men, was hiding in a small village called Raon l'Etape when it was attacked by superior forces and, after a brisk engagement in which the officer was wounded, the whole party was taken prisoner.

The unit which captured them belonged to the SS, but for some reason which remains a mystery the prisoners were handed over to the Wehrmacht after interrogation, instead of being shot in accordance with the Commando Order.

This greatly incensed the local SS commander when it came to his ears. Steps were at once taken to recover the prisoners, and within forty-eight hours this had been done, and they were safely

---

[1] Sergeant-major.
[2] Lit., water police. This was used as a cover name for a branch of the Gestapo.
[3] Hereafter referred to as SAS.

confined on a Security Service Camp near Strasbourg. The next week all the prisoners were taken to a selected spot in the surrounding country, made to dig their own graves, and then shot. In 1945 their bodies were discovered by a British War Crimes Investigation Unit and exhumed. Each prisoner had been shot in the back of the neck.

In other similar incidents large numbers of SAS were murdered after being taken in battle, contrary to the Prisoner-of-War Convention of 1929.

A party of thirty-two prisoners of war belonging to the 1st SAS Regiment, all in uniform, were captured in the Vienne Département by the German LXXXth Corps and taken to Poitiers prison. Whilst there they were interrogated by members of the SIPO under the command of a Dr Herold. Instructions were then received to hand the prisoners over to the SD in compliance with the Commando Order. Dr Herold, to his own credit and to everyone else's surprise, refused to hand them over. The Corps Chief of Staff, Colonel Köstlin, warned Herold of the serious consequences which non-compliance with the order might entail, but the Herr Doktor stood firm in his refusal.

The decision as to what fate should befall these prisoners was left, therefore, to the Corps Commander, General Kurt Gallenkamp, and the Chief of Staff was told to have them shot, and an officer from Corps Headquarters was detailed to see that this order was carried out.

Two days later, as dawn broke, Lieutenant C., and twenty-nine of his men were taken from Poitiers in a truck to the place of execution. On arrival there, the Corps representative, Captain Schönig, told the officer that he and his men would all be shot 'on the orders of Hitler'. Schönig also said that at that moment he was ashamed to be wearing the uniform of a German officer. Nevertheless he remained throughout the shooting, collected the prisoners' identity discs, and duly reported to the Red Cross authorities *that they had been killed in action.*[1]

About the same time another party of British paratroopers was dropped from an aircraft near their objective in the neighbourhood of Paris. They were also in full battledress.

Shortly after landing they were surrounded by some local

[1] General Gallenkamp, Colonel Köstlin Captain Schönig, and others were tried by a British Military Court in Germany in 1946 upon a charge alleging that they were concerned in the killing of these prisoners of war. They were all found guilty. General Gallenkamp was sentenced by the Court to suffer death by being hanged but the sentence was commuted to life imprisonment; Colonel Köstlin was sentenced to imprisonment for life, and Captain Schönig to imprisonment for five years.

German troops and after suffering a few casualties seven were captured and taken to the ill-fated Gestapo Headquarters in the Avenue Foch, Paris. There they were questioned.

Subsequently a doubt seems to have arisen as to whether they should be handed back to the Wehrmacht, who had captured them, or dealt with under the Commando Order. A report of their interrogation was, therefore, sent to RSHA, Berlin, together with a request for instructions for their disposal. As no reply was received, two reminders had to be sent.

Eventually, about a month later, a reply was received. This stated that the prisoners were to be shot within twenty-four hours and 'in civilian clothes'. The following day they were made to change into civilian clothes and then put into a truck outside the Gestapo Headquarters. They were given sandwiches and told that they were 'going on a long journey'. The drive lasted four hours and ended in a field near Noailles. The prisoners were then made to leave the truck and were marched to a clearing in a nearby wood. Their escort, who were armed with sub-machine-guns, placed the prisoners in a line and the firing party took up its position opposite them.

The leader of the German party took out a piece of paper and reading from it told the British soldiers, through an interpreter, that they had been found guilty of collaborating with the French Maquis and condemned to death by shooting. There had, indeed, been no trial of any kind and any such finding would, in any event, not have been in accordance with the facts. Furthermore, the British party had made a legitimate airborne landing, carrying arms and dressed in uniform.

What then happened is best told in the words of two men who survived. One of them was a Czech serving in the British Army. 'I opened my handcuffs with my watch key,' he said, 'and ran away down the hill. I was not hit. Later I made my way to a French village and after spending a few days in hiding joined the French Resistance.'

The other, a Trooper Jones, said, 'I made a run for it. When I had gone about fifteen yards I fell as I lost my balance through being handcuffed. A lot of firing broke out but I was not hit. After a little while I crawled to some trees and stood behind one of them. I saw the bodies of four of my comrades lying on the ground but no sign of the Germans, but there was a lot of firing near the road one hundred and fifty yards away. I hid in the woods for a time. I was then able to get away to a French village.'

Those directly responsible for this shooting well knew that the Berlin order was illegal beyond all doubt, for it had clearly stated that the prisoners were to be shot in civilian clothes so that they might be mistaken for members of the Maquis. Furthermore, the execution took place in a wood over four hours' journey from Paris and all were fully aware that their victims were British prisoners of war captured in fair fight while wearing uniform.

In 1943, as the Allied bombing of Germany grew in intensity, orders were given by the Commander-in-Chief of the Luftwaffe that prisoner-of-war camps should be established in the residential districts of large cities as it was thought that in this way the inhabitants might obtain a measure of protection. Failing that, there would at least be the consolation of knowing that if the residents in those areas were killed a number of Allied airmen prisoners of war would die with them.

From the Führer's Headquarters,
    3rd September 1943.
    The Supreme Commander of the Luftwaffe proposes to establish camps for Air Force prisoners within the residential quarters of big cities, which will constitute at the same time a protection for the population of the towns, and to transfer all existing camps containing about 8,000 British and American Air Force prisoners to larger towns threatened by enemy air attacks.

This order was clearly contrary to the spirit of Article 9 of the Prisoners-of-War Convention of 1929, which provided that prisoners of war should not be used so as to render by their presence certain points or areas immune from bombardment.

Furthermore, Article 2 provided that prisoners of war 'are in the power of the hostile government but not of the individuals or Corps who have captured them. They must at all times be humanely treated and protected, particularly against acts of violence, insults, and public curiosity. Measures of reprisals against them are prohibited.'

In flagrant violation of these provisions many Allied airmen who had baled out of disabled aeroplanes over Germany were not treated as prisoners of war, but ill-treated, beaten, and murdered by German civilians, often incited and always condoned by high officials.

Göring, Himmler, and Kaltenbrunner held a series of important conferences during which a list was made of air operations which constituted 'acts of terrorism' as opposed to normal acts of warfare. All bombardment of the civil population was to be regarded as terrorism and it was decided that 'lynch law should be the rule'.

In an order issued on 10th August 1943 by Himmler to all senior executives, SS and police officers, and transmitted orally by them to their subordinates, the following appears: 'It is not the task of the police to interfere in clashes between Germans and the English and American terror flyers who have baled out.'

The German people were also incited to punish Allied airmen shot down over Germany. In an article in the *Völkischer Beobachter* of 29th May 1944 Goebbels wrote:

> It is only by the use of firearms that we can protect the lives of enemy pilots shot down during bombing attacks. Otherwise these men would be killed by the sorely tried population.
>
> Who is right here? The murderers who, after their cowardly misdeeds expect humane treatment from their victims, or the victims who wish to defend themselves on the principle of 'an eye for an eye and a tooth for a tooth'. This question is not difficult to answer. It appears to us intolerable to use our soldiers and police against the German people who are only treating child murderers as they deserve.

Martin Bormann, too, circularized all Reichleiters, Gauleiters, and Kreisleiters on this subject in May 1944.

After stating that women and children had frequently been fired at on the roads by English and American airmen, he wrote:

> Several instances have occurred where members of such aircraft, who have baled out or have made forced landings, were lynched on the spot immediately after capture by the populace which was incensed to the highest degree. No police measures were invoked against German civilians who had taken part in these incidents.

After receipt of this circular, the Gauleiter of South Westphalia, Albert Hoffman, issued the following instructions to all county representatives, mayors, and police officials in his district:

> Fighter-bomber pilots who have been shot down are in principle not to be protected against the fury of the people. I expect all police officers to refuse to lend their protection to such gangsters. Authorities acting in contradiction to the popular

sentiment will have to answer to me. All police and gendarmerie officials are to be informed immediately of my views.

The Gauleiter of Baden and Alsace, the ill-famed Robert Wagner,[1] issued an order throughout his Gau that all Allied airmen who were brought down or who had baled out were to be killed. He said that they were causing great ravages in Germany, that it was an inhuman war, and that no captured airman should be treated as a prisoner of war nor did he deserve any mercy.

Such incitements were not without results. During 1944 and 1945 numerous attacks were made by German civilians on Allied airmen entitled to be treated as prisoners of war, and many were lynched by the populace or shot by the police or the Volkssturm.[2]

A German named Grüner, who was a subordinate of Wagner, described in a statement made to an American war crimes investigator how he noticed, when passing through Rheinweiler, four British airmen who had been rescued from the Rhine by some German soldiers. The soldiers refused to take charge of the prisoners and Grüner then decided that he would execute them himself in obedience to Wagner's orders. He shot all four in the back with a tommy-gun and then threw them back into the Rhine.

On 21st June 1944, two Liberators were brought down near Mecklenburg. The two crews, totalling fifteen men, were uninjured. All were shot on the usual pretext of 'attempting to escape'. This crime was confirmed by a document found in the files of the headquarters of the 11th Luftgaukommando. The document states that six members of the crew were shot while attempting to escape and the other nine handed over to the police in Waren. Seven of these were shot *en route* for a prison camp whilst attempting to escape, and the two officers, Lieutenant H. and L., were shot later that day on the same pretext.

One of the most cowardly of these attacks was carried out jointly by the Allgemeine SS and Hitler Jugend.

In February 1945 the town of Pforzheim in Southern Germany was heavily bombarded by Allied aircraft and badly damaged. There were many fatal casualties and a large number of homeless people had to be evacuated to the nearby town of Huchenfeld.

Some three weeks afterwards, a Flying Fortress manned by a British crew was returning from a raid on Leipzig when it was hit

[1] Robert Wagner was tried by the French Permanent Military Tribunal at Strasbourg in 1946 and sentenced to death for the murder of Allied airmen and many other war crimes.
[2] The Volkssturm was an auxiliary military organization somewhat resembling the Home Guard in this country.

by flak near Baden-Baden. The crew, consisting of ten officers and warrant officers, baled out and all landed safely. Seven were made prisoners and taken to the civil prison in Buhl, where they were temporarily confined.

The next morning they were marched through the streets of Pforzheim, where they were maltreated by the local inhabitants, and then taken to Huchenfeld. There they were lodged in the boiler house in the cellar of the new school and made preparations to settle down for the night. But before they could do so, a crowd of Germans burst open the door and swarmed into the cellar. With them was the Burgomaster, who had been interrupted while attending a wedding reception.

The guards left their prisoners to the mercy of the angry crowd which first roughly handled them and then dragged them outside into the street and towards the cemetery.

On the way there, three of the airmen succeeded in escaping, but one of these, a flying officer, was later recaptured and confined in a neighbouring police station. The following day he was taken from his cell and led past a crowd of Germans who were standing outside an air-raid shelter. He was set upon, beaten almost to a pulp, and finally shot by a sixteen-year-old member of the Hitler Youth who, in his own words, 'gave the officer a *coup-de-grâce* shot in his head from my pistol'. The German police took no steps to restrain the crowd and no arrests were made.

The remaining four prisoners, who had not managed to get away, were taken by the crowd to the cemetery and there shot.

The Hitler Youth played a major role in this affair. As one of them wrote afterwards: 'The Bannführer[1] made a short speech which made our young blood boil, then he distributed weapons and ammunition. We were told that there were seven British airmen in the Huchenfeld school and that we were to take them away and shoot them.'

When the crowd had rushed into the school cellar they had clearly intended to kill the prisoners there, and it was only through the intervention of the Burgomaster that the airmen were taken to the cemetery. But his anxiety was not for the air-crew. He objected vehemently to the idea of their being shot in the school cellar. 'It would,' he said, 'be a continual horror for our children who have to go inside.'

Shortly after the airmen had been shot, the Burgomaster

---

[1] A junior commissioned rank in the SS.

returned to the wedding party from which he had been so abruptly dragged away earlier in the evening.

On the night of 24/25th March 1944, seventy-six Air Force officer prisoners of war escaped from Stalag Luft III at Sagan in Silesia. Fifteen were quickly recaptured and taken back to camp, three made successful escapes, eight were detained by the Gestapo after recapture, and the remaining fifty were shot by the Germans.

The first intimation of their fate was given on 6th April when the acting Commandant read to the senior British officer in the camp a statement issued by OKW to the effect that forty-one had been shot, 'some of them having offered resistance on being arrested, others having tried to escape on the transport back to camp'. No names were given.

Nine days later the British officer was handed a list containing the names of forty-seven who had been shot and a month later three more names were supplied. In each case the same reasons were given.

It was quite untrue that these men had been shot resisting recapture or attempting to re-escape. They had all been shot by the Gestapo on the direct orders of Hitler.

The first information to reach the outside world was a communication which was handed in June to the Swiss Minister in Berlin, Monsieur Naville, in reply to an inquiry he had made as the representative in Germany of the Protecting Power. This Note stated that thirty-seven prisoners of British nationality and thirteen not of British nationality, escaped from Stalag Luft III, had been shot when offering resistance to recapture or whilst attempting to escape after recapture, and that urns containing their ashes has been sent to Sagan for burial.

M. Naville, however, was not deceived by the German Note. In his reply he described the cremation as 'most unusual, the normal custom being to bury a prisoner in a coffin with military honours' and pointed out that if, as the Germans alleged, these fifty officers who were recaptured in widely scattered parts of Germany had resisted or attempted a second escape, it was probable that some would have been wounded and most improbable that all would have been killed.

It was as stupid of the Germans not to have seen this flaw in their story as it was wise of them to refuse to give the Protecting Power, as was the usual custom, details of the true circumstances in which these officers lost their lives. Let Keitel himself continue the narrative: 'One morning it was reported to me that the escape had taken place and that about fifteen of the officers had been recaptured in the vicinity of the camp. I did not intend to report this case at the midday conference at Berchtesgaden as it was the third mass escape within a very brief period.'

But Himmler forestalled him and announced the incident to his Führer in Keitel's presence. Hitler was furious, and said that the prisoners were to remain with the SD after recapture and not to be returned to the custody of the Armed Forces. He ordered Himmler to see that this was done.

After the conference, Keitel sent for the head of the department of OKW which was responsible for prisoners of war, and also for General von Grävenitz. When they entered Keitel's office he seemed excited and nervous and said that Göring had just reproached him in the presence of Hitler for having let some more prisoners of war escape. 'These escapes must stop,' said Keitel. 'We shall take very severe measures. . . . The men who have escaped will be shot, probably the majority of them are already dead.' General von Grävenitz at once protested, saying that this could not be done and that it was expressly laid down in the Geneva Convention of 1929 that escape was not a dishonourable offence. This protest had no effect.

The shooting was carried out by the Gestapo. After Hitler's morning conference Himmler had set the wheels in motion and orders had been sent by Kaltenbrunner to the appropriate departments for a nation-wide search to be instituted.[1] Within a few days all save three of the escaped officers had been recaptured, most of them in Silesia, though a few had managed to get as far as Kiel and Strasbourg.

The Gestapo then went into action. The following is an account of the shooting of one of the victims, Flight Lietenant H., as presented by the prosecution at the trial of Max Wielen and seventeen members of the Gestapo for their part in these crimes.

Flight Lieutenant H. had reached Alsace before he was recaptured by the KRIPO and taken to Gestapo Headquarters at Strasbourg. At that time the orders for the shooting had not been received in Strasbourg but later in the day the following teleprint was received from RSHA:

To Gestapo, Strasbourg.
    The British prisoner of war who has been handed over to the Gestapo by the Strasbourg Criminal Police, by superiors orders,

[1] Grossfahndung, hue and cry: lit., widespread search.

45

is to be taken immediately in the direction of Breslau and to be shot *en route* while escaping. An undertaker is to be directed to remove the body to a crematorium and have it cremated there. The urn is to be sent to the head of the Criminal Police Headquarters RSHA. The contents of this teleprint and the affair itself are to be made known only to the officials directly concerned with the carrying out of this matter, and they are to be pledged to special secrecy by handshake. The completion of this task is to be reported immediately. This teleprint is to be destroyed at once.

It was arranged that Flight Lieutenant H. was to be killed on the way to Natzweiler Concentration Camp and that the body should be cremated there. The prisoner was taken away in a car by two Gestapo men named Driesner and Hilker, a third member was the driver. On the way, H. was allowed to get out of the car to relieve himself in a wood and during the halt, while Driesner kept him in conversation, Hilker shot him from behind. The corpse was taken to Natzweiler, where the Commandant was informed that it was the body of a prisoner of war who had been shot whilst attempting to escape.

Much the same procedure was adopted in relation to another of the prisoners who had the misfortune to be recaptured when only half a mile from the Swiss-German frontier.

As previously, Natzweiler was chosen for the cremation. Just before they arrived there the man in charge of the escort stopped the car on the pretence that he wanted to relieve himself, and the prisoner, who was handcuffed, was asked whether he too would like to get out. He did, and in the same way as Flight Lieutenant H. was shot.

Four other escaped officers were recaptured near Kiel and the following account of their murder was given by Oscar Schmidt, an official of the Gestapo at Kiel who took part in the crime. 'One morning I was sent for by my chief together with six others, Post, Kahler, Jacobs, another Schmidt, Denkmann, and Struve. We were told to drive to Flensburg where we would receive four British officer prisoners of war. We were to take them away and to use our firearms in the event of the slightest attempt being made to escape.'

It was then explained to them that this meant that these four officers must be 'liquidated' and that non-compliance with this order would be punished by death and family dishonour, and

46

that a similar fate would befall those who talked about the matter. These orders had come from Kaltenbrunner.

Post was put in command of the party which arrived at Flensburg shortly before noon and after lunch took over the four officers. Their hands were then manacled behind their backs and they were led to two cars which were standing in the courtyard of the KRIPO Headquarters ready to take them away. Post took one of the officers with him in his car and the other three went in the second car in which were also the driver, Jacobs, and the two Schmidts.

The method of shooting must have been decided at a high level because in this case too, like the murders in Alsace and near the Swiss border, it was arranged that the officers were to be given an opportunity to relive themselves on the journey, at a place to be indicated, and that the shooting was to commence on a signal to be given by Oscar Schmidt. When the second car arrived at the scene of the crime, Post's car was already there and Denkmann was standing in the road and gave the driver of the second car a signal to stop. Oscar Schmidt then gave the prisoners an order to get out and relieve themselves. They did so and were led into a field, Schmidt following a few paces behind. Schmidt's account continues:

When I came to within about six paces of the group, one of the officers suddenly let out a shout and they all scattered; at the same time shots were fired and the officers fell and lay with their faces to the ground. I saw Franz Schmidt and Jacobs at that moment directly behind the officers with their pistols in their hands. I also had a pistol in my hand; it was loaded and the safety catch released. . . . At this moment Post shouted to me, 'You did not fire, the man is alive.' One of the officers then raised himself and Post, who had snatched a rifle out of Kahler's hands, fired two shots at the officer as he lay on the ground. I never had a chance to fire at this officer as he had thrown himself on the ground immediately the first shots were fired. After Post had fired two shots into this officer's back he fired another rifle shot into the head of each of the other officers who were lying on the ground apparently dead. He then removed their handcuffs. I was ordered to wait for a hearse to arrive and then to take the bodies to the crematorium for cremation. This I did.

About three months later these Germans were informed by

their Chief that a Red Cross Commission was coming to investigate the affair. They were all taken again to the scene of the shooting and told that if interrogated they were to say that the officers had attempted to escape to the hedges in order to get possession of the cars and had been shot so doing. Their attention was once more drawn to the dire consequence which would ensue if any of them were to say what really happened.

Thus fifty British officer prisoners of war were murdered in cold blood, and in each case an official report was sent to RSHA that they had been killed while attempting to escape.

This crime, when it became known, shocked the civilized world; and it was described by the International Military Tribunal at Nuremberg in their judgment as 'plain murder in complete violation of International Law.'

In November 1944 OKW issued instructions regarding the transfer of certain categories of prisoners of war to the SD. The Bullet Decree,[1] as these orders were called, provided that the following prisoners of war were to be handed over to the SIPO and SD:

(1) All recaptured Soviet prisoners of war.

(2) All Soviet officer prisoners of war who refused to work.

(3) All Soviet prisoners of war who had been specially selected by the screening detachments of SD stationed in prisoner-of-war camps (Einsatzkommandos).

(4) Any prisoner of war confined in a prison camp who had committed an offence for which the Commandant considered he had not got adequate disciplinary powers.

(5) Any prisoner of war in respect of whom a special order had been issued by OKW.

All these categories were handed over to the Gestapo for 'special treatment'. This consisted of being deprived of prisoner-of-war status, sent to the concentration camp at Mauthausen, and shot with a bullet in the neck.

At Mauthausen they were known as 'K' prisoners.[2] When they arrived at the camp they were not registered as were ordinary prisoners, and their names remained unknown except to the members of the 'Politische Abteilung'.[3]

[1] The 'Kugelerlass'.
[2] K for Kugel, meaning bullet.
[3] The Political Department, i.e. the branch which looked after so-called 'political' prisoners.

48

They were at once taken to the detention block, where they·were undressed and then taken to what, for camouflage purposes was called the bathroom but which was, in fact, a room in the prison cells near the crematorium especially designed for execution by shooting or gassing.

One of the methods of shooting these 'K' prisoners has been described by a French officer who was himself confined in Mauthausen. 'The shooting was done by means of a measuring apparatus, the prisoner being backed towards a vertical measuring standard with an automatic contraption which shot a bullet into the back of his neck as soon as the wooden bar which determined his height touched the top of his head.'

Sometimes they were marched down in batches to the quarry dressed only in shirts and pants and mowed down by machine-gun fire. Death certificates were prepared in every case and endorsed, 'Killed while attempting to escape'.

From the very outset of the Russian campaign it was evident that the Germans intended to disregard all the laws and usages of war appertaining to prisoners.

The USSR was not originally a party to the 'Geneva Convention relating to Prisoners of War' but it was to the 'Convention relating to the Sick and the Wounded'. It was also a signatory to the Hague Convention. It was argued at the trial of the major war criminals at Nuremberg that this Convention did not apply to the Russian campaign, but the International Tribunal held that it did.

As long ago as the end of the last century the Hague Convention established certain rules regarding the rights and responsibilities of belligerents in regard to prisoners of war, and the High Contracting Parties at that convention stated that 'in cases not covered by rules adopted by them, the inhabitants and the belligerents remained under the protection and governance of the principles of the law of nations derived from the usages established among civilized peoples, from the laws of humanity, and from the dictates of public conscience. . . . The Contracting Powers shall issue instructions to their armed land forces which shall be in conformity with the Regulations respecting the laws and customs of war on land annexed to the present convention.'

In these annexed regulations the following Articles appear:

Article 3. The armed forces of the belligerents may consist of combatants and non-combatants; in the case of capture by the enemy, both have the right to be treated as prisoners of war.

Article 4. Prisoners of war are in the power of the hostile government, not of the individuals who capture them. They must be humanely treated.

Article 6. The state may employ the labour of prisoners of war, other than officers, according to their rank and capacity. The work shall not be excessive and shall have no connection with the operations of war.

Article 7. The government into whose hands prisoners of war have fallen is charged with their maintenance. In default of special agreement between the belligerents, prisoners of war shall be treated, as regards rations, quarters, and clothing, on the same footing as the troops of the government which captured them.

Article 23. It is particularly forbidden to kill or wound an enemy who, having laid down his arms or no longer having any means of defence, has surrendered at discretion.

From the beginning of the war with Russia, Germany was, at the very least, under international obligation to regard all captured members of the armed forces, combatant or non-combatant, as prisoners of war; to treat them humanely whilst in captivity; adequately to house, clothe, and feed them; not to work them excessively nor to employ them in connection with the operations of war. The enemy could not be refused quarter nor could they be put to death after they had surrendered. This was well known to every German soldier, for included in the 'Ten Commandments' printed in his pay-book were the words; 'No enemy who has surrendered will be killed.'[1]

In a new edition of the German Army Manual which was issued on 1st August 1939, exactly one month before the invasion of Poland, many of the above provisions were quoted; but from the very moment of their attack on Russia the Germans flagrantly violated each and every one of them, and the atrocities committed against these helpless prisoners were reminiscent of the barbarous Middle Ages. They treated their prisoners with extreme brutality. They starved them; they let them remain in the open throughout the long severe Russian winter; they worked them to death; they employed thousands of them on work directly connected with the operations of war, often under enemy artillery

[1] See Appendix I.

fire; and they shot all political commissars and politruks[1] after capture.

All these violations of International Law had been planned before the campaign began. Prior to the attack on Russia, Hitler had told his generals that different methods would be used in the new war, and that as the Russians were not signatories to the 'Prisoners-of-War Convention' the treatment of Russian prisoners did not have to follow its provisions.

Several months before the invasion began, Lieut.-General Reinecke, head of the prisoners of war section of OKW, gave orders to the appropriate authorities that open-air camps, surrounded only by barbed wire, should be constructed for Russian prisoners, if there was no time to build 'roofed-in camps', and issued instructions directing all those responsible for guarding them to shoot 'without warning' any prisoners who might attempt to escape.

The German Commander-in-Chief, in a pamphlet entitled *The Conduct of the Army in the East* which was issued before the invasion started, stated that to supply captured Russian soldiers with food was 'misconceived humanitarianism'.

Finally, it was decided at the highest level that political commissars of the Red Army would not be recognized as prisoners of war or evacuated to the rear areas. They would be 'liquidated', *at the latest in the prisoner-of-war transit camps*.

Only one important voice in the whole of Germany was raised in protest against all these decisions; that of Admiral Canaris. He wrote to OKW:

> The Geneva Convention for the treatment of Prisoners of War is not binding in the relationship between Germany and the USSR. Therefore only the general principles of International Law regarding the treatment of such prisoners apply. Ever since the eighteenth century these have gradually been established along the lines that war captivity is neither revenge nor punishment, but solely protective custody, the only purpose of which is to prevent the prisoners of war from further participating in the war. This principle was developed in accordance with the view held by all armies that it is contrary to military tradition to kill or injure helpless people. . . . These decrees for the treatment of Soviet prisoners are based on a fundamentally different point of view.

[1] See page 52.

51

This still small voice remained unheard and unheeded; for Keitel, to whom the protesting memorandum was submitted, merely endorsed the document with this note: 'These objections arise from the military concept of chivalrous warfare. *This* is the destruction of an ideology; therefore I approve and support these measures.'

In March 1941, three months before Hitler invaded Russia, he held a conference in the Reich Chancellery in Berlin at which he told a distinguished military audience including Field-Marshals Keitel and von Leeb, and Generals Halder, von Manstein and Hoppner, his general idea of the new war against Russia, its objective, and the methods by which it would be waged. It would be an ideological war, he told them, for the extermination of 'Asiatic barbaric Bolshevism'. Thus it would differ from the war in the West, and chivalry and military honour would have no place in it. Bolshevism in the Red Army, he said, was kept alive by the political commissars who were present with every Soviet formation. These must, therefore, be liquidated. The commissars, said Hitler, would not fight cleanly and their fate would not be left to the jurisdiction of any military court.

Thus did Hitler condemn to death all Soviet political commissars three months before the Russian war began.

In the Red Army in 1941 there was a political commissar on the strength of every formation and all major units. They were of officer status. Amongst the rank and file were officials with similar functions known as politruks.

Both of these categories were members of the Russian armed forces and entitled, if captured, to be treated as prisoners of war.

By June, OKW had issued a 'Directive for the Treatment of Political Commissars'.

The preamble of this directive began with the prophecy that these political commissars would be dirty fighters and would maltreat German prisoners of war: that they were not to be treated as soldiers or have the protection of International Law. 'They must therefore be proceeded against with all possible severity at once and without further ado. Thus if they are captured they are to be liquidated at once when fighting or offering resistance.'

The order went on to point out that all political commissars wore a particular emblem on their uniform sleeve; that they were to be segregated from other prisoners of war immediately after capture and then 'they will be eliminated'. In deciding the question whether a suspected commissar was guilty or not guilty 'the personal impression and the attitude of the commissar will on principle be considered of greater importance than the facts of the case, *which cannot possibly be proved*'. If commissars were caught in the rear areas they were handed over to a Sonderkommando[1] of the SD, where their rate was automatic.

This order, which was issued by Keitel on the instructions of his Führer, was promulgated to the German Army by Field-Marshal von Brauchitsch, the Commander-in-Chief, over his signature and with a foreword which stated that the elimination of political commissars with the troops was to be carried out on the order of an officer after their separation, outside the fighting area proper, and inconspicuously.

Thus was this directive distributed throughout the German Army. No one, from the generals who issued it to their troops down to the junior officers who had to put it into execution, can have been in any doubt of its criminality. But Hitler cared not whether they understood it or not. He did not expect, he once said, the officer corps to understand his orders, but he demanded that it should unconditionally obey them.

The Commissar Order has been branded as an illegal order by several war-crime tribunals, including the International Military Tribunal at Nuremberg, who in their judgment called it 'a systematic plan to murder', and so it was. In obedience to it the killing of commissars went on throughout the duration of the Russian campaign along the entire battle front.

With such precision were these instructions carried out during the first three months of the campaign that towards the end of September 1941 one German general protested to OKW that its enforcement was impeding the advance.

It is significant that this protest, like that of General von Falkenhausen in Belgium with regard to the shooting of hostages,[2] was made not for the reason that the order was inhumane or a breach of the laws of war, but solely upon grounds of expediency.

By that time it was common knowledge throughout the Red Army that prisoner-of-war status would not be granted to political commissars who were captured. This knowledge gave them the best of all possible reasons for urging their men to fight it out to the bitter end. Consequently, Russian resistance had stiffened, Germany's advance had slowed down, and their casualties had

[1] Special detachment of the Sicherheitsdienst.
[2] See Chapter IV.

increased. The Commissar Order was therefore, to say the least of it, short-sighted, but Hitler would not rescind it and the slaughter continued.

In the Eleventh German Army, from the time when Field-Marshal von Manstein took command in September 1941 until he relinquished it in November 1942, there is evidence that large numbers of commissars were 'liquidated' in pursuance of this order.

This general does not appear to have made a single written protest against the order, although he has admitted that when he received it he was very indignant as, in his view, it ran counter to all military tradition.

He stated at his trial, however, that he was not concerned with its legality but only with the honour of his troops and that he approached Field-Marshal von Leeb, who was then Commander-in-Chief of the Army Group, and told him that he could not carry out the order. Leeb appeared to share von Manstein's views.

When the field-marshal gave evidence before the International Military Tribunal at Nuremberg he said, with reference to his receipt of the Commissar Order, 'It was the first time I found myself involved in a conflict between my soldierly conception of honour and my duty to obey. . . . In practice the order was not carried out. My Divisional Commanders who had already received the order independently before leaving Germany, shared my view. The troops disliked the order intensely.'

How did the troops know of this order? When issued it was only for distribution down to Commanders-in-Chief of Armies and Air Fleet Chiefs and was to be communicated *orally* to lower formations. It is surely a reasonable inference that if the troops knew its contents it must have reached them, and it can only have done so through their commanders.

The fact remains, and there is evidence to prove it, that large numbers of commissars were murdered by the German Armies in Russia during their advance in 1941 and 1942, and that the numbers of victims only began to diminish later when the Nazis were in retreat and the commissar was no longer the pursued but the pursuer.

Article 6 of the Hague Regulations provides that the State having the custody of prisoners of war whom its troops have captured, may employ their labour, excepting officers, according to their rank and capacity. The work must not be excessive and 'shall have no connection with the operations of war'.

The interpretation of what is meant by prohibited work presents certain difficulties. Under the appropriate Article of the Hague Regulations the prohibition is not confined to dangerous work. The element of danger is prohibited by implication from the necessity for humane treatment but it is not specifically mentioned.

In Article 6, the words 'no connection with the operations of war' are so embracing that in the conditions in which modern wars are conducted, in which almost the whole manpower of the State is harnessed to meet military requirements, it would be difficult to name any work which could properly be said to have no such connection.

Article 31 of the Geneva Convention of 1929, however, which was not binding upon Germany in her war with Russia, provided that the work done by prisoners of war must have no *direct* connection with the operations of war. It is impossible to lay down any precise criterion as to whether work is directly or indirectly connected with military operations, but there can be little or no doubt that the construction of entrenchments in the battle zone is directly connected with the operations of war and that the clearing of minefields generally involves a degree of danger.

In the High Command Trial[1] the Tribunal regarded the employment of prisoners of war by combat troops in the combat areas for the construction of field fortifications as constituting 'dangerous employment under the conditions of modern war'; and further, that the use of prisoners on such work and for mine clearing was clearly prohibited by International Law and constituted a war crime.

In November 1941 the German High Command issued a directive to all Army Groups and Armies in Russia on the subject of 'Prisoner of War Battalions'.

The following is an extract:

The exigencies of war economy demand that a German

[1] Generalfeldmarschall von Leeb and thirteen other former high-ranking officers in the German Army and Navy were tried by a United States Military Tribunal at Nuremberg from 30th December 1947 to 28th October 1948. The charges alleged their participation in numerous crimes against prisoners of war and the civilian population of the occupied territories.

One of the accused, Generaloberst Blaskowitz, committed suicide in prison on 5th February 1948, during the trial. Of the remainder, two were acquitted, whereas eleven were convicted of the counts charging war crimes and crimes against humanity and were sentenced to terms of imprisonment from two years up to life imprisonment.

should, if possible, only be employed when he cannot be replaced by a foreigner or a prisoner of war. A number of duties in the army and in the field to which many German soldiers have so far been tied down can be undertaken by prisoners of war if they are strictly and efficiently incorporated within the military framework. The High Command will, therefore, form prisoner of war battalions.

This directive was implemented by all subordinate formations on the Russian front, who issued orders based on it.

Even prior to the directive from OKW, orders for the formation of labour companies had been promulgated by subordinate commanders. A directive on the subject had been sent out from the Eleventh Army over the signature of the Chief of Staff, Wöhler. It stated that prisoners were valuable labour forces, and it provided for the creation of labour companies so that prisoners could speedily be utilized 'for the military purposes of the troops in the zone of operations'.

Prisoners were sent from the cages to artillery, engineer, and signal units for employment in the forward areas. Infantry regiments were authorized to retain those they needed for labour in the front line from the prisoners they captured. Drivers of horse-drawn supply columns and artillery ammnunition columns were replaced by Soviet prisoners and sent to fighting units.

All this was clearly contrary to the Hague Regulations, but from the very start of the campaign it was the manifest intention of the German High Command to employ Russian prisoners in violation of the laws of war. In July 1941 an order had been issued by OKW that certain classes of prisoners must not be evacuated to Germany but employed in the theatre of operations, and the Eleventh Army's directive of 3rd August 1941, which has been quoted above, was in implementation of that decision.

Within a month, 43,000 such prisoners were being employed in the forward supply services and 13,000 on the construction of defence positions. This work was clearly of a military nature and in the combat zone and Army rear area. They handled military stores, equipment, and ammunition for the forward troops, and constructed defence positions. The Germans themselves described the work as of 'the greatest importance for the conduct of operations'.

That this policy was systematically carried out is beyond question. There are entries in the War Diaries of German formations at all levels regarding the employment of prisoners of war on the construction of fortifications in large numbers throughout 1942 and 1943.

Nor was this all. Prisoners were largely used for the clearing of minefields. An order issued by the German XXXth Corps referring to a directive from OKW reads: 'Stress is laid on the Commander-in-Chief's decision that *in order to spare German blood* only Russian prisoners will be used for detecting and clearing mines, except in action or if danger is imminent. This ruling applies to German mines too. For this purpose, special prisoner of war units will be formed.'

Still more reprehensible was the use of prisoners as guides to precede German troops attacking through enemy minefields. Had they been used in this connection merely to guide the German soldiers through known gaps in the minefields little criticism could be made of the practice, even though it would have been a technical breach of the Hague Regulations. They were not, however, used for that purpose, but as a human screen to set off the mines so as to render them harmless to the advancing Germans. The orders regarding the selection and use of prisoners for mine exploding directed that they should be closely watched so that they would not 'evade the mines by taking longer steps'.

Many instances of brutality towards Russian prisoners of war have been investigated and confirmed. Some were tortured with bars of red-hot iron; their eyes gouged out, their stomachs ripped open; their feet, hands, fingers, ears, and noses hacked off, mutilation more suited to Mau-Mau savagery than German Kultur.

After the Germans had retreated on the Dnieper, the bodies of a Russian battalion commander and his commissar were found. Their arms and legs had been nailed to stakes and on their bodies five-point stars had been cut, apparently with knives; lying near them was the body of another Russian soldier, his feet had been burnt and his ears cut off.

Captured female hospital nurses and orderlies were frequently abused and violated. Large numbers of wounded Russian prisoners near Smolensk were bayonetted or shot where they lay awaiting treatment.

During the winter the German troops and their officers used to divest all prisoners of their warm clothing, including women prisoners, and even stripped the dead, leaving them stark naked.

In the little village of Popovka in the Tula region, German troops drove 140 Red Army prisoners of war into a barn and set fire to it, and near Leningrad the Germans in the course of their retreat used explosive bullets to kill 150 Soviet prisoners of war whom they had first beaten and tortured. They then mutilated the bodies.

In December 1941, again near Smolensk, the Germans executed 200 prisoners of war whom they had marched through the town of Kovdrovo naked and barefoot, shooting on the way any who were too exhausted to take another step, as well as some of the local inhabitants who had offered them bread on their way through the streets.

Orders were also given for the branding of prisoners. 'Soviet prisoners of war will be branded with a distinct and lasting mark. The brand will consist of an acute angle of about 45°, one of its sides being about a centimetre in length, pointing downwards on the left buttock about a hand's breadth away from the rectum. Indian ink will be used for colouring.'

The conditions of the German prisoner-of-war camps in Russia baffle all description. Their occupants were killed by the thousand. Those who were sick never received medical attention. In one camp, near Smolensk, two hundred died daily from starvation, typhus, dysentery, or freezing to death. Emaciated sick prisoners were forced to work in the Smolensk power station and those who collapsed from exhaustion were shot out of hand by their guards. The camp hospital was nothing but a shambles. A doctor who worked there during the early months of 1942, in the depths of the Russian winter, stated that it was unheated, that the wounded lay unbandaged on the bare boards, and their clothing and bedding was covered with pus and excreta.

One prisoner-of-war camp was established in the civil jail at Orel. When the Germans retreated, a Commission of doctors took evidence from some of the medical officers in the camp. The prisoners' daily diet consisted of 200 grammes of bread and a litre of soup made from rotten soya beans and mouldy flour. The flour from which the bread was made was mixed with sawdust. The maximum dietetic value of the daily ration was 700 calories.

On such a diet the prisoners were expected to work eleven or twelve hours a day. They were, of course, unable to do so and many of them died of sheer physical exhaustion. Hundreds of the prisoners in this camp suffered from oedema due entirely to this process of deliberate starvation; but no such diagnosis was allowed in the camp. The swelling was always put down to heart or kidney trouble, and the very mention of 'hunger oedema' was forbidden.

Fuel and fresh water were completely lacking, and the camp was infested with vermin. Mortality assumed mass proportions and at least three thousand died solely of malnutrition. Prisoners died at the rate of six a day, and the living slept with the dead.

Nor was this camp worse than any others, for in the early months of the campaign the German High Command cared not whether their Russian prisoners lived or died. It was only later, when their importance as slave labour was realized, that greater efforts were made to keep them alive.

The bare minimum ration laid down by OKW for a prisoner of war for a period of twenty-eight days does not appear to have been excessive. This scale was as follows: bread 6 kilos, meat 400 grammes, fat 400 grammes, sugar 600 grammes. For prisoners doing especially strenuous work the scale was slightly higher.

The prisoners were also deprived of their clothing. An administrative order issued by one German Division headed 'Situation with Respect to Clothing' laid down that all boots which were serviceable should be removed from Russian prisoners without hesitation. Half-starved, stripped of their clothing, and left to live out in the open in the freezing cold of the winter of 1941/42, it is small wonder that they died like flies.

But it was not solely from starvation, neglect, and exposure that they perished. On 24th July 1941, a month after Hitler's armies had invaded Soviet territory, the German High Command issued a basic order on the treatment of Russian prisoners of war in the theatre of operations. It dealt with their screening, collection, and disposal. For this purpose they were to be divided into five categories, one of which was described as consisting of 'elements which are politically insupportable; suspects, commissars, and agitators'. All such were to be dealt with in accordance with 'Special Instructions'. This meant that the Sonderkommandas[1] of Gestapo and SD which were attached to each prisoner-of-war camp selected these 'politically insupportable elements'. In the phraseology of the order itself, these SD units were to operate 'as unobtrusively as possible', and the liquidations were to be carried out without delay at such distances from transit camps and villages as would ensure their not becoming known to other prisoners of war or to the civilian population.

---

[1] Special Detachments.

Such were the instructions; but in practice the prisoners were nearly all sent off to concentration camps. For their last journey they were packed into closed trucks like so many carcases, often without food and water, and shut in for three or four days.

On one occasion, when a prisoner-of-war train, consisting of fifty trucks, arrived at its destination and the trucks were opened, the stench of dead bodies was overpowering; half the prisoners were dead, many on the point of death, and the few who still had the strength to make a dash for water were shot by the guards. Another train full of prisoners, made up of thirty trucks, at the end of its journey was found to contain not a single living soul, and 1,500 dead bodies were unloaded from it.

CHAPTER III

WAR CRIMES ON THE HIGH SEAS

AT the outbreak of war between England and Germany in 1939, it had been settled practice for over three centuries that an enemy merchant ship might be captured by a warship of the other belligerent and brought into port so that a Prize Court could, in appropriate circumstances, condemn the vessel and its cargo.

A neutral vessel might likewise be stopped and searched for contraband, and if found with contraband it was subject to seizure and confiscation by the Prize Court.

It was also established international practice, amounting to a usage of war, that save in the case of vessels sailing in previously declared 'war zones' the destruction of a vessel, if permissible at all, could only take place after capture except where visit and search was forcibly resisted.

It was presumed that when ships were sailing in convoy they were forcibly resisting visit and search by the enemy's warships, and they were, therefore, liable to be sunk on sight: but no merchant ship which was not sailing in convoy might be sunk without being warned to stop and submit to visit and search.

The breaches of this well-established international maritime law were so frequent in the First World War that it was considered most desirable that the position should be restated, and this was done in Article 22 of the London Naval Treaty of 1930 between the United States, Great Britain, France, Italy and Japan.[1]

Article 22 provided that:

(I) In action with regard to merchant ships, submarines must conform to the rules of International Law to which surface vessels are subject.

(II) In particular, except in the case of persistent refusal to stop on being duly summoned, or of active resistance to visit and search, a warship, whether surface vessel or

---

[1] This brief statement of the legal position in regard to the sinking of enemy merchant vessels in war is paraphrased from a Foreign Office memorandum of 8th October 1940

submarine, may not sink or render incapable of navigation a merchant vessel without having first placed passengers, crew, and ship's papers in a place of safety. For this purpose the ship's boats are *not* regarded as a place of safety, unless the safety of the passengers and crew is assured in the existing sea and weather conditions by the proximity of land or the presence of another vessel which is in a position to take them on board.

These rules were clear and unequivocal and there could be no valid excuse for not understanding them, but it was manifest within a few hours of the outbreak of the Second World War that the Germans intended entirely to disregard them, for on the evening of 3rd September 1939, SS *Athenia*, outward bound for America, was sent to the bottom by a German U-boat with the loss of about one hundred lives.

The Nazi Party paper, the *Völkische Beobachter*, in its issue of 23rd October 1939 carried this glaring headline:'Churchill sank the *Athenia*.'

Below a picture of the ship the following appeared:

The above picture shows the proud *Athenia*, the ocean giant which was sunk by Churchill's crime. One can clearly see the big radio equipment on board the ship. But nowhere was an SOS heard from her. Why was the *Athenia* silent? Because her captain was not allowed to tell the world anything. He very prudently refrained from telling the world that Winston Churchill attempted to sink the ship through the explosion of a time bomb. He knew it well but he had to keep silent. Nearly 1,500 people would have lost their lives if Churchill's original plan had turned out as the criminal wanted. Yes, he longingly hoped that the 100 Americans on board the ship would find death in the waves so that the anger of the American people, who were deceived by him, should be directed against Germany as the presumed author of the deed. It was fortunate that the majority escaped the fate intended for them by Churchill. Our picture on the right shows two wounded passengers. They were rescued by the freighter *City of Flint* and, as can be seen here, turned over to the American coastguard vessel *Gibb* for further medical treatment. They are an unspoken accusation against the criminal Churchill. Both they and the shades of those who lost their lives call him before the tribunal of the world and ask the British people: 'How long will the office, one of the richest in tradition known to Great Britain's history, be held by a murderer.'

Fine words or humbug and bravado from the nation which has since had to answer at the bar of history for a dozen million murders.

The facts were very different. SS *Athenia* was torpedoed during the late hours of the evening of 3rd September 1939 by the U-30, commanded by Oberleutnant Lemp, who was killed in action later in the war. No warning shot was fired. The U-boat waited until darkness before surfacing.One of the crew who had witnessed the sinking was made to sign a declaration under oath that he would 'erase from his memory all the happenings of the day'.

As soon as the sinking became known, Admiral Raeder and the German Admiralty officially denied that any U-boat could have been in the area concerned at the time of the attack.

Admirals Raeder and Dönitz both knew in the middle of September 1939 that it was Oberleutnant Lemp's submarine which had sunk the *Athenia*, for Lemp himself reported the occurrence. An attempt was then made to make it appear that the submarine commander had mistaken the ship for an armed merchant cruiser on patrol. Dönitz said that he had told all his submarine officers to keep a sharp look out for such vessels but had not told them what type of vessel might be so used or mentioned the names of particular ships.

It is most improbable that there was any truth in the suggestion that the U-30 had sunk the *Athenia* in mistake for a merchant cruiser, for an order of 22nd September 1939 had laid it down that in all cases the practice was to be that the 'sinking of a merchant ship must be justified in the War Diary as due to possible confusion with a warship or an auxiliary cruiser'. This directive was issued five days before U-30 returned to base at Wilhelmshaven, so that it was clearly in Dönitz's mind to make this excuse at least five days before he had the opportunity to question Lemp about the incident.

It was also significant that no disciplinary action was taken against the commander. OKM[1] 'considered that a court martial was unnecessary as the captain had acted in good faith'. In any event, Dönitz himself took the view that a court martial would only acquit Lemp and 'would entail unnecessary publicity and *loss of time*'.

[1] Oberkommando der Marine—Navy GHQ

In the War Diary kept by the Chief of the Submarine Command the following entry was made for 27th September 1939: 'U-30 comes in. She had sunk: SS *Blairlogies* and SS *Fanad*.' Furthermore, U-30's log book was forged. The first page was removed and a new one substituted. The forgery was not as carefully done as German thoroughness would have led one to expect. Whereas the dates on the original pages of the log were all in Roman numerals, those on the first and substituted pages were in Arabic figures. All reference to the sinking of SS *Athenia* was duly omitted from the forged page.

The *Athenia* was sunk less than twelve hours after the declaration of war between Germany and Great Britain. The Germans had not waited long to let the world know that she intended to disregard the Protocol of 1936[1] and revert to her piratical practices of the First World War.

But there was worse to come.

At the commencement of the war Dönitz was commander of the U-boat arm of the German Navy. This was the principal weapon of the fleet, and millions of tons of Allied and neutral shipping were sunk by his submarines during the course of the war.

With Dönitz in control, it was not reasonable to expect that the U-boat commanders would be over-scrupulous in their methods of submarine warfare. He was the most ardent of Nazis and was described in the 1944 edition of the Diary for the German Navy as always 'a leader and inspiration to all the forces under him'. His public utterances prove his fanaticism, and that he successfully indoctrinated his subordinates with his own beliefs is demonstrated by the ruthless policy of unrestricted submarine warfare carried out by them throughout the war.

A memorandum prepared in October 1939 by Admiral Raeder and the German naval war staff entitled *Possibilities of Future Naval Warfare* clearly defined the course set for naval strategy. After stating that the most ruthless methods would have to be adopted in the attack on British sea communications and that it was desirable to base all action taken upon existing International Law, the document went on to point out that any other measures which were 'considered necessary from a military point of view,

[1] When the London Naval Treaty was allowed to expire on 31st December 1936, Article 22 remained binding on the Parties by virtue of Article 23. Nevertheless, in London on 6th November 1936, the United States and Great Britain (including the Dominions and India) signed a Protocol which incorporated verbatim the provisions of Article 22. Provision was made for the accession of other States. Germany acceded in 1936 and Soviet Russia in 1937.

provided a decisive success can be expected from them, will have to be carried out even if they are not covered by *existing* International Law. In principle, therefore, enemy resistance should be based on some legal conception even if that entails the creation of a new code of naval warfare.' The end, once again, was clearly to justify the means.

The course of submarine warfare against Allied and neutral merchant shipping followed the ruthless pattern set by Admiral Raeder's observations. From the first, the merchant ships of belligerents and neutrals were sunk without warning and apart from some exceptions no attempt was made to rescue passengers or crew. Later in the war, when a system of proclaiming operational danger Zones had come into force, submarine attacks without warning still continued outside those zones.

The first sinking of a neutral merchantman by a German submarine without warning was on 30th September 1939, when the Danish steamer *Vendia*, bound for the Clyde in ballast, was torpedoed. Two perfunctory warning shots were fired by the U-boat but these were followed almost immediately by the firing of the torpedo which sank her, although the ship's captain had already signalled that he would comply with the submarine's orders regarding search, but had not had time to abandon ship.

Before the end of November the sinking of neutral shipping in similar circumstances had become the general practice. On 12th November a Norwegian ship named *Arne Kjode* was sunk by a German submarine in the North Sea. No warning of any kind was given. The vessel was a tanker and was proceeding from one neutral port to another. The captain and four of his crew were picked up by another vessel after spending many hours in open boats. The submarine commander himself made no attempt to rescue the Norwegian crew.

In January 1941 Hitler announced that every ship whether in convoy or nor 'which appears before our torpedo tubes' would be torpedoed. From the threats which preceded this announcement it would appear to have been intended principally for American consumption, and when it aroused much condemnation on the other side of the Atlantic the Germans contended that the order referred only to ships which entered the 'war zone'.

That a ship was outside the war zone was no guarantee of immunity from unlawful attack, as the sinking of the *City of Benares* on 17th September 1940 clearly proved. This liner of 11,000 tons carried about four hundred people, passengers and crew, of whom

65

nearly a hundred were children. She was sunk outside the 'war zone' without warning, and two hundred and fifty-eight passengers, including seventy-seven children, lost their lives. The attack took place in shocking weather, hail and rain squalls and a big sea running. She was torpedoed at about 10 p.m. and in the confusion due to darkness and the gale four of the ship's boats capsized on being launched, and others were swamped later by heavy seas. Many of the children died from exposure.

The toll of innocent victims of German 'ruthlessness' mounted throughout that first winter, crews and passengers drifting for days in open boats in the teeth of an Atlantic gale; clinging to rafts until they dropped off into the water one by one, their fingers too numb with cold to grip the rail longer; crews machine-gunned from the submarine while still lowering the boats, or afterwards when drifting aimlessly about on the oily sea.

Was this, then, the 'ruthless' new code of naval warfare 'born of military necessity' which Admiral Raeder mentioned in his 1939 memorandum? Those whose memories could go back to the grim days of 1917 knew that at least it was no novelty.

The torpedoing of the British steamer *Sheaf Mead* on 27th May 1940 with the loss of thirty-one of her crew was characterized by the extraordinarily callous behaviour of the submarine commander towards many of the crew who, after their ship had sunk, were clinging to spars and upturned boats.

The commander's name was Kapitänleutnant Ochrn and his vessel U-37. The chief engineer of the *Sheaf Mead* gave this description of him: 'Young, about twenty-eight, well built. He had fair hair and was rather good-looking. He spoke good English with a very deep voice.'

From the following entry in this young man's diary[1] on the date in question he appears to have enjoyed himself:

27th May.

1252 Steamship sighted, steering west, about 5,000 tons. Speed 10 knots. Start tracking.

1444 Boat now in position ahead of steamer. Dived. Swell hinders depth-keeping and observation . . . at full speed, keeping abreast . . . only a short time now before we fire . . . the distance is narrowing. Tube ready—shall I or not? The gunnery crews are also prepared. . . . Hurrah! a gun at the stern, an AA gun perhaps. FIRE! It cannot

---

[1] This was found in his possession when he was later taken prisoner.

miss. Periscope up, observation. . . . Hit scored aft 30. Distance 320 metres. Stern sinks considerably. The crew jump into the boats. Her bow rises. I have a look round.

1554   Surface—stern under water. Bows rise higher. The boats are now on the water. Lucky for them. A picture of complete order. The bows rear up quite high. Two men appear from somewhere in the forward part of the ship and rush along the deck towards the stern. The stern disappears. A boat capsizes. Then a boiler explosion, two men fly through the air limbs outstretched . . . then all is over. A large mass of wreckage floats up. We approach to identify the ship. The crew have saved themselves on wreckage and capsized boats. We fish out a buoy, no name on it.

1648   I ask a man on the raft. He says, hardly turning his head, 'Nix name'. A young boy in the water calls, 'Help, help please'. The others are very composed. They look damp and tired. An expression of cold hatred is on their faces . . . On to the old course.

Having sunk his quarry, the submarine commander cruised round the area for half an hour. Two men stood on deck with boat-hooks to keep off the ship's boats. The crew, too, remained on deck taking photographs of the survivors but said nothing. The submarine later submerged without offering the survivors any assistance.[1]

In January 1940 the High Command of the Armed Forces had issued a directive to the effect that the Navy was henceforth authorized to sink by U-boats all vessels in waters near enemy coasts in which the use of mines was possible, and U-boat commanders were told to adapt their behaviour and employment of weapons to give the impression that the hits were caused by mines.

Instructions regarding the abandonment of the crews of sunk merchant ships first appear to have been issued in May 1940.

[1] But some German submarine commanders at first behaved very differently. In one case the crew of a British trawler had been ordered to take to their boats as their ship was to be sunk. When the commander saw its condition he said, 'Thirteen men in that boat! Fancy sending a ship to sea with a boat like that. You English are no good!' The skipper of the trawler was then told to re-embark his crew and make for a home port with all speed, and was presented with a bottle of German gin with the 'commander's compliments'.

67

Standing Order No. 154 of the U-boat Command contained the following:

> Do not pick up men or take them with you. Do not worry about the merchant ship's boats. Weather conditions and distance from land play no part.[1] Have care only for your own ship . . . we must be harsh in war. *The enemy began the war in order to destroy us, so nothing else matters.*

When the United States of America entered the war and Germany was forced to face the fact that there would now be a large increase in tonnage available for immediate use and an almost inexhaustible ship-building capacity, more drastic orders still were given. U-boat commanders were enjoined not merely to abstain from rescuing crews but to exterminate them.

Less than a month after the Japanese attack on Pearl Harbour, Hitler had an opportunity of explaining this new phase to their ambassador in Berlin. He said that no matter how many ships the Americans built, lack of suitable crews would be their main problem and that it was his intention that *all* merchant ships would be sunk without warning. Germany was fighting for her very existence and humane feelings could not enter into it. He would give the order that U-boats were to surface after torpedoing and shoot up the lifeboats. According to the shorthand note which was taken of this exchange of views, 'Ambassador Oshima heartily agreed with the Führer's comments and said that the Japanese too were forced to adopt these methods'.

In the following September a 'Top-Secret' order was issued to all U-boat commanders from Dönitz's headquarters:

> No attempt of any kind must be made at rescuing the crews of ships sunk. This includes picking up persons in the water and putting them in lifeboats, righting capsized lifeboats, and handing over food and water. Rescue runs counter to the rudimentary demands of warfare for the destruction of enemy ships and crews. . . . Be harsh, bearing in mind that the enemy takes no regard of women and children in his bombing attacks on German cities.

On the same day as the above order was despatched this entry appeared in Dönitz's War Diary:

---

[1] It will be remembered that the Naval Protocol of 1936 provided that ship's boats are not regarded as a place of safety, unless the safety of the passengers and crew *is assured in the existing sea and weather conditions by the proximity of land*, or the presence of another vessel which is in a position to take them on board.

The attention of all commanding officers is *again* drawn to the fact that all efforts to rescue members of the crews of ships which have been sunk contradict the most primitive demands for the conduct of warfare for annihilating ships *and their crews*.

The commander of the 5th U-boat Flotilla at Kiel,[1] Heinz Möhle, considered that the order was ambiguous and sought clarification from a senior officer on Dönitz's staff. The intention of the order was explained to him by two examples. The first concerned a U-boat in the Bay of Biscay. It was on patrol when it sighted a rubber dinghy carrying the survivors of a British plane. As the submarine was on an outward mission, fully stocked and provisioned, there could be no question of taking the aircraft crew on board. The U-boat commander therefore gave the dinghy a wide berth and continued his patrol. When he reported the circumstances on his return to base he was told that as he was unable to bring the survivors back for interrogation he should have sent them to the bottom so that they 'would not live to fight another day'.

The second example given was this: that during the first month of the U-boat campaign against the United States shipping a very considerable tonnage had been sunk in shallow waters off the American coast and the majority of the crews were rescued because of the proximity of land. The view at Dönitz's headquarters was that this was most regrettable.

The International Military Tribunal at Nuremberg held that the 'Laconia Order', as it was called, did not deliberately order the killing of survivors of vessels sunk by U-boat attack, but they said in their judgment that its terms were undoubtedly ambiguous and deserved the highest censure.

When it was passed on by Möhle, however, while briefing U-boat commanders prior to their proceeding on a mission, he read them the order without comment and amplified it by giving the two examples just mentioned. The commanders could then have only been under the impression that the policy of the Naval High Command was to kill ships' crews. Perhaps to salve his conscience a little, Möhle then used to say, 'U-boat Command cannot give you such an order officially: everybody must handle this matter according to his own conscience'.

[1] Korvettenkapitän Karl Heinz Möhle. This officer was tried by a British Military Court at Hamburg in October 1946 upon a charge alleging that he passed these orders on to his U-boat commanders. He was found guilty and sentenced to five years' imprisonment.

The Germans have always contended that the sole object of the 'Laconia Order' was to prevent submarine commanders from hazarding their craft by standing by to rescue the survivors of their attacks. Had that been so, it could have been effected by inviting their attention to Standing Order 154.[1] Furthermore, in that event the order would not have left the matter in doubt, for in drafting such instructions special attention is given to the possibility of their capture by the enemy.

What were really the Grossadmiral's views on the subject at the time appear from a speech which he made early in October 1942 when he inspected the 2nd U-boat Training Division.[2] Addressing the officers then attending courses, he told them that U-boat successes had declined. After promising the students that there would shortly be an improvement, he said that the Allies were having great difficulty in manning their ships. Allied seamen considered the route across the Atlantic dangerous because German submarines were still sinking their ships in large numbers. Many of these sailors had been torpedoed more than once and were reluctant to go to sea again. Dönitz then said that he could not understand how German U-boats could still rescue the crews of merchant ships they had sunk, thereby endangering their own ships. By so doing they were working for the enemy, since the rescued crews would sail again in new ships. They had now reached a stage in the war, he continued, *in which total war had to be waged also at sea. The crews of ships like the ships themselves were a target for U-boats.*

The students who listened to that speech gathered that total war had now to be waged against both the ships and their crews—and who shall blame them? The decision of the Nuremberg Tribunal upon the allegation of the prosecution that the Grossadmiral deliberately ordered the killing of survivors of torpedoed vessels certainly did him no injustice.

Six months after the issue of the 'Laconia Order', SS *Peleus*, a Greek ship chartered by the British Ministry of War Transport, was sunk by U-852, commanded by Kapitänleutnant Heinz Eck, in the Atlantic Ocean.

SS *Peleus* was bound in ballast for the Plate, having left Freetown on 8th March, and by the evening of 13th March 1943

---

[1] See above, page 68.
[2] Evidence of this speech was given at the Nuremberg Trial of Major War Criminals by former midshipman Peter Josef Heisig.

she was steaming west just south of the Equator and about 300 miles from the nearest point on the African coast. She had a crew of thirty-five, most of whom were Greeks. There were only three survivors.

About 5.50 p.m. two torpedoes were observed on the port bow, both of which struck the ship, and she sank in under three minutes. Most of the crew managed, nevertheless, to get clear and were clinging to wreckage and rafts that were floating about.

The submarine then surfaced and closed up to one of the *Peleus*'s boats in which there were three survivors, and one of the submarine's officers who spoke English was ordered by his captain to find out the name of the ship they had torpedoed. One of the survivors was then brought aboard U-852 and supplied the required information: the name of the ship, the captain's name, cargo, port of sailing and destination, and whethether there were any other vessels in the vicinity.

The officer detailed to get this information returned to the conning-tower to report to the commander, who then informed him that they had decided to eliminate all traces of the sinking by killing the survivors.

Meanwhile, the Third Officer of SS *Peleus*, who had been brought on board the submarine, was deprived of his lifebelt and put back on the raft from which he had been taken.

Eck then opened fire on the rafts with machine-guns, and the crew threw hand grenades among the survivors. As far as is known, all but three were killed. These men remained on their rafts in the open for twenty-five days until picked up by a Portuguese vessel. They have all sworn affidavits giving their experiences on this occasion.

One of them, a Greek named Liossis, stated that he was on watch when he saw the tracks of two torpedoes approaching the port beam, and at once ordered the helmsman to comb[1] their tracks.

Nevertheless both torpedoes struck the *Peleus* and Liossis found himself in the water and swam around until he found some wreckage to which he could cling. He was soon joined by another Greek member of the crew and together they made for a raft they could see ahead. After a short while the submarine surfaced, circled round the wreckage, and hailed the Third Officer's raft. He was ordered aboard and questioned as described above.

[1] i.e. to turn the ship to a course as near as possible parallel to the after torpedo. See page 12 of *The Peleus Trial* by J. Cameron (William Hodge and Co.).

Meanwhile, Liossis lashed his raft to another on which were more of the shipwrecked crew, and the submarine then appeared and hailed them to go nearer. Thinking that perhaps they were going to be picked up, Liossis and his companions approached the German U-boat, which suddenly opened fire on them with a machine-gun. One of his friends was hit in several places and the rafts were riddled with bullet holes but did not sink. The Germans then threw hand grenades. The submarine kept on firing with machine-guns and throwing grenades at the wreckage for a long time, and just before dawn moved off.

The commander of U-852 at his trial[1] said that he decided to sink the rafts by machine-gun fire and did so, but he swore that at that time there were no members of the *Peleus's* crew to be seen and that he never gave the order to fire at the survivors. He agreed that his Chief Engineer remonstrated about the decision to destroy all traces and that because of it 'the possibility of saving lives disappeared' as it was against his orders to take survivors on board. He said that he had received the 'Laconia Order'.

There is little doubt that unlike the commander of U-156, Korvettenkapitän Hartenstein, who six months earlier had sunk SS *Laconia*, Kapitänleutnant Eck would have received the congratulations of the Grossadmiral on his return to base for his realistic ruthlessness. But it was not to be. The patrol on which he sunk the *Peleus* was his first and last as a U-boat commander and instead of returning to Kiel at its termination to receive the thanks of his admiral and his Führer he beached his vessel on the coast of Somaliland after an air attack on 2nd May 1944 and was made a prisoner of war.

The commander who had sunk the *Laconia*, however, rescued a number of survivors and received, for his consideration, a mild reprimand for having risked the loss of his vessel. As the Grossadmiral wrote in his report on Hartenstein's operation, 'the incident is proof again of what a handicap humane feelings towards an enemy may prove to be'.

On 5th July 1944 a steam trawler, the *Noreen Mary*, was sunk by U-247 eighteen miles west of Cape Wrath. She was at the time engaged in fishing on the west coast of Scotland and had on board a catch of 325 boxes of fish. She had left Ayr four days earlier and steamed to the fishing grounds off the Butt of Lewis.

[1] The commander and four members of his crew were tried by a British Military Court in Hamburg in October 1945 for being concerned in the killing of members of the crew of the *Peleus* by firing and throwing grenades at them. All were found guilty of the charge, and the commander and three others sentenced to suffer death by shooting.

At about 8 p.m. a deckhand named James MacAlister saw two torpedoes pass down on their port side, about eight feet apart and ten feet from the ship's side. At the same moment he saw a conning-tower about 150 yards away and dead astern.

MacAlister called all hands on deck, but by the time they arrived the submarine had submerged and the mate refused to believe MacAlister's story.

About an hour later, however, the U-boat surfaced on their starboard beam and at once opened fire on the *Noreen Mary* with a machine-gun. The trawler was making three knots and the weather was fine with good visibility and the sea smooth. She immediately increased speed to ten knots, but the submarine gave chase and continued firing. The first few rounds killed three of the crew, including the skipper.

The U-boat then opened fire with a heavier gun which was mounted on the conning-tower; the first shell hit the boiler, stopping the ship and enveloping her in steam.

The remainder of the crew, seven in number, had now taken cover, but three others were soon killed and the submarine circled round ahead of the trawler and passed down her port side firing both guns.

MacAlister and the mate tried to launch the boat, but the latter was killed during the attempt and the former then went below to shelter in the pantry, which was under the water-line. The trawler now had a big list to port and at 10.10 p.m. capsized and sank. The four survivors were thrown into the sea. MacAlister swam around until he came across the upturned bow of the lifeboat, on to which he was able to climb.

The submarine had still not submerged and steamed in the direction of the upturned lifeboat, firing a short burst at it. When she was about seventy yards away, MacAlister slipped off into the water and remained there until the U-boat ceased firing and submerged.

About 5 a.m. the next day, HMT *Lady Madeleine* picked up the only two survivors, MacAlister and the trawler's Second Engineer. Of the other eight members of the *Noreen Mary*'s crew, six had been killed and two were missing, believed drowned.[1]

U-247 was one of the latest German submarines and was on her first operational patrol. She carried two big guns, one on her after-deck, the other on the fore part of her conning-tower, and a

[1] This account of the action was taken from a Deposition sworn by James MacAlister before a Notary Public in Edinburgh on 21st December 1945.

small gun which looked like an Oerlikon was mounted on the fore-deck. The *Noreen Mary* was an ordinary fishing trawler going about her lawful occasions, but like all other small ships during the war she carried a Lewis gun on an anti-aircraft mounting to protect her from the attentions of German planes who were prepared to attack all and everything.

This unlawful attack was reported in the 'Commander's War Diary' as follows:

1943   Fishing vessel. Two-fan from tubes I and IV. Vessel turns away to starboard shortly after the shot and takes up a position of 180°. The sea being as smooth as a mill-pond, she probably saw the tracks.

2055   Surfaced. Fishing vessels. Engaged the nearest. She stops after three minutes. T3a sinking shot fired from tube III at the *Noreen Mary* as she lay stopped. A miss, misfired, did not clear.

2151   Sunk by flak with shots into her side. Sunk by the stern.

The Chief of the Operational Division BDU seems to have been well pleased with this gallant action, for he made the following comment on the entry in the War Diary: 'The sinking by flak of the fishing vessel in this area testifies to *great offensive spirit and verve*. . . . Operation well carried out in difficult conditions.' In fact, it was murder most foul.

From the first day of the war until the last, this murder on the high seas went on night and day. As in the First World War, Germany carried on unrestricted submarine warfare against both belligerents and neutrals in disregard of the Protocol of 1936 and the usage and custom of the civilized world.

CHAPTER IV

ILL-TREATMENT AND MURDER OF THE CIVILIAN POPULATION IN OCCUPIED TERRITORY

IN former times belligerents had complete power over territory under their occupation. They could devastate it, kill the inhabitants or carry them away into captivity, and appropriate all property. Great changes took place, however, during the eighteenth and nineteenth centuries, culminating in the 'Hague Regulations Respecting the Laws and Customs of War on Land' which were adopted by the Hague Peace Conference of 1907.

Article 46 of these Regulations provided that 'family honour and rights, the lives of persons and private property, as well as religious convictions and practices must be respected'. Throughout the territories occupied by the Germans during the Second World War there were wholesale breaches of that Article.

Millions were deported from their homes as slaves; thousands of hostages and reprisal prisoners were put to death; hundreds of unjustified reprisals were carried out; scores of towns and villages were razed to the ground; thousands of fertile acres were ruined by the scorched earth policy; millions of Jews were exterminated; hundreds of thousands of innocent civilians were killed in mass executions; ghettos were destroyed and their occupants killed or carried off to concentration and annihilation camps. All raw materials, scrap, and machinery were taken away and used for the German economy; there was wholesale seizure of art treasures, furniture, and textiles from all the invaded territories.

Addressing a conference of German occupation authorities in August 1942, Göring said: 'God knows you are not sent there to work for the welfare of the people in your charge but to get the utmost out of them so that the German people can live. That is what I expect of your exertions. This everlasting concern about foreign people must cease now, once and for all. It makes no difference to me if your people starve.'

The deliberate policy of the occupation authorities was to

terrorize the inhabitants and ruthlessly exploit everything and everybody for the German war effort.

Although in certain circumstances the taking of hostages was, before the Geneva Convention of 1949, permitted under International Law, their subsequent execution, except for capital offences of which they had been properly convicted, was clearly forbidden by Article 50 of the Hague Convention of 1907, which reads: 'No collective penalty, pecuniary or other, can be decreed against populations for individual acts for which they cannot be held jointly responsible.'

Lord Wright, discussing this question in an article in *The British Year Book of International Law* in 1948, wrote: 'My own settled opinion, based both on principle and on authority, is that the killing of hostages (which includes reprisal prisoners) is contrary to the law of war, and that it is not permissible in any circumstances, and that it is murder.'

Furthermore, this would appear to have been established as long ago as the seventeenth century by no less an authority than Grotius in his *De Jure Belli ac Pacis*, and Lord Wright in his article quoted this passage:

> Hostages should not be put to death unless they themselves have done wrong . . . in former times it was commonly believed that each person had over his own life the same right which he had over other things that came under ownership, and that this right by tacit or express consent passed from individuals to the State. It is then not to be wondered at if we read that hostages who were personally guiltless were put to death for a wrong done by their State. But now that a truer knowledge has taught us that lordship over life is reserved for God, it follows that no one by his individual consent can give to another a right over life, either his own life or that of a fellow-citizen.

The practice of shooting hostages and reprisal prisoners[1] was habitually carried out by the German authorities in every country under military occupation.

After the Armistice was concluded with France in June 1940,

---

[1] There is a distinction, though of no interest to the victim, between hostages and reprisal prisoners. The former are taken into custody in order to guarantee with their lives the future good conduct of the community to which they belong; the latter are arrested after some incident has taken place, and are put to death by way of retaliation or reprisal. In either event innocent victims forfeit their lives for offences committed by others.

the attitude of the German occupation authorities was at first conciliatory. They hoped to draw the French into their war against England and later the United States of America, and tried by every means in their power to gain the maximum co-operation and collaboration of the French people.

It was but a pious hope, and this mild approach was doomed to end in failure. With increased resistance from the French, the mask of sweet reasonableness was quickly dropped, it had never been more than a sham and a shallow pretence, and the Nazis reverted to type. The execution of hostages at Dinant, at Laon, and at Senlis, which in 1914 had shocked the civilized world, paled into insignificance besides the massacres at Oradour-sur-Glâne, at Lidice, in the Balkans, in Warsaw, in Russia and the Ardeatine Caves.

Before the end of 1940 the red posters edged with black were common sights in France, pasted on the walls of Paris and the towns and villages throughout the country. These announced the first shootings of hostages carried out in reprisal for anti-German incidents.

In September 1940 the Commander-in-Chief of the German Army in France had defined hostages as 'inhabitants of a country who guarantee with their lives the impeccable attitude of the population. The responsibility for their fate is thus placed in the hands of their compatriots. Therefore the population must be publicly threatened that hostages will be held responsible for hostile acts of individuals.'

The responsibility of the innocent for offences committed by others was the official policy and attitude of the occupation authorities, and steps were taken by them to ensure that these threats were carried into execution. 'Threats which cannot be realized,' the order stated, 'give the impression of weakness.'

This doctrine was given the highest official approval in September 1941 by the issue of a General Order over Keitel's signature. It remained in force throughout the war and was addressed to the German military commanders in France, Belgium, Norway, Holland, Denmark, the Ukraine, Serbia, Salonika, Greece, and Crete, all of which were under German occupation.

In its application to Russia it ordered that 50 to 100 Communists were to be put to death for each German soldier killed. This order was confirmed later in the same month, and adapted by Stülpnagel in his famous order known in France as the 'Hostages Code'.

This order is of great importance as it clearly demonstrates the attitude of the German military command in France towards the hostages policy. The following are extracts from it:

I. On 22nd August 1941 I issued the following announcement: 'On the morning of 21st August 1941, a member of the German Armed Forces was killed in Paris as a result of a murderous attack.' I therefore order that:

(1) All Frenchmen held in custody of any kind by the German authorities, or on behalf of German authorities in France, are to be considered as hostages from 23rd August.

(2) If any further incident occurs, a number of these hostages are to be shot, to be determined according to the gravity of the attempt.

III. On the basis of my notification of 22nd August 1941 and of my order of 19th September 1941 (which was set out in paragraph II), the following groups of persons are therefore hostages. (Six such groups were then set out.)

VI. *Lists of hostages.*

If an incident occurs which according to my announcement of 21st August 1941 necessitates the shooting of hostages, the execution must immediately follow the order. The district commanders, therefore, must select from the total number of hostages in their own districts, those who from a practical point of view may be considered for execution and enter them on a list of hostages. These lists will serve as a basis for the proposals submitted to me in the case of an execution.

According to the observations made so far, the perpetrators of those outrages originate from communist or anarchist terror gangs. The District Commanders are, therefore, to select from those in detention those persons who, because of their communist or anarchist views in the past or their positions in such organizations, are most suitable for execution. In making the selection it should be borne in mind that the better hostages to be shot are known, the greater will be the deterrent effect on the perpetrators themselves, and on those persons who in France or abroad, bear the moral responsibility for acts of terror and sabotage.

A list of hostages is to be prepared from prisoners with De Gaullist sympathies.

A pool of hostages was also established.

The lists must contain about 150 for each district and about 400 for the Greater Paris Command. The district chiefs should always record on their lists those persons who had their last residence or permanent domicile in their own districts, because persons to be executed should, as far as possible, be taken from the district where the act was committed.

Instructions were then given for the actual execution, and the final paragraph ends thus:

When the bodies are buried, the burial of a large number in a common grave in the same cemetery is to be avoided, in order not to create places of pilgrimage which, now or later, might form centres for anti-German propaganda. If necessary, therefore, burials must be carried out in various places.

Similar orders were issued in Belgium by General von Falken-hausen, in Holland by Gauleiter Seyss-Inquart, and in Norway by General von Falkenhorst.

The effects of this policy were not always those which its authors had expected and from Belgium Falkenhausen sent this letter to Keitel criticizing the principle, not for humanitarian reasons but on the grounds of expediency:

Enclosed is a list of the shootings of hostages which have taken place up till now in my area and the incidents on account of which these shootings took place. In a great number of cases, particularly in the most serious, the culprits were later appre-hended and sentenced.

The result is undoubtedly very unsatisfactory. The effect is not so much deterrent as destructive of the feeling of the population for right and security: the cleft between the people influenced by Communism and the remainder of the population is being bridged: all circles are becoming filled with a feeling of hatred towards the occupying forces and effective inciting material is given to enemy propaganda.

Signed: von Falkenhausen.

Falkenhausen complained more than once to OKW about the deplorable effects of Keitel's order. He pointed out again that in several cases the saboteurs were discovered after the innocent hostages had been shot, and that the real culprits often did not belong to the same circles as the executed hostages. This led to resentment on the part of sections of the population who had previously shown a passive attitude.

Towards the end of 1942 a further warning reached Keitel from the Wehrmacht Commander in Holland. After reporting the shooting of a number of very distinguished hostages in Rotterdam, he stated that public opinion had been greatly affected. Nothing which the Germans had done since the occupation began, and there were few enormities which they had not committed, had created such an impression or aroused so much resentment. Many letters had been received at the German Headquarters, some signed and some anonymous. The report ended: 'In short, such disapproval even in the ranks of the very few really pro-German Dutch had never before been experienced, or so much hatred felt.'

But Keitel cared for none of these things. His order of 16th September 1941 was never countermanded throughout the whole war, and over 29,000 hostages were executed in France alone.

From time to time appeals were made by the German occupation authorities to the general population to desist from resistance, and to potential French traitors and informers to denounce their loyal compatriots.

The following is the text of such an appeal which was issued in September 1941:

I recognize that the great majority of the population is conscious of its duty, which is to help the authorities in their unremitting effort to maintain calm and order in the country in the interest of the inhabitants.

But among you there are agents paid by Powers hostile to Germany, Communist criminal elements, who have only one aim, to sow discord between the Occupying Power and the French population. . . . I will no longer allow the lives of German soldiers to be threatened by these murderers. I shall stop at no measure, however rigorous, in order to fulfil my duty. . . . I appeal to you all, to your administration and to your police to co-operate by your extreme vigilance and your active personal intervention in the arrest of the guilty. It is necessary, by anticipating and denouncing these criminal activities, to avoid the creation of a critical situation which would plunge the country into misfortune.

He who fires in ambush on German soldiers, who are only doing their duty here, and who are safeguarding the maintenance of a normal life, is not a patriot but a cowardly assassin and the enemy of all decent people.

Frenchmen! I count on you to understand these measures which I am taking in your own interests.

Signed: von Stülpnagel.

It is a matter for wonder that the nation that had invaded France thrice in seventy years should know so little of its enemy's psychology.

It was during the month of October 1941 that the 'executions of Châteaubriant and Bordeaux' took place. On 21st October the following notice appeared in the newspaper *Le Phare*:

Notice. Cowardly criminals in the pay of England and of Moscow killed the Feldkommandant of Nantes yesterday morning by shooting him in the back. So far the assassins have not been arrested. As expiation for this crime I have ordered that fifty hostages be shot to begin with. Because of the gravity of the crime, fifty more hostages will be shot in case the guilty should not be arrested by midnight the 23rd October 1941.

A list of sixty Frenchmen, held in custody at Châteaubriant, who were all supposed to be dangerous Communists was prepared by the Vichy Minister of the Interior, Pucheu,[1] and handed to General von Stülpnagel.

Twenty-seven of these were shot at Châteaubriant, and the Abbé Moyon, who was present, wrote this report of the execution on the day after it occurred:

It was a beautiful autumn day. The temperature was particularly mild. There had been lovely sunshine since morning. Everyone in town was going about his usual business. There was great animation in the town, for it was Wednesday, which is market day. The inhabitants knew from the newspapers, and from information received from Nantes, that a senior officer had been killed there but refused to believe that such savage and extensive reprisals would be carried out. At Choiseul Camp the German authorities had, some days previously, put into special quarters a number of men who were to serve as hostages in case of attacks against the Occupation Forces. It was from these men that those who were to be shot that evening were chosen.

---

[1] Pucheu was tried by a French Military Tribunal in Algiers in 1944. He was sentenced to death and subsequently executed.

The Curé of Bère was just finishing lunch when Monsieur Moreau, Chief of Choiseul Camp, arrived at the presbytery and in a few words explained the object of his visit. He had been sent by Monsieur Lecornu, Sous-Préfet of Châteaubriant, to inform the Curé that twenty-seven men selected from the 'political prisoners' of Choiseul were to be executed that afternoon and to ask him to go at once and attend them.

The priest agreed to go and went immediately to the camp. The Sous-Préfet was already there to announce to the prisoners their terrible fate. . . . Suddenly there was the sound of motorcar engines. The door which I had shut when I entered the room, so that we might be more private, was abruptly opened and French constables with handcuffs appeared. A German Army Chaplain arrived. He said to me, 'Monsieur le Curé, your mission has been accomplished and you must withdraw immediately.'

Access to the quarry where the execution took place was absolutely forbidden to all Frenchmen. I only know that the hostages were executed in three groups of nine each, that all the men who were shot refused to have their eyes bound, that young Mocquet fainted and fell, and that the last cry which sprang from the lips of these heroes was an ardent 'Vive la France'.

A police officer named Roussel saw the condemned men driven through Châteaubriant in the afternoon in four German trucks, preceded by a German officer in a staff car. The men were handcuffed and were singing patriotic songs such as the 'Marseillaise' and the 'Chant du Départ'. In one of the trucks was a party of armed German soldiers.

About two hours later the convoy returned from the quarry where the execution had taken place and drove into the courtyard of the Château, where the bodies of the hostages were put into a cellar until coffins could be made.

The following day, the 23rd October, according to Roussel's statement, 'the bodies were put into coffins without any French persons being present, and all entrances to the Château were guarded by German sentries. The dead were then taken to nine different cemeteries in the surrounding Communes, three coffins to each. The Germans were careful to choose places where there was no regular bus service, presumably to avoid the population going *en masse* to the graves of these martyrs.'

Only two days later fifty more reprisal prisoners were shot by the Germans in Bordeaux. These were taken from a batch of a hundred persons who were known to be sympathizers with the Communist Party or the De Gaullist movement and who had been arrested on 22nd October. These reprisal measures were announced to the Préfet of the Gironde in a letter from General von Faber Du Faur:

Bordeaux, 23rd October 1941.

To the Préfet of the Gironde, Bordeaux.

As expiation for the cowardly murder of Councillor of War, Reiners, the Military Commander in France has ordered fifty hostages to be executed. The execution will take place tomorrow.

In case the murderers should not be arrested in the very near future additional measures will be taken, as in the case of Nantes. I have the honour of making this decision known to you.

Signed: von Faber Du Faur.
Chief of the Military Regional Administration.

There were many other shootings of hostages as reprisal measures. In September 1942 an attack was made on a number of German soldiers at the Rex Cinema in Paris, and 116 hostages were shot in reprisal.

The Fort of Romainville in the suburbs of Paris has since the war become a place of pilgrimage for Parisians. During the occupation it became a depot for hostages where a pool was kept from which victims were selected to be shot in reprisal for some act against the Occupying Power.

One of them, Monsieur Rabate, who had the good fortune to survive, has given an account of the fate of some of these prisoners:

Some of us were transferred to the German quarter of the Santé [a prison in Paris] but the majority of us were taken to the military prison of Cherche-Midi [also in Paris]. We were questioned in turn by a Gestapo officer in the Rue des Saussaies. Some of us were tortured to such an extent that our limbs were broken. While questioning me, the Gestapo officer said, 'Rabate, here you will have to speak. Professor Langevin's son-in-law, Jacques Solomn, came in here arrogant. He went out crawling.'

After a short stay of five months in the Cherche-Midi, we were transferred on 24th August 1942 to the Fort of Romainville. We were not allowed to write or receive letters and on the doors of our cells was written, 'Alles verboten' (Everything is forbidden). All we had to eat was three-quarters of a litre of vegetable soup and 200 grammes of black bread per day. The biscuits sent to the prison for the political prisoners by the Red Cross and the Quaker's Association never reached us. In Romainville we were confined as 'NN' prisoners.[1]

In Northern France, which was administered in conjunction with Belgium by General von Falkenhausen, it was the same. It was the same in Holland and in Norway. In all the Western European countries the Germans carried out systematic executions of hostages in reprisal for acts of resistance.

In no case were these executions according to law; they were always carried out before any effort had been made to discover and arrest the real culprits, and in many cases the perpetrators were arrested shortly after the innocent hostages had given their lives to 'expiate', as the Germans called it, the resistance of their compatriots.[2]

By the end of 1941 Hitler had already come to the conclusion that the measures taken to punish those who committed offences against the German Occupation were inadequate. He decided, therefore, that in future the only cases to be brought to trial before the German Military Courts would be those which could be presented within eight days of the commission of the offence and in which a sentence of death was certain to be awarded.

Accordingly he issued the 'Night and Fog'[3] decree of 7th December 1941. Its object was to ensure that non-German civilians in occupied territories, alleged to have committed offences against the Occupation Forces, were taken *secretly* to Germany, hence its name, unless it could be guaranteed that a death sentence would be passed if tried by a Military Court in their own country.

Hitler took the view that in such cases any lesser sentence would be regarded by the occupied as a sign of weakness, and that the

[1] See page 85.
[2] It is hardly surprising, therefore, that by Article 3 of the 'Geneva Convention of 1949' the taking of hostages 'at any time and in any place whatsoever' has now been expressly forbidden.
[3] Nacht und Nebel.

only way, short of a death sentence, to deter a potential offender was to take such measures as would leave his family and the local population uncertain of his fate.

In a secret letter forwarding the Führer's instructions in respect of the decree to the Abwehr,[1] the new plan for dealing with such prisoners was thus described: 'The prisoners are, in future, to be transported to Germany secretly . . . these measures will have a deterrent effect because (a) the prisoners will vanish without leaving a trace, and (b) no information may be given of their whereabouts or their fate.'

This idea was later carried a step further by the application of what was officially described as the 'collective responsibility of members of families of assassins and saboteurs'. Whenever any member of the Occupation Forces was assassinated, or sabotage was done to important installations, not only were the culprits to be shot, but their kinsmen and their female relatives over the age of sixteen were to be sent to concentration camps, and if the culprits themselves were not apprehended their relatives could be punished in their stead.

It should not be assumed that under this decree all NN prisoners, as they were called, were brought to trial after reaching Germany. In the majority of cases no trial was ever held. When brought before the civil or OKW courts under the NN procedure they were usually denied the right of being confronted by the witnesses upon whose evidence they had been charged, and were not allowed to call witnesses in their defence. Often no charge was ever preferred and the accused only learned a few minutes before the trial opened of the nature of the charge for which he was to be tried. The proceedings were held *in camera*. Such trials were farcical and were intended to be nothing else.

In 1944 the NN proceedings were, on Hitler's orders, transferred from the courts to the Gestapo, and it is not disputed that under this procedure many thousands of the civilian population in the occupied territories were arrested, deported to Germany, tried, sentenced to death, and executed, or imprisoned under inhuman conditions in prisons and concentration camps from which they seldom returned.

One of the war crimes which will be longest remembered was the destruction of the village of Lidice, in Czechoslovakia, and the massacre of a large number of its inhabitants as a reprisal for the

[1] The counter-intelligence.

shooting by partisans of the Protector of Bohemia and Moravia, Reinhard Heydrich.

The Germans arrived in the village late on the night of 9th June 1942 and all the inhabitants were at once ordered to leave their houses, taking with them money and other valuables, and to assemble in the square. All obeyed, but a woman and her child who tried to escape on the way were shot down. The women and children were taken by the Gestapo to the school, where they spent the night.

When day dawned on 10th June, all the men of the village were collected in the barns and stable yard of one farm and from there were led into the garden and shot in batches of ten. The shooting went on until 172 male adults had been killed. The executioners were then photographed with the corpses at their feet, like the members of a pheasant shoot with their bag.

A number of the women were taken to Prague and shot there. The remaining 195 were sent to Ravensbrück Concentration Camp, where 42 died of ill-treatment, seven were gassed, and three were never seen again. Four women with newly born children were also taken off to a concentration camp after their babies had been murdered.

All the children were separated from their mothers a few days after the destruction of the village. Ninety of them were sent to a concentration camp at Gneisenau and have never been seen again. The younger children were taken to a German hospital in Prague and after being examined by 'racial experts' and measured to see whether they were up to Nazi Master-Race-Aryan standards and fit for adoption into German families, those who passed this pseudo-scientific test were sent to Germany to be brought up as Germans under German names. All trace of them has been lost. Those who failed were sent to Poland for Sonderbehandlung.[1]

The village priest, named Sternbeck, who was seventy-three years of age, was offered his freedom if he would renounce his congregation. When he refused he was tortured and his church was desecrated before his eyes. He was shot with the rest of his male parishioners, having declared that he had lived with his flock for thirty-five years and proposed to die with them.

By the evening of the 10th June not a living inhabitant remained in the village. The men were thrown into a common grave; the houses first plundered, and then burned. When only the empty

[1] Special treatment, i.e. extermination in the gas chambers of Treblinka.

shells remained standing, they were demolished so that not one stone should remain on another. The rubble was cleared away, the ground ploughed up and surrounded by a barbed wire fence to remain for ever a barren waste as a warning to the Czechs.

The Germans published an official announcement of this outrage in the paper *Der Neue Tag*[1] on 11th June 1942:

In the course of the search for the murderers of SS Obergruppenführer Heydrich, incontestable proof was found that the population of Lidice near Kladno gave support and assistance to the perpetrators of the crime. The relevant evidence was, in spite of interrogations, collected without the co-operation of the inhabitants. The attitude to the crime revealed hereby is still further emphasized by other activities hostile to the Reich, by stores of seditious matter, dumps of weapons and munitions, an illegal radio transmitter, and also rationed goods in great quantity, and by the fact that inhabitants of the village are in active service with the enemy abroad. Since the inhabitants of this village have, in the most uncompromising manner, opposed the published laws through their activity and support in the murder of Heydrich, the male adults have been shot, the women sent to a concentration camp and the children placed in suitable educational institutions. The buildings have been razed to the ground and the name of the place has been erased from the records.

What began in France in 1940 as a mere trickle of blood became during the last three years of occupation a raging torrent. And as oppression was intensified, resistance to it grew. When collaboration proved a failure, terrorism took its place.

By 1943 no pretence was even made by the Germans that offenders against their regulations should be first tried and then punished. In January 1943 von Falkenhausen, who was responsible for part of Northern France as well as Belgium, issued an order that anyone found in possession of explosives, ammunition, or firearms of any description without valid authorization would be 'liable in future to be shot immediately without trial'.

It might, therefore, be thought that the Germans regarded the 'Maquis' as *francs-tireurs*: but it is manifest that the French Forces of the Interior, to give them their proper name, were considered to be irregular troops and therefore a legitimate component of the French Armed Forces.

This would appear from the following extract from a memorandum to the Wiesbaden Commission entitled 'Terrorist Action Against Patriots':

> On the enemy side we have organizations which absolutely refuse to accept the sovereignty of the French Government of Vichy and which from the point of view of numbers as well as of armament and command should almost be designated as troops . . . these revolutionary units regard themselves as being a part of the forces fighting against Germany. General Eisenhower has described the terrorists who are fighting in France as troops under his command. It is against such troops that repressive measures are directed.

But they were not granted the protection or treatment after capture which is the right, under International Law, of every member of the belligerents' armed forces who is made a prisoner of war.

Orders were issued by Keitel from OKW that they were to be shot on the spot if caught in the *act* of sabotage—there can be no complaint about that—but if captured they were then to be transferred to the nearest local office of the SIPO or SD. Any women who sympathized but took no actual part in hostilities were 'to be assigned to work'. This masterly euphemism meant that they were to be deported to Germany like cattle, sent to a slave labour camp, and worked until they died or became unfit for further exploitation. What happened to them then is told in another chapter.[1]

All civilians in the occupied territories who were considered a danger to security, instead of being interned in their own country in accordance with the usually accepted practice, were to be 'turned over to the SD'. That, too, sounds innocent enough to anyone ignorant of what the SD was and stood for, or of what happened when the 'turning over' had been accomplished. But it meant the lash, the thumb-screw, the head-screw, the extraction of finger-nails, and toe-nails, the concentration camp, the gas chamber.

In pursuance of Keitel's order, the SIPO and SD were given authority to execute without trial. These orders were of general application throughout the occupied territories in Western Europe.

[1] See Chapters V and VI.

Let free people consider what this meant. It was summary police jurisdiction: anyone living in any of those countries under German occupation without rhyme or reason could be summarily sentenced to death and executed by a comparatively junior official of the local Sicherheitspolizei. No charge, no evidence, and no defence. It was done daily, it was done everywhere, and it was murder.

In Holland, after an attempt to kill Rauter, Gauleiter Seyss-Inquart proclaimed 'for the Occupied Netherlands Territory in its entirety, summary police justice which shall enter into force immediately'. It is known that by this procedure more than four thousand Dutch citizens were put to death.

In Belgium, at the time of its liberation in September 1944, the crimes committed by German troops against civilians and members of the official Resistance Forces which were fighting against the German Army reached their peak.

At Graide a Resistance Forces camp was attacked. The Germans were entitled to do this and to make prisoner those who were not killed in fair fight during the operation. After the German troops left, however, fifteen corpses were found terribly mutilated. The Germans had used bullets with sawn-off tips.[1] Two of the prisoners had been beaten with cudgels before being finished off with a pistol shot in the back of the head.

On 6th September 1944 several hundred members of the Belgian Secret Army were quartered in the Château de Forêt. The Germans had received reports that this detachment was about to move and the Château was surrounded. Some of the partisans were killed trying to break through the cordon of German troops but others were taken prisoner. The German troops then advanced on the Château using these prisoners as a screen. After two hours the fighting stopped for lack of ammunition, and those Belgians who were still holding out were told that their lives would be spared if they surrendered. This promise was not honoured. Many of the survivors were first tortured and then killed. The corpses were then sprinkled with petrol and the Château set on fire.

In December 1944 von Rundstedt turned round and made a

---

[1] Every literate German soldier knew that this practice was forbidden. In his 'Soldbuch' (Pay Book) were set out the 'Ten Commandments for the German Soldier Regarding Warfare'. The fifth commandment stated: 'Dum-Dum bullets are prohibited, also no other bullets may be transformed into Dum-Dum.' See Appendix I.

last and desperate counter-offensive before retreating over the Belgian-German frontier. In its early stages the German troops reached the Marche-Bastogne road and occupied the village of Bande. These soldiers, who belonged to the Wehrmacht, were well behaved and gave no trouble.

Further down the road, however, was a control post set up by the SD, and on Sunday morning, 24th December 1944, a detachment of Gestapo arrived in the village and arrested about seventy male inhabitants. They even entered the church during High Mass and took into custody some of the congregation. The officer in command of this detachment said that he was only taking them to the control post to check up their identity cards and that they would all be returned to their homes in time for Christmas.

Simultaneously a number of arrests had been made in the neighbouring village of Grune by another detachment of SD. All those apprehended in both villages were then taken to a burnt-out sawmill on the outskirts of Bande in which the control post was situated. There they were interrogated.

After the questioning was over the older men were released, but the younger were taken to a shed where they were relieved of all their personal belongings except that they were allowed to retain their handkerchiefs. They were then lined up in three ranks and marched with hands behind their heads along the Grand Route until they reached the burnt-out shell of a house belonging to a Monsieur Bertrand.

Here they were halted and turned with their faces towards the road and their backs to the houses. They remained like this for some time, standing in the snow and guarded by seven SS men, armed with tommy-guns. One officer remained in command of the escort; he who had conducted the interrogation.

The massacre soon began A Feldwebel[1] came up to the left-hand man of the rear rank, placed a hand on his shoulder and led him just inside the doorway of Monsieur Bertrand's house. As soon as each prisoner entered the doorway the SS officer, who was posted at the entrance in such a way that he could not be seen from the road, shot the victim in the back of the neck and with a jerk of his knee sent the body hurtling into the cellar which was open to the air as the ground floor had fallen in when the house was burnt down.

The condemned men numbered thirty-three. When twenty had been killed in this way the next to be shot was a young Belgian

[1] Sergeant in the Wehrmacht.

named Léon Praile. He was a tall, strong youth with broad shoulders. Praile, noticing that the German sergeant was weeping, turned round and struck him full in the face and knocked him down. In the confusion Praile managed to escape, and after spending a night in the woods hid in a barn on the farm of his uncle who was the Burgomaster.

He was, however, the only one to get away, and the other thirty-two were all murdered. The whole countryside this time was under snow and the Germans covered up the bodies with planks which they found in one of the ruined houses. No one was allowed to pass that way, and except for Praile, no one even suspected what had happened. The villagers all thought that their friends and neighbours had been taken off to Germany as slave labour.

On 10th January 1945, the Germans evacuated Bande and British troops moved in the next day. The Burgomaster, who had learned the truth from his nephew, called on the British commanding officer and asked him to come to the scene of the crime. When the planks and snow which covered the bodies were removed, thirty-one corpses were found. Each had a bullet wound at the base of the skull.

This crime was carried out as a reprisal. In September 1944, when the Germans had previously been in Bande before withdrawing eastward in front of the advancing Allies, three of their number had been killed in the adjacent woods. A German officer, Lieutenant Spaan, who was billeted in Bande at the time of the massacre, told his landlady that orders had come 'directly from Himmler' that thirty men should be executed to avenge the three Germans who had been killed in September by members of the Belgian Resistance.

That was doubtless the truth, for the Burgomaster, after the Germans had gone, himself found written in chalk on the door of a shed behind the Café de la Poste: 'This is to avenge the heroes shot by terrorists in September.' No attempt had been made to discover who these 'terrorists' were, there had been no real investigation. Thirty-three young Belgians of military age had been selected at random and, after a perfunctory interrogation and without trial, put to death.

But to return to France. Although the French Forces of the Interior consisted largely of properly organized units of varying sizes which received orders through their own channels from regular military commanders, there were undoubtedly acts of sabotage and ambushes carried out during the first few weeks after the Allied landing in Normandy by individuals and small parties whom the Germans were entitled to regard as *francs-tireurs*. If captured, these members of the Maquis could have been brought before German military courts and condemned to death.

But they were not; they were, all too often, first brutally tortured and afterwards murdered without trial.

At Rodez, the very day before it was liberated, the Germans shot thirty members of the Maquis whom they had captured, after torturing them. They were shot by tommy-guns and to finish them off the Germans crushed their skulls in with large stones.

In the forest of Achères many members of the Maquis were killed by the Gestapo. Their bodies were eventually discovered and a report of what was found was made by the Commissaire de Police of Pau. Several of the corpses had broken limbs and deep wounds in the lower part of their legs which appeared to have been caused by the cords, with which they had been tightly bound, biting into their flesh.

Two younger men who had been wounded in a skirmish with German troops in Provence were dragged from a ward in the hospital in Nîmes, where their wounds were being cared for, and shot. Their bodies were mutilated and round their necks was hung a placard: 'Thus are French terrorists punished'.

Throughout August 1944, when the Germans were in full flight from Northern France, the tally of atrocities mounted. On the afternoon of 30th August part of the Adolf Hitler Division arrived in the little village of Tavaux in the Département of the Aisne; and a patrol went to the house of the local resistance leader, whose name was Maujean.

The door was opened by his wife, whom the soldiers immediately shot, wounding her in the thigh and breaking her jaw. They then dragged her into the kitchen where, in front of her five young children, one of whom was but a baby, they broke an arm and a leg, poured petrol over her and set her on fire. The children were then told that if they would not disclose where their father was hiding they would be shot. They refused to say where he was, whereupon the Germans locked the children in the cellar, poured petrol over the floors of the house, and set it on fire. They then left. The fire was put out and the children were saved and it was by the eldest, a boy of nine, that the account of the atrocity was given.

There were numerous other instances of reprisals being taken on near relatives of men who were fighting in the French Resistance Forces. At Oyonnax a youth of eighteen, whose brother was in the Maquis, disappeared one night. Three days later his body was found at Siège terribly mutilated. His nose and tongue had been cut off and there were marks of blows all over his body and cuts on his legs. By his side were the bodies of four other young men who had been so mutilated that they could not be identified. None of the bodies showed any signs of gun-shot wounds and all five young men had clearly died from their ill-treatment.

At Prestles in the South of France during the summer of 1944 a detachment of SS men visited a farm where two members of the Maquis were supposed to be hiding. They were not there, so the SS, deprived of their prey, arrested the farmer and his wife. The Germans shot the husband, raped his wife, then killed her, and after torturing their little son aged three, crucified him on the farmyard gate.

At Ascq another German unit, by way of reprisal for the destruction of the railway line, massacred seventy-seven men including twenty employees of the French State Railways. They were taken indiscriminately and had no direct connection with the incident which provoked the reprisal. One victim was a retired business man of seventy-four and another was a schoolboy of fifteen. This outrage was officially reported by the Vichy Government to Field-Marshal von Rundstedt, then Commander-in-Chief in Northern France, who replied, 'The population of Ascq bears the responsibility for the consequences of its treacherous conduct, which I can only severely condemn.'

General Bérard, who was President of the French Mission attached to the German Armistice Commission, wrote to General Vogl, its Chairman, about the unsatisfactory reply given by von Rundstedt. He pointed out that between 10th October 1943 and 1st May 1944 more than 1,200 people had been victims of such atrocities.[1] He pointed out that all these measures of repression struck mainly at the innocent. Reprisals were carried out on persons supposed to be connected in some way with the Maquis without any effort having been made to find out whether there was any foundation for such assumption.

In regard to the particular outrage which appeared to have caused the German Commander-in-Chief no concern, General Bérard protested that all these innocent people paid with their lives

---

[1] This was before the massacre of Oradour-sur-Glâne. After the Allied landing in Normandy the number of atrocities greatly increased.

for an attempted attack which had not caused the death of a single German soldier. This protest was summarily rejected.

On the day following the Allied landings in Normandy considerable numbers of the French Forces of the Interior attacked in Tulle the Vichy French forces who were employed in maintaining order in the district, and after a long day's fighting seized most of the town. A few hours later German armoured vehicles came to the assistance of the hard-pressed Vichy garrison and entered the town, from which the FFI then withdrew.

The German commander decided to carry out reprisals. The FFI having withdrawn without leaving any prisoners, the reprisal was made upon the civilian population, one hundred and twenty of them. The following passage is from an official report:

The victims were selected without any investigation or questioning, haphazardly: labourers, students, professors, artisans, and tradesmen. There were even some Milice[1] and Waffen-SS recruits among them. The one hundred and twenty bodies which were hanged from the balconies and lamp-posts of the Avenue de la Gare, for a distance of 500 metres, were a horrible spectacle that will remain in the memories of the unfortunate people of Tulle for a long time.

During April and May of 1944, the campaign against the French Resistance Movement in central and south-west France was intensified. The Maquis, in preparation for the Allied invasion of Normandy, were constantly harrying the German lines of communication and orders from the High Command had been given authorizing those responsible for internal security to take *any* measures they considered necessary to break down the resistance of the French people.

To perform this task the SS 'Das Reich' Panzer Division was allocated to the German General in command of the Limoges military district.

The Maquis themselves were difficult to round up. They had no supply problems, and knew the country like the back of their hands; they only emerged from their lairs to make some lightning raid on an enemy convoy or a military encampment, and then returned to hiding. The Germans, therefore, found it easier to take reprisals on innocent people, and when a successful Maquis

[1] Milice. A voluntary police force recruited by the Vichy Government for collaboration with SD and Gestapo.

operation had taken place, wreaked their vengeance on the local population of rural France.

A deserter from the 'Das Reich' Division who was with them during those months has given this brief account of some of the atrocities committed:

During these operations the officers wore no badges of rank, not wishing to be recognized. First we cleaned up the country around Agen within a radius of seventy kilometres. The population of many villages were searched and massacred and the officers raped the youngest women. After the operation was over, the officers searched the soldiers and took away all objects of value from them. All cattle were taken by the Divisional Supply Column, as supplies from Germany had been cut off.

Some kilometres from Agen when we were passing through a small hamlet of some twelve houses a woman about thirty years old was watching us from a window. Seeing a lorry halted by the roadside, our company commander asked her, 'Are there any Maquis here?' 'No,' she answered. 'Then whose is this lorry?' 'I don't know,' she replied. Without further questioning she was dragged down from the first floor, undressed, beaten with cudgels, and hanged bleeding from a nearby tree.

Further on, our convoy stopped in front of a large house over which the tricolour was flying. Our company commander opened fire on the front of the building and the owner came out: the officer immediately shot him in the chest. All the occupants were made to come out and five young women were taken away in one of our vehicles. The convoy then left, all the men singing and firing their rifles as they drove through the village. Passing through the country after leaving the village, we fired at anyone working in the fields, and their horses, cows, and dogs were all machine-gunned.

From there we went to Limoges and the next day we continued cleaning up in the Haute-Vienne. Everything in our path was killed; and the women undressed, raped, and hanged from trees. On 6th June we arrived at St Junien. That evening, while the company were searching for provisions, I managed to get away, unable any longer to endure such sights.

On 6th June, the invasion of Normany had begun, and with it the tempo of Maquis operations heightened. In order to prevent German reserves being rushed from the south and south-west to reinforce their hard-pressed comrades in the north, the Maquis made persistent attacks on road and rail communications causing great confusion. Meanwhile the 'Das Reich' Division continued its march through central France spreading death and destruction.

Some twenty-two kilometres north-west of Limoges, and in the Canton of St Junien which the division had reached on the 6th June, lies the village of Oradour-sur-Glâne, situated on the north bank of the little river Glâne not far from the main Limoges-La Rochefoucault-Angoulême road.

Oradour-sur-Glâne was a largish rural 'Commune' in the Haute-Vienne Département. With the neighbouring hamlets of Brandes, Lapland, Bellevue, Le Repaire, La Fauvette and a number of others, its total population in 1936 was about 1,500. The population of the village itself, however, was much less as the greater part was dispersed amongst a number of adjacent hamlets and isolated farms.

Since the commencement of the war the population of the village had been somewhat enlarged by the arrival of a number of refugees from Lorraine, and people from Limoges who found existence in the country easier in war time than life in the town.

The 10th of June 1944 was a Saturday, and Oradour-sur-Glâne full and busy. In addition to the inhabitants themselves there was the usual number of week-enders from Limoges, and as it was the beginning of a new ration period for tobacco, dealers from all parts of the Commune had come to Oradour to get their allocation.

All were still lingering over déjeuner when at 2.15 p.m. a large convoy of German troops swept into Oradour from the Limoges road and parked in the lower part of the village. The soldiers were wearing steel helmets and were dressed in the well-known green and yellow camouflaged denims worn by so many Waffen-SS units. Some vehicles proceeded higher up the village and parked there.

Shortly after their arrival the town crier passed through the streets reading out an order to the effect that everyone without exception, men, women, and children, must parade at once with their identity cards in the village square. At the same time each house in the village was visited and all the occupants brought out and marched to the square; those still in the fields were also rounded up, many being shot dead in the process. Others living in isolated farms and nearby hamlets were also brought in.

It also happened that all the school children were assembled that afternoon for a medical inspection, 191 children in different school buildings. The detachment commander said that they feared there might be a skirmish in the village and they would, therefore, take all the children to the church for safety. Thus assured, the children and their teachers were escorted there without any trouble. All save one. One young boy, a refugee from Lorraine, had experienced German troops before and said to one of his friends, 'These are Germans, I know them, they'll do us harm, I am going to try to get away.'

Somehow or other, this boy, whose name was Roger Godfrin, escaped from the others and after hiding for a time in the school garden managed to reach the surrounding woods. Six hours later, of all those children, he alone was alive.

By a quarter to three all were assembled in the square; the young and the old, invalids and cripples, fathers and sons, mothers and daughters, pupils and teachers, infants in arms and babies in their perambulators; the Maire, the notary, the blacksmith, the chemist, shopkeepers, artisans, and peasants—not less than six hundred souls.

The German officer in command then called on the Maire to name thirty hostages, but these were firmly refused.

The German troops had now closed in, and their intended victims were surrounded and separated into two groups, the one consisting of the women and young children, the other of the men. The former group was marched off under escort to the church. Their fate will be described later.

The men were then addressed by the German commander. He told them that he had information that there was a secret store of Maquis arms in the village and he proposed to make a thorough search. During the search, the male inhabitants would be taken to six of the village barns and there kept under guard. Accordingly they were formed into six parties and marched away to the farms of a like number of local residents.

Of all these men, only five survived, and it is from them that the fate of the others is known. Let one of them tell his story.[1]

Yvon Roby in June 1944 was eighteen years old and then lived with his parents at Forêt-Basse in the Commune of Oradour-sur-Glâne.

The group locked in the barn with me included Brissaud, the blacksmith, Compain, the confectioner, and Morlières, the

[1] This deposition is taken from the *Dossier d'Oradour-sur-Glane* and was subsequently published in an official pamphlet, *Crimes ennemis en France*.

hairdresser. We had hardly arrived when the Germans made us move two carts which were in the way; then, having forced us inside, four soldiers posted at the door covered us with their tommy-guns to prevent our escaping. They talked and laughed among themselves as they inspected their firearms. All of a sudden, five minutes after we entered the barn, the soldiers, apparently in obedience to a signal fired from the square, opened fire on us. The first to fall were protected from the bursts of fire which followed by the bodies of the others who fell on top of them. I lay flat on my stomach with my head between my arms. Meanwhile the bullets ricocheted off the wall nearest me. The dust and grit hampered my breathing. Some of the wounded were screaming and others calling for their wives and children.

Suddenly the firing stopped and the brutes, walking over our bodies, finished off with their revolvers at point-blank range those who still showed signs of life.

I waited in terror for my turn to come. I was already wounded in the left elbow. Around me the screams died down and the shots became less frequent. At last silence reigned, a heavy depressing silence only broken from time to time by smothered groans.

The soldiers then covered us with anything they could find which would burn; straw, hay, faggots, wheel spokes, and ladders.

All those around me, however, were not dead and the uninjured began whispering to those who were wounded but still alive. I turned my head slightly and next to me saw one of my friends on his side lying covered with blood and still in his death throes. Would my fate be the same?

I heard footsteps; the Germans had returned. They then set fire to the straw which covered us and the flames quickly spread through the barn. I tried to get away but the weight of the bodies on top of me hampered my movements. Furthermore, my wound prevented me using my left arm. After desperate efforts I finally managed to get clear. I raised myself gently, expecting to receive a bullet, but the murderers had left the barn.

The air was becoming stifling. I suddenly noticed a hole in the wall some way up from the ground. I managed to squeeze through it and took refuge in an adjoining loft.

Four of my friends had gone there before me, Broussaudier,

Darthout, Hebras, and Borie. I crawled under a heap of straw and dried beans. Borie and Hebras hid behind a pile of sticks. Broussaudier was huddled up in a corner. Darthout, with four bullet wounds in his legs, asked me to make room for him beside me. We lay close together side by side and waited anxiously, listening intently to every sound.

Alas, our ordeal was not over. Suddenly a German entered, stopped in front of our pile of straw and set fire to it. I held my breath. We avoided making the slightest sound or movement, but the flames began to scorch my feet. I raised myself on top of Darthout, who did not move, and I risked taking a quick look; the SS men had gone. At this moment Broussaudier came across the loft. He had discovered another means of escape. I followed close behind him and, pursued by the flames, found myself outside, near a rabbit hutch which Broussaudier had just entered.

I went in after him and without losing a moment scraped a hole in the ground in which I lay crouching. Then I covered myself with rubbish which was lying all round me. There we remained for three hours until the fire at last reached the rabbit hutch and the smoke got in our throats. I held my hands over my head to keep off the sparks which were falling from the roof and burning my hair.

Yet a third time we managed to escape from the flames. I noticed a narrow gap between two walls. We managed to crawl up to it, still crouching, and breathe a little fresh air, but it was impossible to remain in such a position for long. We got up, therefore, and cautiously made our way towards the square. We had to make quite certain that there was no German soldiers left on guard there. Broussaudier went on ahead as scout. There was no one in sight. We reached the square. Dare we cross it?

One last glance to right and left and we made off as quickly as we could in the direction of the cemetery. At last we gained the shelter of a coppice. We embraced each other, so great was our joy at having regained our freedom.

We then separated. I had to spend the night in a field of rye and on the following morning at about eleven o'clock finally reached my home in Forêt-Basse.

Whilst this butchery was going on, the party of women and children numbering some four hundred had reached the church.

It consisted of all the women in the village, many of them carrying babies in their arms or wheeling them in perambulators, and all the children of school age.

Of these, but one survived, Madame Marguerite Rouffanche, a native of Limoges, who this day lost her husband, a son, two daughters, and her little grandson of seven months.

For nearly two hours, packed in the church, these wretched people waited with mounting anxiety wondering what was to be their fate. What that fate was has been told by Madame Rouffanche in the following words.[1]

About 4 p.m. a number of soldiers, all about twenty years of age, entered the church with a kind of packing case which they carried up the centre aisle and placed at the head of the nave near the choir. From this case there hung what looked like lengths of cord[2] which were left trailing on the ground. These cords were lit and the soldiers moved away. When the fire reached the packing case the latter exploded and produced clouds of thick black suffocating smoke.

The women and children, gasping for breath and screaming with terror, fled to other parts of the church where it was still possible to breathe. It was then that the door of the vestry was broken open by the sheer weight of a mass of panic-sticken people. I followed in and sat down on a step resignedly to await my fate.

The Germans, realizing that this part of the church was overrun, brutally mowed down all others who tried to reach it. My daughter was killed at my side by a shot fired from the outside. I owe my life to having the presence of mind to close my eyes and feign death.

A volley rang out in the church. Then straw, faggots, and chairs were thrown on top of the bodies which were lying strewn all over the stone floor. Having escaped this slaughter and received no wound, I took advantage of a cloud of smoke to hide behind the high altar.

In this part of the church were three windows. I went towards the centre one which was the largest and with the help of the small stepladder used for lighting the candles, I tried to reach it. I do not know how I managed to do so but somehow extra strength was given me. The glass was broken and I jumped through the frame. The drop was over three metres.

[1] *Crimes ennemis en France.*
[2] They were, in fact, fuses.

I looked up and saw that I had been followed by a woman whom I knew and who was holding out her baby to me from the open window. She let herself drop beside me. The Germans, whose attention had been attracted to us by the child's screams, then machine-gunned us. My friend and her baby were killed and their bodies were subsequently discovered where they had fallen.

I then proceeded to the vicarage garden, being wounded on the way. There, hidden amongst rows of green peas, I anxiously waited for some one to come to my aid. I lay there wounded until 5 p.m. the following day when at last I was discovered.

The very ruins of the church themselves provided silent but striking corroboration of Madame Rouffanche's testimony. The roof was burnt out, much of the nave which was spared by the fire has since collapsed and the blakened walls to this day remain gaunt witnesses of the crime. The high altar was practically destroyed and the communion table torn away from its seating and twisted.

A subsequent inspection of the ruins revealed that the Germans fired many of the shots from inside the church where large numbers of empty cartridge cases were found. It also confirmed that they fired low, doubtless to make more certain of hitting the children.

Two or three days later the site was inspected by the District Inspector from the Ministry of Health. When he made his first inspection the church floor was littered with ashes, human debris, and sickening heaps of flesh and bones. Amidst this indescribable mess lay many half-charred unrecognizable bodies. He reported finding, close to the high altar, many bones and charred remains, including the foot of a child of about six years of age. In the vestry, into which, according to Madame Rouffanche's account, large numbers of women and children had rushed after the explosion, the charred remains of bodies were recovered in large quantities. In a chapel on the south side of the church was a small door leading into the churchyard. Many of those who had not been wounded by the first volley of shots made for this door, doubtless hoping that they might be able to escape through it. But it must have been locked, for near it a large pile of ashes and charred bodies was found. The inspector's report stated that there were sufficient bodies to fill a large farm wagon, and from the quantity of wedding rings and trinkets found, and police estimated the number of victims amounted to several hundred, all of whom were burnt alive. People living two kilometres away have testified that they heard screams coming from the direction of the church.

Having annihilated its inhabitants, the German troops systematically pillaged the village and its environs, then drove away.

No official pretext for these outrages was ever given by the German military authorities. On the day following the massacre, it was merely reported without comment that in the course of military operations the locality of Oradour-sur-Glâne had been 'reduced to rubble and ashes'.

A member of the Sicherheitsdienst, however, who visited the Préfecture of the Haute-Vienne to obtain a statement from the Préfet after his visit to Oradour following the outrage, told him that a German officer and his driver, who had been captured by the Maquis and were being led through the village, were attacked by some women who bound their wrists with wire: that they were then taken away to be shot but the officer managed to escape. He returned at once to Limoges where he organized a punitive expedition against the village by way of reprisal and in which he himself took part.

Exhaustive inquiries have never produced any corroboration of such an incident and it is more than doubtful whether it ever happened. In no circumstances, however, would it have justified so terrible a reprisal. Had such an incident taken place the persons responsible could, without great difficulty, have been discovered and brought to trial in accordance with International Law; but this massacre of hundreds of innocent people was an outrage on humanity and, when the details became known, horrified the civilized world.

A report of this outrage was sent by the Vichy Government to the German Commander-in-Chief in the West, who was requested to communicate the facts to the German High Command in France because of the 'political importance which they will assume from their repercussion on the minds of the French people'. The investigation made by the French established that no member of the FFI was in the village nor within seven kilometres of it, and that the unit which committed this atrocity did so as an act of vengenance on this harmless community because of some attack made on one of its soldiers fifty kilometres away.

In June 1940 Italy came into the war on the side of Germany and fought as her ally until the armistice of September 1943, when a National Government was formed in Southern Italy under King Victor Emmanuel.

After the Allied forces landed in Italy a Republican Government was set up in the north under Mussolini.

During the winter and spring of 1943/4 partisan activity became widespread along the German lines of communication, and drastic steps to suppress resistance were taken by the Supreme German Commander, Field-Marshal Albert Kesselring.

Kesselring himself said this about the German attitude to the Italians after the armistice:

Italy entered the war against Germany's wish, and the support of the German Army, Air Force, and Navy was required for the Italian forces. German armies came and fought for Italy's vital interests. German sacrifices in Africa, Tunisia, Sicily, and Southern Italy were immense, but they were borne. Though numerically far superior, the Italians fought less strenuously than the Germans but this was tolerated for the sake of Italian friendship. This feeling changed into hatred when Italy, betraying the Axis policy, started partisan warfare.

In the afternoon of 23rd March 1944 an incident happened in Rome which led to fearful reprisals being taken by the Germans and the intensifying of terrorist measures against the civilian population in Occupied Italy.

Each afternoon about three o'clock it was customary for a detachment from one of the German Polizei regiments to march along the Via Rasella. As it did so on that day a bomb exploded causing thirty-two fatal casualties amongst the Germans and wounding many others. Obersturmbannführer Kappler of the SD soon reached the scene of the explosion and started making an investigation.

Meanwhile, the incident had been reported through the usual military channels to Hitler's headquarters, whence orders were at once received by Field-Marshal Kesselring to shoot within twenty-four hours ten Italians for every German policeman killed. No details were given as to how these reprisal prisoners were to be selected.

This order was passed on through General von Mackersen, Commander of the Fourteenth Army, to General Maelzer, the Military Commander of the city of Rome, with instructions to ascertain whether there were enough prisoners under sentence of death to make up the required number.

Kappler informed the German garrison commander that in order to find the requisite total he would have to draw up a list of 280 people whom he described as 'worthy of death'.[1] This qualification was a wide one and included not only those who were undergoing long sentences of imprisonment, but many in arrest for alleged partisan activities and acts of sabotage, and all Jews who were in the custody of the SD in Rome at that time.

Kappler went round his prison in the Via Tasso but was unable to make up the numbers. He therefore obtained from another Roman jail other prisoners who were awaiting trial by German military courts.

The number finally put to death was 335. It included an old man of seventy, a boy of fourteen and a half, once man who had already been acquitted by a German court and, for good measure, fifty-five Jews, none of whom had any connection with the partisans and some of whom were not even Italian nationals. The victims were assembled in the Ardeatine Caves on the outskirts of Rome and the execution was carried out there by Kappler's Sicherheitsdienst, the Wehrmacht having declined to perform it.

At the trial of Field-Marshal Kesselring in the Tribunale di Giustizia in Venice in February 1947,[2] Kappler described the shooting of these unfortunate people. They were made to kneel down, five at a time, their hands were bound behind their backs and they were then shot in the back of the head. There were sixty-seven batches of five and all afternoon the slaughter went on. There was no medical officer present to see that one batch were all dead before the next came along. When the last victim had been despatched the cave was blown in to conceal all trace of the crime.

The Germans never even pretended that most of these people had anything to do with the bomb incident. Some had already been held in custody for a long time; many of them did not live near the Via Rasella; some did not even live in Rome at all, and fifty-five of them had merely had the misfortune to be born Jews.

The bombing of the German police detachment was, of course,

[1] Totwürdig.
[2] He was found guilty on all charges and sentenced to death by shooting, but the sentence was commuted by the confirming officer to one of life imprisonment and he was released in 1953, 'as an act of clemency'. He is now President of the Stahlhelm.

an offence against the Occupying Power and those responsible for it could have been tried by a German military court and doubtless sentenced to death. None of those who were put to death in the Ardeatine Caves had been even tried, let alone convicted. They were all shot as a reprisal. The word 'reprisal' can be widely interpreted but it cannot be properly contended that the arbitrary killing of innocent inhabitants becomes justifiable merely by calling it a reprisal.

The massacre in the Ardeatine Caves was only a precursor of what was to follow. On 17th June 1944 the Field-Marshal issued another order. It was drafted by Kesselring himself and was addressed, *inter alia*, to the Tenth and Fourteenth Armies, HQ Luftwaffe, and the Supreme Head SS and Police Italy, who was General Wolff.

It announced new measures in connection with operations against partisans and stated that the partisan situation in the Italian theatre, particularly in central Italy, had so deteriorated as to constitute a serious danger to the fighting troops and their lines of communication. 'The fight against the partisans must be carried on with every means at our disposal and with the utmost severity. I will protect any commander who exceeds our usual restraint [SIC], in the choice and severity of the methods he adopts against partisans. In this connection the old principle holds good, that a mistake in the choice of methods in executing one's orders is better than neglect or failure to act.'

The order then went on to describe certain action which should be taken whenever a civilian implicated in partisan operations was apprehended. If shooting ten Italians for every German killed by the civilian population was their 'usual restraint', this new order was indeed an invitation to greater terrorism.

About the same time Kesselring issued an appeal to the Italians which is set out below.

The Supreme Commander of the German Armed Forces states:

Up to now the German Armed Forces have done all that they have had to do by the necessities of war, correctly and with the greatest consideration for the population. This friendly attitude is dependent upon absolute reciprocity on the part of the population. If criminal assaults and attacks by partisans until now isolated and individual should increase, then the attitude of the Supreme Commander of the German Armed Forces must, perforce, change immediately. The people themselves will be responsible for the consequences of such a decision.

To guarantee the security of rear areas and lines of communication, I order at once that:

1. Anyone found in the possession of arms and explosives which have not been declared to the nearest German Command WILL BE SHOT.

2. Anyone giving shelter to partisans or who protects them, or who assists them with clothing, food, or arms WILL BE SHOT.

3. If any person is discovered who has knowledge of a group of rebels or even of a single rebel without giving such information to the nearest HQ, he WILL BE SHOT.

4. Anyone giving information to the enemy or the partisans of the locality of German Commands or military installations WILL BE SHOT.

5. Every village where it is proved there are partisans or in which the assaults against German or Italian soldiers have been committed or where attempts to sabotage warlike stores have occurred WILL BE BURNED TO THE GROUND. In addition all male inhabitants of such a village over eighteen years of age WILL BE SHOT. The women and children will be interned in labour camps.

ITALIANS.

The welfare of your country and the fate of your families are in your hands. The German Armed Forces as stated in this order will act with justice but without mercy, and with such severity as the case may indicate.

Referring to this appeal in a further teleprint order dated 1st July 1944 the Supreme Commander said:

In my appeal to the Italians I announced that severe measures are to be taken against the partisans. This announcement must not represent an empty threat. . . . Whenever there is evidence of considerable numbers of partisan groups, a proportion of the male population of the area will be arrested, and in the event of any act of violence being committed these men will be shot. . . .

Should troops be fired at from any village it must be burnt down and the ringleaders will be hanged in public.

Nearby villages will be held responsible for any sabotage to cables or damage to tyres.

After this clear incitement to murder and arson the order sanctimoniously stated that plunder was forbidden and that all counter measures must be hard but just, because 'the dignity of the German soldier demands it'.

The German forces needed little encouragement to exceed their 'usual restraint'. Within ten days the following proclamation was pasted all over the walls of the little town of Covolo.

The Town Major of Covolo makes it known that:

For every member of the German Armed Forces, whether military or civilian, who becomes injured FIFTY men, taken from the place where the act was committed, will be shot.

For every soldier or civilian killed, ONE HUNDRED men, also taken from the place where the incident occurred, will be shot.

Should several soldiers or civilians be killed or wounded ALL THE MEN OF THE PLACE WILL BE SHOT, THE PLACE SET ON FIRE, THE WOMEN INTERNED, AND CATTLE CONFISCATED FORTHWITH.

Nor were the German troops slow to implement such orders, and during the month of August a series of appalling reprisals were taken against the Italians.

In Borgo Ticino four German soldiers were wounded one morning by unknown people. A reprisal was immediately carried out by the German troops who first posted road blocks in the village streets. In an inn a game of boccia was in full swing attended by many from the neighbouring village as well as the local inhabitants.

The Germans surrounded the inn, arrested a large number of men, and selected thirteen of them, all under thirty years of age, to be shot. An Italian officer tried to intervene, but he was only successful in obtaining the release of two Black Shirts who were amongst the intended victims. The reprisal prisoners were then shot, including a Fascist who had returned wounded from the Russian front and was only visiting the village by chance to see his fiancée. The village was blown up and set on fire.

Two days later the German Commander in Brescia sent a detachment of the Feld-Gendarmerie[1] to Bovegno, where it was suspected that there was a secret meeting of the partisans in the Hotel Brentana. As the detachment reached the outskirts of the village it was fired upon and three men were wounded.

By way of reprisal the detachment entered the village square and fired indiscriminately at everyone. None of those in the square can have been in any way responsible for the ambush of the German troops a few minutes earlier. During the firing at least six people were killed and others wounded. Amongst the dead were a member of the Republican National Guard and another member of Mussolini's Republican Party, both of whom were still on the side of the Germans.

Several houses were set on fire, including the local co-operative store and the bakery. Food in apartment houses, shops and hotels was seized and during the night eight more Italians were shot by German troops who remained in the village until dawn, when they withdrew. It was definitely established that all save two of the victims were ordinary peaceful citizens in no way connected with the partisan movement.

At this time a number of Russians were serving with the German forces in Italy. Four of them had deserted from their units which were stationed in the Region of Vicenza and had joined the partisans in the mountains of Posina. The inhabitants of Posina were totally unaware of this but the German Commander of the Russian Company at Mavano nevertheless decided to hold them responsible. He issued a proclamation warning the people of Posina that if the four Russians did not return by 17th August to their service the village would be shelled and then destroyed by fire. He also took about twenty hostages from Posina and the outlying district of Fusine. These included the parish priest, the Commissioner-Prefect and the secretary of the Commune.

The Russian deserters had not returned by the evening of the 17th and the centre of Posina was shelled for twenty minutes, and seven days later many houses were set on fire. Over 100 houses were destroyed and 120 families were rendered homeless and lost all their belongings.

Another outrage in Vicenza was committed a few days later in the little village of Valli di Pasubio, where one of the inhabitants found at his place of work a letter written in Russian. As the

[1] The Field Police, cf. Divisional Provost Company.

finder could not read Russian he gave it to another Russian soldier to read. The letter, it appeared, had been written by one of the Russians serving nearby with the German forces and was an incitement to some of his comrades to desert and come and join him with the partisans.

The innocent Italian was at once arrested and his house burned to the ground, and that same day the neighbouring village of Cortiana was set on fire. Thirteen families were rendered homeless and fifteen men taken away and never seen again.

On 1st September 1944, in the Padua district, a clash took place between three German soldiers and a like number of partisans near Montecchia di Crossara. Two of the Germans were killed, and vengeance was wreaked on the village. All the houses were searched and the contents of any value removed: clothing, bedding, wireless sets, typewriters, bicycles, and livestock.

The German troops then set fire to the houses which they had looted. Forty houses were thus completely destroyed and in one were found the charred remains of a young woman and a child of three, both of whom had first been shot. Amongst the other victims were a girl of nine and an old woman of eighty-four.

Throughout the month of August this reign of terror continued in the Province of Venezia. But perhaps the most terrible of all these reprisals was made at Torlano, near Udine, after a lively skirmish between German troops and partisans had taken place not far from the outskirts of the village.

Some of the people who had been working in the fields when the fight began took cover in the village itself, which the German troops then entered. They found several Italians hiding in the cellars, killed them all, and set fire to the houses after looting their contents. Thirty-two men, women, and children were murdered in this way, and ten members of one family, named De Bortoli, were all shot in one house: Virginio De Bortoli, the head of the family; his son Silvano, who was a war cripple; another son; a daughter; and six grandchildren between the ages of two and fourteen. Several more young children were also shot. Many of the corpses were charred by fire and some could not be identified.

These atrocities made a deep impression in northern Italy and the Duce himself complained bitterly to Dr Rahn, who was the Ambassador and Plenipotentiary of Germany with the Italian Republican Government. On receipt of the Duce's letter Dr Rahn forwarded a copy to Kesselring, who replied that *in future* offenders would be dealt with by court martial.

Reprisals should not be undertaken before there has been an inquiry and a genuine effort made to apprehend those responsible for the incidents which justify reprisals being taken. They must never be excessive and should not exceed the degree of violation committed by the enemy.

All the above reprisals were undertaken arbitrarily without any adequate steps being taken to discover the offenders, and far exceeded in their severity what was either proper or necessary. They were not really reprisals as the term is understood by international jurists. They were nothing more nor less than brutal acts of indiscriminate vengeance which both violated the unchallenged rules of warfare and outraged the general sentiment of humanity.[1]

From the first moment of their invasion of Polish territory, the German armies committed a succession of atrocities on the civilian population. Within four days of the outbreak of war, two hundred Polish citizens were shot or burnt to death at Sosnowiec by German troops of Army Group South. The Germans entered the village without any resistance, no Polish troops being there. Unarmed inhabitants were fired at indiscriminately, some were dragged out of their houses and shot outside in the village square. The synagogue was burned to the ground and twelve Jews shot after having first been forced to dig their own graves.

The following day at Kajetanowice about eighty Poles were shot to death by other units of the same German formation. The Germans fired into the houses, set fire to them, and then fired on their occupants as they ran for safety.

Two days later at Pinczow 300 more Poles were either shot or burned to death. On this occasion the troops set fire to the houses, throwing grenades into them: 500 houses were demolished in this way. There was no reason for such barbarity. The Polish troops had already retreated before the Germans arrived and there was no local resistance of any kind.

On 10th September, 112 Poles in another village, including a number of children, were shot to death or killed by hand grenades. The German troops had entered the village on the Saturday without meeting any resistance and on the Sunday morning some Polish soldiers were seen in the fields advancing towards the village. Before they reached it they were shot down.

The Germans then collected a number of civilians and led them

[1] See *Oppenheim's International Law*, Vol. II, Section 253, 6th edn., 1940. Ed. Lauterpacht.

to a barn, where they were made to kneel down with their hands above their heads and were shot. The bodies were put into a barn which was set on fire. One hundred and twelve skulls were later found in the ashes.

During the same period, 160 Polish citizens, men, women and children, were shot or burned to death at Kilejoweic. When the Germans arrived they herded together a number of civilians into a meadow and fired into them, killing about thirty. Later they drove another batch into a house, locked it, set it on fire, and shot at those who tried to escape through the windows. For two or three days whilst the German troops remained in the village these incidents continued and when at last they left, 160 dead Poles were counted and the whole village had been burned to the ground save for one farm.

These terrible crimes were committed daily by the German troops as they advanced victoriously through Poland. A full account of them would be nothing less than a tedious catalogue of rapine, arson, and murder.

Within a few short weeks the battle was over: the Polish Army had capitulated, and the 'General Government' was set up under Hans Frank. The aim was that Poland should become a mere colonial possession of the Third Reich; and the policy of terror, starvation, slave labour, eviction, and extermination began.

Between September 1939 and the beginning of 1945 there were 2,332 executions in Poland with a total of 34,098 victims. Eight thousand of these were killed in the last four months of 1939 when the German police, supported by local Germans, began to eliminate the Polish population. Out of the total number of executions, 57 per cent were of men; 20 per cent men and women; 12 per cent men, women, and children; and the remainder unknown. Some of these executions were of persons who had been sentenced to death by a German military court in accordance with International Law, but 84 per cent were put to death without trial, verdict, or sentence.

Many of these executions took place in the course of terror raids on towns and districts in Poland which the Occupying Power called 'pacification'. The method of 'pacifying' the district was to shoot a number of its inhabitants.

The raids were usually made by the SS or Gestapo, and the following is an account of an execution in Sroda on 17th September 1939:

Gestapo agents surrounded a block of houses, where they started a manhunt. Passers-by in adjacent streets were also seized. As a result of this raid eighteen men were arrested and assembled in the prison courtyard. Later, a group of twenty-one men was taken from the prison and all the condemned were marched through the town to the place of execution. They were ordered to keep their hands clasped behind their necks. During their march through the town, their Gestapo escort beat and tortured them.

Arrived at the place of execution, they were forced to dig a ditch with their bare hands. This was to be their grave. When the grave was ready, the SS men made them stand in line along the edge of the ditch and shout 'Heil Hitler'. They were then mowed down by machine-gun fire. All were not, of course, killed outright and the firing-party finished off those still alive with spades and then threw the bodies into the ditch and trampled them down until the surface was level.

The victims of one mass execution in the Bilgoriz district were disinterred in 1944 and this report on the condition of the corpses was made by the medico-legal experts who conducted the exhumation: 'Before the murder the condemned men had been tied with thick wire. Several knots were made on their forearms and wrists. ... They were beaten and tortured in a most cruel and bestial way. This is proved in several cases by a crushed face or a broken lower jaw and upper jaw: in one case by a large split in the skull.'

Another 'pacification' in the Radonnsko district was supposedly carried out as a reprisal on the local population for having aided the partisans. An eye-witness saw the Germans drag adults and children from three farmhouses, shut them up in a barn and then open heavy machine-gun fire upon it. The barn caught fire and the occupants were burnt alive. The German troops then went to another farm, and the story of what happened there has been told by a youth named Wladyslaw Pietras, who was the sole survivor:[1]

My parents implored them to spare our lives but they took no notice and began firing on us. At the first shots we all fell on the floor but the Germans continued. One bullet hit me in my left side. When the Germans left the cottage I decided to run for it. My parents and my brothers and sisters lay motionless on the

[1] Wladyslaw Pietras's deposition was made before the Central Commission for the Investigation of German War Crimes in Poland, and is published in the Commission's official report, *German Crimes in Poland*, Vol. 1 (Warsaw, 1946).

The Village of Lidice
(By courtesy of the Lidice Society)

Cremating oven at Belsen where 12 or more bodies were burned at a time

Patriots hanged at Tulle
(By courtesy of the Presidence du Conseil, Direction de la Documentation)

The leader of the "Grossaktion"
Major-General Stroop

une chambre de malades au Revier (lazaret) où l'on devait descendre les
morts de la nuit, des étages supérieurs.....

Removing the dead from Ravensbrook sick quarters

At Birkenau before the crematorium was built bodies were burned in pits
(By courtesy of the Polish Cultural Institute)

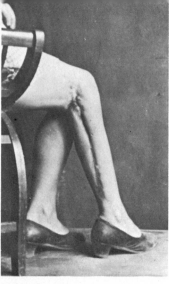

A Polish woman's leg disfigured by human guinea-pig operations *(By courtesy of the Polish Cultural Institute)*

Ilse Koch, wife of the Commandant of Buchenwald

Above: Spectacles taken from prisoners before execution
Below: Corpses in Bergen/Belsen

New arrivals at a concentration camp being paraded for medical inspection
From a photograph found on a German prisoner

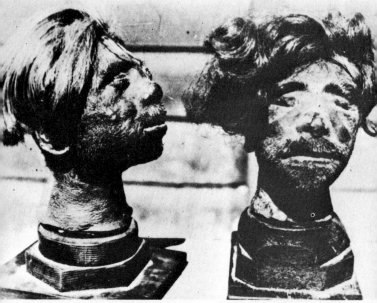

Shrunken heads. A present from a jail keeper to his wife

Joseph Kramer's driving licence

Thumb-screw used by the Gestapo in Belgium
(By courtesy of the Belgium Government)

THE WARSAW GHETTO
The people are driven from the shelter of the bunkers

THE WARSAW GHETTO
The victims are lined up before being searched
(By courtesy of the Polish Cultural Institute)

floor. Only my little niece Teresa, three months old, was still crying in her cot. I managed to reach the woods and waited hidden in the undergrowth, and from there I saw our house in flames. During this raid I lost my father and mother, my grandmother, two brothers, and three sisters. My little niece Teresa was burnt alive. Our village consisted of only four farmsteads. All were demolished by fire and all the inhabitants except myself either murdered or burnt.

Atrocities of this kind were commonplace in 1939 when the Nazis' plan to 'eliminate' the population of Poland was being put into execution.

Hitler had said that in the forefront of his programme was 'the destruction of Poland.' 'The aim,' he said in a speech on 22nd August 1939, 'is the elimination of living forces, not the arrival at a certain line . . . the destruction of Poland shall be the primary objective.'

And so the awful holocaust went on for five long years. To give a detailed account of its progress would be tedious and nauseating, but the following description by an eye-witness of a typical mass execution which took place in November of 1941 will suffice as a specimen of them all:

At 4 a.m. the Gestapo entered my cell and told me they had come to fetch me. I was handcuffed and taken to a motor-car with two other prisoners. We were all placed in the back of the car and our feet chained together. After motoring some distance we turned up a bridle path in the middle of a forest. We were then unfettered, pulled out of the car, and taken to a clearing where mass graves had been dug. Large numbers of Jews were sitting all around, women and children and babies-in-arms. The Gestapo ordered the Jews to undress, beginning with those near the larger of the two graves, and then jump into it. Those who hesitated were beaten and pushed in. On the bottom of the grave was a layer of quicklime. Some of the women who were carrying their babies jumped in with them; others first threw their babies in. We three prisoners were ordered to collect the Jews' shoes and clothing. The Gestapo took all valuables, watches, rings, and other jewellery, and put them in heaps. The order was then given that no more were to get undressed. The grave was packed almost to the limit. Meanwhile, I and my two companions went on collecting the scattered clothing, valuables, blankets, and other belongings, and this took until about noon,

when a lorry drove up with four large tanks on it. The Germans
then fitted up a small motor pump and pumped the contents of
the tanks, which appeared to be water, into the grave. . . .[1]

The following morning the grave was filled in.

The enormity of the German war crimes in Poland cannot be
appreciated unless the objective of German Government in that
country be understood.

Hans Frank's original directive when he took over the administration of that unhappy country was, so he has said, to turn
Poland's 'economic, cultural, and political structure into a heap
of rubble'. He had little doubt that his instructions meant what
they said, for he wrote in his diary: 'If I were to come to the
Führer and say "My Führer, I have to report that I have annihilated another 150,000 Poles", he would reply, "Magnificent, if it
was necessary".'

In Nazi eyes, military necessity excused any breach of the laws
of war.[2]

The crimes committed by the Germans against the laws and
usages of war and against humanity in Poland had no justification.
They were the natural outcome of Nazi ideology and Nazi planning, and put their authors beyond the pale of European civiliza-
tion.

When Hitler marched into Russia in June 1941, the well-known
slogan of German imperialism had come once again into its own
—the 'Drang nach Osten'.[3] 'If new territory is desired,' Hitler had
once written in *Mein Kampf*, 'it can be secured at the expense of
Russia. The new empire must move along the paths trodden by the
Teutonic Knights, this time to acquire soil for the German plough
by means of the German sword.' Wheat, coal, and oil from the
Ukraine and the Caucasus, nickel from the Kola Peninsula, all
these vital sinews of war were there for the taking and Germany
needed them badly.

That Nazi aggression did not start in the East only came about,
as Hitler told his generals at a conference in November 1939, 'by
force of events'. But the prize was still there to be won and the
moment for so doing had only been postponed.

The war against the Russians was fought with more savagery

[1] The rest of this witness's description is too horrible to print.
[2] 'Kriegsräson geht vor Kriegsmanier', which may be translated as 'Necessity in war
overrules the manner of warfare'. See *Oppenheim's International Law*, Vol. II, p. 184,
6th edn.
[3] The 'Drive towards the East'.

114

and barbarity than anywhere else, and it has been contended by German counsel at a number of war crime trials that the Hague Conventions did not apply to the war between the USSR and Germany. The argument put forward and supported by two obscure Russian writers on International Law is that the idea that there was any natural law having international force had for many years been under an official ban in the USSR merely on the grounds that such law represented 'the thinly veiled instrument of capitalist expansion'. Nevertheless, all modern Russian jurists have stressed both the reality and the enforceability of International Law.

Furthermore, no State has ever recognized the fact that Russia was entitled to repudiate any of the obligations of the Tzarist Government and particularly not such a one as Hague Convention IV, which required a specific form of notice for the purpose of withdrawing from it. Nor has such notice ever been given to the Netherlands Government, which kept the register of adherents, and as late as 1939 that government circularized to all concerned, including the German Reich, a list of adherents which included the USSR and which was never challenged.

When this question was raised before the International Military Tribunal at Nuremberg, they disposed of it in these words:

It is argued that the Hague Convention does not apply in this case because of the general participation clause in Article II of the Hague Convention of 1907. In the opinion of the Tribunal it is not necessary to decide this question. The rules of land warfare expressed in the Convention undoubtedly represented an advance over existing International Law at the time of their adoption, but the Convention expressly stated that it was an attempt to revise the general laws and customs of war which it thus recognized to be then existing. But by 1939 these rules laid down in the Convention were recognized by all civilized nations and were regarded as being declaratory of the laws and customs of war.

The Barbarossa Jurisdiction Order of 19th May 1941, issued to the German commanders a month before the offensive against Russia began, left them in no doubt of the methods by which the invaded territory was to be subjugated. It provided that alleged offences by enemy civilians were to be relentlessly liquidated, *suspected* offenders were to be brought before an officer on whose

115

decision depended whether or not they were to be shot, and collective reprisals were to be made against localities where partisan attacks had been made.

This order was liberally interpreted and there was one occasion on which, in pursuance of it, a Russian girl of sixteen was shot for singing an anti-German song.

From the moment the German troops entered Russia until the last Nazi had been driven out, from the Russo-German border to Smolensk, from Smolensk to Stalingrad, from Stalingrad to the Crimea, and from thence to Kharkov, wherever the German soldier or the SS men set foot, crimes of unimaginable brutality were committed against old men, women, and children in their thousands. The paraphernalia of murder was extensive, the technique varied but it was patiently organized and directed at a high level.

As one of the Russian prosecutors at the Nuremberg trial told the Court, when the sites where the Germans buried their victims were opened up and the bodies exhumed and examined by experts in forensic medicine, it was evident that the methods of killing were identical although the burial grounds were often thousands of kilometres apart and the executions had been carried out by different people. The wounds were invariably inflicted in the same parts of the body.

Nor was this all. The precautions taken to camouflage the mass graves as anti-tank ditches or trenches were also identical, and when the victims arrived at the place of execution they were invariably ordered to undress and lie face downwards in pits already prepared. As soon as the first layer of human bodies had been shot it was covered with quicklime, and the second batch of victims was made to undress and lie down on top of it. Whether it was in the swamps of Bielorussia or in the foothills of the Caucasus, the drill was the same.

This wholesale slaughter was not the result of the excesses of undisciplined German units or formations, still less of individual officers and soldiers, but was the considered policy of Hitler's Cabinet deliberately planned before the outbreak of hostilities and faithfully carried out in obedience to orders.

To implement this policy and execute these plans, it was not only necessary that the Nazis should encourage the lowest instincts of their troops and incite them to murder innocent civilians and treat them with every kind of brutality and violence; it was also necessary to train special units to do the work and to make it known that such crimes would go unpunished.

116

The task ahead was so abhorrent and revolting that only those without feeling, without pity, and without conscience could perform it. Much had been done in Germany before the war to free its people from what Hitler called 'the humiliating restrictions imposed by the chimera of conscience and morality'; but not enough, and formations of perverted creatures, the Einsatzkommandos, accompanied the Wehrmacht throughout Russia to do the latter's filthy work.

According to an order issued by Hitler, a German soldier could not be brought to trial by court martial for any act committed against Soviet citizens. He could be punished by his commanding officer *if necessary*.

Local commanders were often given extensive powers to undertake collective punitive measures against the civilian population. They could burn down villages and towns, seize without normal requisitioning procedure supplies and livestock, and arrest any inhabitant and have him deported to Germany for slave labour.

It has already been stated that whatever form of reprisal may be sanctioned by International Law, it should only be made after all other methods have been tried to obtain satisfaction and after consultation at a very high level; no reprisals should ever be undertaken on the responsibility of a subordinate commander. From the beginning of the Russian campaign, however, local commanders were given very wide powers.

The principle that war crimes against Soviet citizens would involve the perpetrator in no disciplinary action was kept constantly in mind by the German High Command. Hitler, having been informed that certain members of the Wehrmacht, for atrocities committed during operations against partisans, had been called to account for their behaviour, instructed Keitel to issue a further directive on this subject.

This directive stated that if the repression of partisans in the East was not pursued with the most brutal means it would not be long before the menace reached uncontrollable proportions. 'The troops have, therefore, the right and the duty to use in this struggle any and unlimited means, even against women and children, if only conducive to success. . . . No German participating in combat action against guerrillas or their associates is to be held responsible for acts of violence either from a disciplinary or judicial point of view.' This directive gave the German soldier in Russia *carte blanche* to rape and to murder, and he took full advantage of it.

All these orders were passed on to the troops, and subordinate commanders issued their own instructions. On 12th June, von Manstein issued a directive for the behaviour of the troops in Russia as an appendix to one of his operation orders. It urged them to take ruthless measures against 'Bolshevik instigators, *franc-tireurs*, saboteurs, and Jews'.

Courses of instruction in ruthlessness were held in the German Army. A corporal who served in the special battalion 'Altenberg' which took an active part in the atrocities committed by the German troops in the city and region of Kharkov stated that whilst on such a course he attended lectures given by senior officers in the GFP[1] who said that the Russian people were subhuman, that the majority should be destroyed, and that those who were spared would be employed by the Germans as slaves. 'Such instruction,' the corporal continued, 'was in accordance with the policy of the German Government towards the peoples of the occupied territories; and, it must be confessed, was put into practice by every member of the Armed Forces, myself included.'

Special instruction was also arranged for those selected to supervise the machinery of death in extermination camps. In one camp, during the internment there of a Russian named Manusevitch who gave this information, special ten-day courses on corpse-burning were held. The pupils were generally officers and senior NCOs. The chief instructor was a Colonel Schallok, who had great experience of such matters. On the site where bodies were being burned he explained the process and how to set up a bone-crushing machine.

Russian children were even used as live targets for the musketry training of the Hitler Jugend. A Frenchwoman named Ida Vasso, who was manageress of a hostel for aged Frenchmen in Lvov during the German occupation, said that she had seen this happen, and her statement was fully investigated and confirmed. The report of the Commission on the result of their inquiries stated that in Lvov the Germans 'spared neither men, women, nor children. The adults were simply killed on the spot and the children given to the Hitler Youth for target practice'.

On 30th June 1941, the Germans entered Lvov and began their massacre the next day. After hundreds had been put to death they arranged an exhibition of the murdered citizens in an arcade. The mutilated bodies, mostly of women, were laid out along the walls of the houses. The *pièce de résistance* of this macabre show was

[1] Geheime Feld Polizei—the Field Security Police.

118

the corpse of a woman whose baby was pinned to her breast wiht a German bayonet.

It was not only by the Hitler Youth that children were used as practice targets. In one small village in the Krasnya Polyana District a party of drunken German soldiers placed a young boy of twelve on the porch of one of the houses and opened fire on him with an automatic rifle. He fell riddled with bullets.

In another village German troops tied the wrists of the twenty-five-year-old pregnant wife of a Russian soldier and raped her. They then cut her throat and bayonetted both her breasts.

At Rostov, a fifteen-year-old boy was playing in his back yard with his tame pigeons. Some German soldiers who were passing entered and stole the birds. When the boy protested the thieves took him along to the next street corner, shot him, and trampled on his face until it was unrecognizable.

Near Smolensk, when the German troops first arrived, they shot about 200 schoolboys and girls who were in the fields helping with the harvest, after a number of the girls had been taken away to satisfy the appetites of the officers. The brutal assaults made by the troops upon women during the first few months of the invasion were redolent of the days when Attila, the Scourge of God, ravaged Gaul with his hordes of Huns.

In the Ukrainian village of Borodayevka not one woman escaped violation. At Berezovka all females between the ages of sixteen and thirty were carried off like the Sabine women of old, and in Smolensk the German commander opened a brothel for officers in one of the hotels into which large numbers of respectable women were driven and forced into prostitution. In the city of Lvov, thirty-two women in a clothing factory were first raped and then murdered by the attacking troops. Other girls were dragged into the Municipal Gardens and brutally raped: an old priest who tried to intervene had his cassock torn off, his beard singed, and was then bayonetted to death. Near Borissov, in Bielorussia, seventy-five women tried to flee on the approach of the Germans; they were caught and many of them raped. A girl of sixteen was taken into the woods by a party of soldiers and also raped. Her breasts were cut off in the presence of some other Russian women and she was nailed to a tree and left to die.

Such was the outcome of licensing these men in advance to commit crimes without fear of punishment. The results were those which their masters intended and for which they had planned.

But the violation of women is not the whole of the story. In many towns and villages through which the Germans passed in their first lightning break-through, wholesale massacres took place. In one village all the old men and youths were shot and the houses burnt to the ground; in another all the old people of both sexes and the children were driven like cattle into a collective farm barn, locked in, and burnt alive; in yet another, sixty-eight people were crowded into a small hut and the doors and windows sealed up until everyone inside was dead by asphyxiation; and in a fourth, 100 peaceful civilians were locked up in the church with a number of wounded soldiers of the Red Army and the building then blown up.

But these were comparatively minor atrocities compared with the larger massacres, which the Germans called 'Grossaktionen',[1] such as those carried out at Kiev and Rostov.

At Kiev, the capital of the Ukraine, within a few days of its capture, they tortured and murdered 52,000 men, women, and children, large numbers of whom were Jews. Many of these were assembled in the Jewish cemetery, stripped naked, and beaten before they were shot.

In Rostov, during a stay of ten days, the German troops annihilated many thousands of the inhabitants; forty-eight were killed by machine-gun fire outside the State Railway offices; about sixty were shot while walking along the street; and 200 murdred in the Armenian cemetery. When they were driven out of the city by the Russian troops after such a brief occupation, they threatened to wreak bloody vengeance on the population 'when they returned'.

Civilians were also used by the Germans as a screen to cover the advance and retirement of their troops. In August 1941, during an attempt to force a crossing of the River Ipput, the inhabitants of the town of Dobrush were used as a shield against Russian fire, being driven in front of the attacking German units. This practice was continued as long as German troops remained on Soviet soil. Large numbers of civilians were also used to clear mine-fields, although their employment on dangerous work is forbidden under International Law.

It might be supposed that great difficulty was experienced in finding sufficient executioners. The supply was always equal to the demand and it will have been observed that the demand was not small. None seems to have regarded this sinister duty with distaste; not a few relished it and some boasted of their exploits with

[1] Major operations.

pride. One of these, named Le Court, a senior corporal in the German Army proper and not a member of the SS, was, despite his French name, a native of Stargard where he had been born and lived all his life. He owned a cinema and was mobilized with the 4th German Airborne Division, and when serving in Russia was twenty-seven years old.

Whilst employed as a laboratory assistant in the photographic section of the headquarters of Air Field Service, he used to spend his spare time, to use his own words, 'shooting Red Army prisoners of war and peaceful citizens and burning down houses together with their occupants'.

In November 1942 he participated in the shooting of ninety-two Soviet citizens and, a month later, of fifty-five more. 'On both occasions,' he said, 'I did the actual shooting.' He also took part in reprisals on a number of villages and in that way personally set fire to many houses. He had, so he said, shot over 1,000 persons and 'in recognition of good work and service in the German Army received promotion before it was due'.

Doubtless he deserved the reward of his Führer whose advice he had so faithfully followed, for had not Hitler said, 'This gigantic territory [Russia] must be quieted as soon as possible: the best way to attain this objective is to shoot everyone, even those who only cast an ugly look.'

There were, however, some Germans who were horrified by what they saw. One German officer, a Major Roesler, who had previously commanded a battalion of the 528th Regiment, sent a report to the officer commanding the Ninth Military District regarding an outrage which he witnessed near Zhitomir, when his unit was resting in the area in July 1941.

Major Roesler had just moved into his new quarters with his staff when he heard volleys of rifle fire, not far away, followed by pistol shots. He decided to find out what was going on, and started off in the direction of the firing with his adjutant, First-Lieutenant von Bassevitz.

As they approached a railway embankment they were informed that a mass execution was in progress. What they saw when they reached the escarpment is best described in Major Roesler's own words:

When we finally scrambled over the embankment a picture of horror was revealed to us. A pit, about seven to eight metres long and perhaps four metres wide, had been dug in the ground.

121

The upturned earth was piled on one side of the pit and was completely soaked with blood. The pit itself was filled with numerous corpses of both sexes and all ages. There were so many corpses that it was impossible to tell how deep the trench was. Behind the pile of earth stood a detachment of Feld-polizei under the command of an officer. Many soldiers from units billeted in the area stood there, dressed only in shorts, watching the performance.

I approached the grave as near as possible in order to see for myself, and what I saw I shall never be able to forget. In the pit lay an old man with a long white beard, clutching a walking-stick in his left hand. As he appeared to be still alive I ordered one of the policemen to finish him off, and he smilingly replied, 'I have already shot him seven times in the stomach; he can die on his own now'.

The bodies lay in the trench, not in rows, but as they had fallen from the edge when they had been shot. . . . I have never seen anything like this before, neither in the First World War, nor in this. I witnessed many disagreeable things in the Frei-willigen Korps[1] in 1919 but nothing so horrible as what I saw at Zhitomir. . . . I wish to add that according to the testimony of German soldiers who have often watched these executions, several hundred persons are being shot like this every day.

The officer commanding the Ninth Military District sent this report to OKW together with the following typical covering letter:

Subject:—Atrocities perpetrated on the civilian population of the East.

With regard to the numerous mass executions in Russia which are widespread, I was at first convinced that they had been un-duly exaggerated. I forward herewith a report from Major Roesler which fully confirms such rumours. . . . If such things are done *openly* they will become known in the Fatherland and give rise to criticism.

Signed: Schirwindt.

In such a welter of barbarity it is not easy to single out one criminal or one incident for special mention, but crazy sadism

[1] This was founded in 1919 by a number of desperados from the German Army who refused to be bound by the Versailles Treaty and regarded Philipp Scheidemann, who signed it, as a traitor. Their activities were confined to Eastern Germany, principally Silesia and the Baltic Provinces, which they called 'Das Baltikum'. The members of this organization committed many acts of sabotage and murder against the lives and property of those whom they considered collaborators with the Allied Commission and the Government of Friedrich Ebert.

surely reached its peak in the extermination camp of Yanov during the period when Hauptsturmführer Gebauer, Obersturmführer Wilhaus, and Hauptsturmführer Wartzok were, in that order, Commandants.[1]

Gebauer, with his own hands, used to strangle women and children. He froze men to death in barrels; their hands and feet were first tied, they were then lowered into the tubs and left there until they froze to death.

Murder was so monotonous that the staff were officially encouraged to devise new methods, and one of them named Wepke, made a bet that he could cut a boy in half with one stroke of his axe. The bet was taken. Wepke got hold of a ten-year-old boy in the camp, made him kneel down with his head hidden in the palms of his hands, and after taking a practice swing, with one single stroke he cut the boy in two.

Wartzok used to hang the internees up by their feet and leave them hanging until they died. The chief of his interrogation branch, named Heine, stuck bars of iron into the bellies of the inmates and pulled out women's finger-nails with a pair of pliers.

Wilhaus, from the balcony of his office, frequently shot prisoners walking across the parade ground, partly for the sport of it and partly to amuse his wife and daughters. Occasionally he would hand the rifle to his wife so that she could have a shot. To entertain his nine-year-old daughter he sometimes used very young children for 'clay pigeon' practice, having them thrown up in the air so that he could take pot shots at them. His daughter would applaud and say, 'Papa, do it again'. Papa did.

It was this same commandant who on Hitler's fifty-fourth birthday, in substitution for a salute of guns, selected fifty-four internees and shot them himself.

In Yanov the tortures and the murders were carried out with musical accompaniment. An orchestra was formed of inmates and a special tune called the 'Tango of Death' was composed. When this camp was disbanded every member of the orchestra was put to death.

Such is the story of Nazi atrocities in the occupied territories, but it touches merely the fringe. The final score was twelve million murders. Speaking of these crimes in his closing speech to the

[1] This account of some of the atrocities committed in Yanov camp is taken from the testimony of an eye witness named Manusevitch who was employed in the camp. Manusevitch worked in a special squad of prisoners employed for burning the corpses of those murdered in the camp. See the Proceedings of the 59th Day of the Nuremberg Trials of Major War Criminals, Thursday, 14th February 1946.

International Military Tribunal at Nuremberg, Sir Hartley Shawcross said:

> In all our countries, when perhaps in the heat of passion or for other motives which impair restraint some individual is killed, the murder becomes a sensation, our compassion is aroused, nor do we rest until the criminal is punished and the rule of law vindicated. Shall we do less when not one, but on the lowest computation twelve million[1] men, women, and children are done to death? Not in battle, not in passion, but in the cold, calculated, deliberate attempt to destroy nations and races, to disintegrate the traditions, the institutions, and the very existence of free and ancient States. Twelve million murders! Two-thirds of the Jews in Europe exterminated, more than six million of them on the killer's own figures. Murder conducted like some mass production industry. . . .

It may well be that it is because all this slaughter took place at a time when the world was preoccupied with battle, murder, and sudden death that its enormity has never been generally recognized and has so soon been forgotten.

[1] This is the number estimated by the Prosecution. Since then a number of writers have made other estimates, one being as low as a little under nine million, but it remains, like the others, an estimate, and the real number will never be known.

CHAPTER V

SLAVE LABOUR

BETWEEN 1941 and 1945 more than five million foreign workers were deported like slaves to Germany whence a large proportion of them, though the number is not known, never returned. What happened to them is described in this chapter.

It is easier to appreciate the concept of Germany's slave labour policy if it is remembered that it was inherent in National Socialist doctrine which made the State pre-eminent and had no regard for the personal rights of individuals. According to a German writer on National Socialism, 'the relationship of labour is not a simple judicial relationship between the worker and his employer. It is a living phenomenon in which the worker becomes a cog in the National Socialist machine for collective production.'

Compulsory labour was instituted in Germany itself as early as 1935, and from 1939 the general mobilization of workers began under a decree of Göring as part of his Four-Year Plan. Under this decree foreigners resident in Germany were also liable for such service, so the principle of the compulsory recruitment of foreign workers was in existence in Hitler's Germany before the war.

The extension of this principle to the occupied territories in 1941 despite its prohibition by International Law can, therefore, occasion no surprise. It was one of the elementary components of the policy of Nazi domination and proceeded directly from the theory of the 'Master Race' and the conception of total war.

If there was a shortage of labour in Germany which imperilled the war effort, slaves would be brought in from the occupied territories. They would work for a German victory—so long as they were able. When they became too feeble or too ill to work, let them die. If they did not die quickly enough, they would be given assistance; put to death in the gas chambers of the concentration camps and their remains cremated in the camp ovens. But let there be no waste; their by-products must be utilized; their blood and ashes as fertilizer, their hair to make cloth, and the gold in their teeth to swell the coffers of the Reichsbank.

Such was the Nazi view. And as they thought, so they acted.

The International Law regarding forced labour by the inhabitants of occupied territories is set out in Article 52 of the Hague Convention which was binding on the Germans in 1939.

> Requisition in kind and services shall not be demanded from municipalities or inhabitants except for the needs of the army of occupation. They shall be in proportion to the resources of the country, and of such a nature as not to involve the inhabitants in the obligation of taking part in military operations against their own country.

Nor has an Occupying Power any right to deport the inhabitants to its own country and compel them to work there. This was done during the First World War on a comparatively minor scale and large numbers of French and Belgians were sent to Germany to work, but the practice was universally condemned by other nations. In the Second World War, however, the deportation of the inhabitants of occupied territories was carried out on such a vast scale and in circumstances of such brutality and degradation that the practice in the 1914/18 war fades into insignificance.

The Nazi slave labour policy had two objects; one was to use foreign labour to maintain the impetus of the German war machine; the other, a logical outcome of the Nazis racial doctrine, was to weaken by extermination 'inferior' peoples. It was never the intention that the majority of these deportees should ever survive their ordeal and return home. They died or were killed in hundreds of thousands, and many thousands more are still displaced persons.

An integral part of the general Nazi plan of total war, the slave labour programme was formulated and directed by Sauckel and Speer. Both these men were convicted by the Nuremberg International Tribunal; Sauckel was sentenced to be hanged and Speer to twenty years' imprisonment. In dealing with Sauckel's responsibility, the Tribunal in their judgment said that his attitude to the slave labour programme was expressed in one of the regulations which he issued: 'All the men must be fed, sheltered, and treated in such a way as to exploit them to the highest possible extent at the lowest conceivable degree of expenditure.' And so they were.

They were transported from their homes and their country in conditions usually considered quite unsuitable for cattle; they were crowded together in filthy quarters; they were overworked and underfed, and when they were no longer fit for work but refused to die, they were sent to a concentration camp where they were gassed and their bodies cremated in the camp ovens. According to Sauckel the aim of this labour policy was to use all the resources of what he called conquered countries, including all raw materials and human labour power, completely and conscientiously to the profit of Germany and her allies.

Wherever the German armies went the inhabitants were rounded up and sent to the Reich to work. Some attempt was at first made to obtain volunteers, but when this was conspicuously unsuccessful all pretence of voluntary recruitment was abandoned, and the workers were obtained by a combination of fraud, force, and terror.

The first victim, of course, was Poland. Frank, Hitler's Gauleiter in that country, set a target of a million workers and ordered his police to surround Polish villages and use press-gang methods.

'The supply and transportation of at least a million male and female agricultural and industrial workers to the Reich—among them 750,000 agricultural workers of which at least fifty per cent. must be women—in order to guarantee agricultural production and as a replacement for industrial workers lacking in the Reich.' These were his demands.

As early as May 1940 compulsion began to be used as there were insufficient volunteers to satisfy the Reich's requirements. 'The arrest of young Poles when leaving church services or the cinema,' wrote Frank in his diary, 'would bring about an ever-increasing nervousness of the Poles. I have no objection at all to such rubbish, capable of work yet often loitering about, being snatched from the streets. The best method for this would be the organization of a raid.'

Such raids became frequent as more workers were required. A need for more reinforcements of Polish labour had arisen by 1942. Those Jews who were still in employment in Germany were to be evacuated and replaced by Poles. The fate of such Jews will be shown in a later chapter, but an instruction from the Plenipotentiary General for manpower stated that the Poles who were deported to the Reich to replace them would be put into concentration camps and put to work 'in so far as they are criminal or asocial elements'. The remaining Poles would be transported to Germany *without family* and put at the disposal of labour exchanges to work in armament factories. This was in direct contravention of International Law.

As so often happened during the war these arbitrary methods did not always have the effect their authors intended or expected. In the same way as the shooting of hostages later on in France only increased resistance to the German occupation, so this 'wild and ruthless manhunt' for workers in Poland produced a violent reaction. One of Sauckel's deputies at a meeting of Hitler's central planning board reported in the following terms:

> The situation in Poland at the moment is extremely serious. The resistance against the administration by us is very strong . . . for example, fourteen days ago the head of our Labour Office in Warsaw was shot dead. Recruiting [for labour] even if done with the best will, remains extremely difficult unless police reinforcements are at hand.

In the Eastern Occupied Territories, which included Russia, the enforcement of labour was on a much larger scale. In 1942 Sauckel gave orders for two million workers to be drafted from the Ukraine. In forwarding these requirements to Rosenberg, who was then Reich Minister for the Eastern Occupied Territories, Sauckel wrote: 'I do not ignore the difficulties which exist for the execution of this new order but I am convinced that with the ruthless use of all resources and the full co-operation of all concerned the execution of the new demand can be accomplished by the date fixed.' All resources were, indeed, ruthlessly used and there was full co-operation, not least from the Reich Commissioner for the Ukraine to whom these orders were passed on by Rosenberg.

His reaction to these demands was not uncharacteristic.

> We are the master race. . . . I will draw the very last out of this country. The inhabitants must work, work, and work again. Some people are getting excited that the population may not get enough to eat. They cannot demand that. We definitely did not come here to give them manna. We are a master race which must remember that the lowest German worker is racially and biologically a thousand times more valuable than the population here.

Nor was Reichsführer Himmler more considerate. He wrote:

What happens to the Russians does not interest me in the slightest. Whether other nations live in prosperity or starve to death interests me only in so far as we need them as slaves for our culture. If 10,000 Russian females fall down from exhaustion while digging an anti-tank trench interests me not at all so long as the trench is finished for Germany.

As the forced recruitment of workers for Germany mounted to a crescendo, so partisan resistance increased. Many Russians, to escape deportation, left their homes and withdrew to the forests where they joined guerrilla bands. Precisely as Hitler's Commissar Order merely drove the Russian armies to resist with greater determination and to stay and fight it out rather than retreat; so the renewed drive for slave labour led to a shortage of potential slaves and simultaneously to increased resistance by the civilian population.

Still more ruthless steps were, therefore, taken to obtain Russian workers and an intensive manhunt was begun.

Amongst the papers found in Rosenberg's files after his capture were cuttings taken by the Nazi censors from letters written by Russians during this period. One of them wrote:

At our place new things have happened. People are being taken to Germany. On October 5th some people from the Kowkaski district were scheduled to go, but they did not want to and the village was set on fire. As not all who were due to leave Borowytski could be found, three truck loads of Germans arrived and set fire to their houses.

Another wrote:

On October 1st a new conscription of labour forces took place. Of what happened, I will describe the most important to you. You cannot imagine the bestiality. You probably remember what we were told about the Soviets during the rule of the Poles. At that time we did not believe it and even now it seems incredible. The order came to supply twenty-five workers, but no one reported. All had fled. Then the German police came and set fire to the houses of those who had fled. The fire burned furiously, as it had not rained for two months. In addition, the grain stacks were in the farm yards. You can imagine what took place. The people who had hurried to the scene were forbidden to put out the flames and were beaten and arrested. Meanwhile the police set fire to more houses. The people fell on their knees and kissed the policemen's hands but they were beaten down with rubber truncheons and the police threatened to burn down the whole village. I do not know how this would have ended had not Sapurkany intervened. He promised there would be more labourers by the next morning.

Describing the hunt in another district a third wrote:

They have already been hunting here for a week and have not got enough. The imprisoned workers are locked in the school-house. They cannot even perform their natural functions, but have to do it like pigs in the same room. People from many villages went the other day on a pilgrimage to the Poczajow monastery. They were all arrested, locked up, and will be sent to work. Amongst them are the cripples, the blind, and the aged.

A district commissioner near Kiev in reporting his activities in 1942 to Minister Rosenberg wrote:

In August 1942 measures had to be taken against two families each of which was to supply one labour recruit. Both had been requested but did not come. They had to be brought in by force but succeeded twice in escaping from the collecting camp in Kiev. Before the second arrest, the fathers of both workers were taken into custody as hostages, to be released only when their sons appeared. I then decided at last to take steps to show the increasingly rebellious Ukrainian youth that our orders must be obeyed. I ordered the burning of the houses of the two refugees.

And then there follows with sickening hypocrisy this sentence:

This harsh punishment was acceptable to the local population because previously both families had treated with contempt and scorn those conscientious people who had voluntarily sent their children to join the labour drafts.

But it was the Plenipotentiary General for Labour himself[1] who said that of the five million foreign workers brought into Germany from the occupied territories not even two hundred thousand came voluntarily.

[1] Sauckel.

However, these harsh and brutal methods had no success. The burning of entire villages produced no more recruits; but though unsuccessful they were, nevertheless, continued, and SS troops were ordered to take part in the raids on villages, to burn them down and impress the entire population for slave labour in Germany.

Nor was this all. In the collecting and transit camps through which these wretched people passed they were subjected to every form of indignity, ill-treatment, and brutality, and the conditions in which they were transported to Germany were truly appalling.

They were generally dragged away from their homes in such haste that they had no time to pack any of their belongings; sometimes they were taken away half-dressed; sometimes in their night attire. They were lodged in cellars, beaten, and kept without food, water, heat, or toilet facilities, and during medical inspection the women were frequently subjected to indecent treatment.

The following account is taken from a captured German document:

> In the women's and girls' shower rooms services were partly performed by men who would even help with the soaping. Men also took photographs in the women's shower rooms. Since most of these women were Ukrainian peasants they were of a high moral standard and used to strict modesty, and they must have considered such treatment as degrading.

The document from which the above passage has been taken stated that these incidents were 'altogether unworthy of the dignity and prestige of the Greater German Reich', but the Greater German Reich appears to have done little or nothing to remove this stain from its reputation.

On their journey, from Russia to Germany, the sick and the infirm were bundled with the others into cattle trucks, fifty to sixty in each truck. No arrangements were made to feed them *en route*. They had no water, and had to perform their natural functions where they stood or lay. Many, when they arrived in Germany, were already unfit for work and trainloads of these were then sent back to Russia in similar conditions.

The circumstances in which these returning deportees were conveyed were well known to Plenipotentiary Sauckel's Ministry, as the following report prepared in Rosenberg's office proves:

> In this train women gave birth to babies who were thrown out

of the windows during the journey, people with tuberculosis and venereal diseases rode in the same car; dying people lay in freight cars without straw; and one of the dead was thrown on to the railway embankment. The same must have occurred in other returning transports.

It was not only from Poland and Russia that slave labour was deported. From France, Holland, Belgium, and later Italy many thousands went to Germany.

In France from 1940 to the end of 1942 the policy was put into force with some discretion. This was in line with the general Nazi approach towards the French whom, with a surprising *naïveté*, for they should have known better, they first tried to appease with blandishments and moderation, instructing their armies to behave 'correctly'.

But the true heart of France was never in Vichy, and as soon as she had regained full consciousness after her stunning defeat in what General de Gaulle called 'the first battle' of the war, it was evident that the Gallic Maid could neither be wooed nor seduced. She would have to be ravished.

During the months which followed, Sauckel's powers were greatly increased by decrees of Hitler and Göring and he was given complete administrative control and even legislative competence in the performance of the task which his Führer had set him, and from his suite in the Ritz Hotel in Paris he sent many a Frenchman to slavery and death.

In his official pronouncements he justified the policy on the basis of National Socialist philosophy with customary rodomontade. The remarkable violence of the war, he said, forced him to mobilize in the name of the Führer, many millions of foreigners to labour for the German war economy. This was necessary for the preservation of the life and liberty of the German people and their Western culture for those who 'in contrast to the parasitical Jews and plutocrats', possessed the honest will and strength to live by their own efforts. He said that there was a vast difference between the work formerly exacted through the Treaty of Versailles and the Dawes and Young Plans— which took the form of slavery for the might and supremacy of Jewry—and the use of labour which he, as Hitler's Plenipotentiary General, had the honour to carry out as a contribution to the fight for the liberty of Germany and her allies.

But the object of the plan was not only to help the German war effort. Extermination by work was a basic element of the policy itself and not merely one of its consequences. For this reason, foreign labour was employed in the German war industry to the utmost limit of each worker's health and strength.

In 1942 Sauckel was given further powers over the civil and military authorities of the territories in the occupation of the German Armed Forces. This enabled him to have his own representatives on the headquarters of military commands, and to give them direct orders over the heads of the military commanders.

General von Falkenhausen, who was the Military Governor of Belgium and Northern France, has testified[1] that when the recruitment of labour was placed under Sauckel's direction the old arrangements were changed. Previously, there was an officer on his staff who was responsible for the hiring of labour which, von Falkenhausen stated, was purely voluntary. Afterwards, orders were given directly by Sauckel to the Labour Branch, and all the Military Governor had to do was to carry them out.

During the entire occupation, local field commanders used conscripted labour for guard duties and work on fortifications. In France they impressed Indo-Chinese and workers from North Africa. In the latter half of 1942, two large contingents of slaves, all conscripted, were drafted to France to work in the Todt Organization;[2] 5,560 Algerians and 1,825 Moroccans.

The Chantiers de Jeunesse[3] were also used from 1943 onwards to supply forced labour. In January 1943 the Labour Office of the German Armistice Commission in Paris announced that the Commander-in-Chief West, then von Rundstedt,[4] was examining whether and in what ways more French labour might be called upon for the accomplishment of tasks 'important to both countries' and that it was intended to recruit members of the Chantiers

[1] General von Falkenhausen was interrogated on 27th November 1945 by the French War Crimes Investigation Section.

[2] The Organization Todt was a labour force employed in the occupied territories on such projects as the Atlantic Wall and the construction of military highways. Albert Speer, the Reich minister for armaments and war production, used compulsory labour service to keep it up to strength. The organization was named after its founder Fritz Todt who died in 1942 and was succeeded by Speer.

[3] This was a Youth organization formed by Marshal Pétain after the armistice and modelled to some extent on the Hitler Jugend. Its marching song contained the refrain 'Maréchale, nous voilà'.

[4] Field-Marshal von Rundstedt was one of the leading generals in the German Army and of the old school. He was later responsible for the Ardennes counter-offensive of December 1944 which was Germany's last hit back. He was to have been tried as a war criminal in 1949 but the proceedings were dropped as he was found by a special medical board to be unfit for trial.

de Jeunesse. Many of these new recruits were used by the Germans for work on the fortifications which formed what came to be known as the 'Atlantic Wall'. It is difficult to understand how the construction of defences to keep out the allied armies then preparing to liberate France could accurately be described as a task 'important to both countries'.

As resistance to labour conscription increased, the occupation authorities promulgated ordinances imposing the death sentence on those disobeying requisition orders. An ordinance of 31st January 1942 decreed the following:

Whoever fails to comply with these requisitions of service or goods imposed upon him by the Military Commander in France, or any authority designated by him . . . shall be punished by penal servitude . . . and in serious cases the death penalty may be inflicted.

These serious violations of the Hague Regulations were the subject of numerous protests by General Doyen, the French Delegate to the German Armistice Commission.

As early as 1941 he drew the Commission's attention to the illegal use of forced labour in the Todt Organization in connection with the 'execution of military work on the coast of Brittany'. He complained that the French civil authorities were forced to provide guards for vulnerable points such as bridges, tunnels, munition depots, and operational airfields and, in an appendix, he gave a list of the services so provided.

General Doyen also protested vigorously against the ordinance of 31st January 1942, and stated that it was in contravention of both International Law and the Armistice Convention.

The German assertion, so often repeated, that recruitment of labour in France was on a purely voluntary basis is without foundation. Those workers who signed German labour contracts were subject to physical and moral pressure at which the Nazis were adept. The pressure was both collective and personal.

It is also beyond doubt that it was planned, as the following extracts from a German directive prove:

Subject:—Increased mobilization of labour for the German Reich from the occupied territories and preparations for mobilization *by force*. The labour shortage renders it necessary for workers for the Reich to be recruited in the occupied territories to a much greater extent than previously. . . . In the first place, this mobilization should be carried out on a voluntary basis as hitherto. If, however, satisfactory results are to be obtained the German authorities in charge of the scheme must be able to exert *any pressure necessary*.

This general directive was faithfully implemented by those to whom it was addressed, namely, Sauckel's representatives in France, Belgium, Holland, Norway, and Luxembourg. Propaganda was carried out to deceive workers of those countries in regard to the material advantages offered by the German employment exchanges. This was done in the Press and on the radio.

Such propaganda produced poor results, for it did not take the French long to realize that these material advantages were nonexistent. The next step, therefore, was to create artificial unemployment and to lower the living conditions of the workers and the benefits of the unemployed. This, too, was a failure and so-called voluntary recruitment was replaced by conscription.

One of the measures taken to obtain French and Belgian slaves was disclosed by Sauckel at a conference which he attended in 1944 in connection with the Four-Year Plan. The passage here quoted is from a shorthand note taken during the proceedings. 'The most abominable point against which I have had to contend is the claim that there is no organization in these districts to recruit Frenchmen and Belgians and despatch them to work. So I have had to train a whole staff of agents of both sexes who for good pay, just as was done in olden times for "Shanghaiing", go hunting for men and dupe them, using liquor as well as persuasion.' There must have been many a Frenchman who, after an evening out, woke up the next morning in a cattle truck *en route* for Germany, with a headache and a single ticket to Dachau[1] via some armament factory in the Ruhr.

The direct pressure put upon the workers was two-fold, moral and material. The Germans promised to offset the deportation of French workers to Germany by releasing a corresponding number of prisoners of war. It then transpired that the number of prisoners to be released was only in the ratio of one for five workers.

The nature of material pressure used is illustrated by the following letter sent to a young Frenchman from the department office of the Reich Labour Minister in the Pas de Calais:

[1] One of the Nazi concentration camps in southern Germany. See Chapter VI.

Sir,

On 26th March last, in Marquise, I ordered you to go and work in Germany at your own job, and you were to have travelled with the convoy which left for the Reich on 1st April. You paid no attention to this summons. I hereby warn you to present yourself with your luggage, next Monday 28th April before 19 hours at 51 rue de la Pomme d'Or in Calais. I call your attention to the fact that you leave for Germany as a free worker and that you will work there under the same conditions and earn the same wages as the German workers. In case you do not present yourself I must warn you that *unfavourable consequences may very well follow*.

The letter was signed 'Hanneran, Delegate for the Labour Ministry of the Reich'.

Whether the recipient of this letter was impelled by the threat of 'unfavourable consequences' to obey the summons or not is unknown; but there were doubtless many others who were. What happened to them when they got to Germany is told elsewhere in this chapter.

In January 1943 Sauckel was in Paris when he received a message from Speer to the effect that the Führer had now decided that it was no longer necessary, when recruiting skilled and unskilled labour in France, 'to have any particular regard for the French'. Recruitment could therefore be carried on with more severe pressure and measures.

Sauckel reviewed the requirements and decided that 150,000 skilled workers were at once required from France for the armament industry in Germany and that another 50,000 should be drafted from Holland and Belgium.

A few days later he attended a meeting of the Central Planning Board in Berlin, and told them that he had successfully persuaded Laval, who had already introduced compulsory labour in France, to extend the present law by the addition of three more age-groups and that these had just been called up.

But this was a mere drop in the ocean. In June 1943 Sauckel sent Hitler a skeleton plan for the coming six months. It provided for the deportation to Germany of 500,000 more slaves by the end of the year. Sauckel requested Hitler's approval and it was given for the asking.

The plan, however, was one thing; its implementation was another. Sauckel returned to the Ritz and, from his luxurious quarters there, began a campaign to force his programme through, but the French had recovered from their stunning blow of 1940 and the scheme met with widespread passive and active resistance from Government officials and militant patriots.

At a periodic conference of the Four-Year Plan in March the following year, Sauckel was forced to admit failure. 'Last autumn,' he said, 'as far as foreign manpower is concerned the labour recruiting programme was sadly battered. I do not wish to elaborate on the reasons here, they have been discussed at length. All I have to say is, the programme has been wrecked.'

Undismayed by this admission and notwithstanding the breakdown of the existing programme which it had disclosed, it was decided to proceed with the plan for the transfer to Germany during 1944 of well over a million foreign workers. These figures had been approved at a conference which Hitler had attended in January. This programme had called for 91,000 per month from France and 250,000 each from Belgium and the Netherlands for the whole year.

Sauckel never ceased to bring such pressure as he was able on the Vichy Government to meet these insatiable demands, and in February 1944 the call-up bracket was extended to subject to compulsory labour all men between the ages of sixteen and sixty and all women between eighteen and forty-five.

Nevertheless, the Plenipotentiary General had to report to Hitler that the aging Marshal of France would not agree to compulsory labour for women in the Reich, but he was able to tell his Führer that the French Government accepted the demand that officials who sabotaged the enforcement of the programme should be liable to the death penalty, and assured him that he had made it abundantly clear that more rigid measures would be taken if the demands for more slaves were not met.

But the sands of time were running out and the impending liberation of France grew ever nearer.

The Germans had decided, in the event of the invasion of France by the Allies, to deport forthwith all male inhabitants fit for work, but the allied armies advanced so rapidly once they had set foot on French soil that these plans could not be carried out.

The promise made to all these workers before they left their homes for Germany, that they would receive the same remuneration as the Germans, was never honoured.

137

They received very little, as the fines which could be imposed by their employers for the slightest breach of discipline often reached the amount of weekly pay due, and the worker received nothing. Those employed in factories were generally confined in labour camps and the Poles who were largely employed on farms were housed in the stables and liable to corporal punishment.

The camps in which the foreign workers lived were often administered by the firm which employed them. One such camp was situated at Schandelah and its inmates were employed by Steinoel & Co. in their factory nearby.

This factory produced oil from slate. In 1943 oil was becoming scarce in Germany and Reich Minister Speer emphasized the necessity of getting more in order to be able to continue the war. The work of Steinoel was given priority and they were supplied with slave labour from the concentration camp at Neuengamme.[1]

The manager of this firm was nominally responsible for the workers who were accommodated at Schandelah, and although he took no active part in its administration he was fully conversant with the general conditions of the camp.

The conditions of life, diet, and hygiene in this camp was atrocious. The diet was barely enough to keep inmates alive. Clothing was rarely washed and still more rarely changed. The camp abounded in fleas and lice. To protect themselves from the cold the prisoners, for that is what they were, began to cover themselves with paper from cement bags on the working site. The civilian administrative staff objected to these bags being put to such use so the prisoners were, upon the orders of the Camp Commandant, beaten for using them. The punishment for this offence was twenty-five strokes administered in public.

There was no medical officer in the camp and the hospital was run by the medical orderly, who in peace-time was a bricklayer by trade. He performed all his operations with a scalpel which he sterilized by dipping it in petrol.

The following is an extract from a description of the medical orderly's operations, given by one of the inmates who acted as his assistant:

Personally I admired the manner in which he set to work, but as he was operating in a haphazard fashion on persons who were already three-quarters dead, it is not surprising that they all died. For example, he operated with my assistance on a

Yugoslav whose stomach was terribly bloated but the remainder of whose body was exceedingly thin. This orderly told me that the stomach was full of pus. He opened it, took out the pus and sewed it up again. I shall never forget to the end of my life how the patient died three days later singing the Yugoslav national anthem. The orderly had a scalpel with which he did all his operations. He disinfected it with petrol which he stole from the garage. He also had some small pincers and a pair of scissors. There were no anaesthetics so nobody gave any. The patient was either held down by me, or bound to the table.

The camp medical officer only visited the camp to inspect the dead and give death certificates. He was never called in for anything else.

The attitude of the camp staff was that it did not matter whether the prisoners died or not. The staff themselves, however, did not die of starvation.

At numerous war crime trials of concentration and labour camp staffs it has been argued in their defence that the chaotic state of Germany in 1944 and the early months of 1945 made it inevitable that conditions in such camps should greatly deteriorate. The clothing of the Schandelah camp staff, however, was quite good and their food adequate. They did not die of starvation. Although the SS kitchen was the same as the workers', a special cooker was used for the SS food. They had 500 grammes of potatoes a day, they had thirty-five grammes of butter. The workers never got butter. The staff had sixty grammes of sausage daily, forty grammes of meat daily and no meatless days. Once a week they had milk soup: for this fifty litres of milk was used. They had 100 grammes of cheese daily; the workers rarely got cheese. The SS staff, moreover, did no hard work.

The real difference between the camp staff and the workers was this: the staff were regarded as human beings; the workers were regarded as expendable animal material.

The work was very hard, particularly for men who were weakened by semi-starvation. If it was not done quickly enough they were reported by the civilian supervisor. When prisoners were so weak that they could no longer work, they were returned in batches to Neuengamme and replaced by fitter men. They were literally worked to death, that is to say, they did work on a starvation diet until they either died at Schandelah or, being unfit for work, were returned to Neuengamme to die there. The Commandant, whose name was Ebsen, was a sadistic brute and the rest of the staff took their cue from him. Before he had joined the SS he had been a gamekeeper, a lay preacher, and interested in young persons who had gone astray.

It was he who gave the guards orders to beat all workers found wearing paper bags to supplement their clothing: these beatings were carried out with a small whip of rubber called a 'Schlag'.

He had complete power of life and death over the prisoners. He used to lecture the staff, telling them they must have nothing to do with the inmates whom he called 'criminals' and 'scum'; and as 'scum' he treated them, beating all and sundry both on and off parade.

Ebsen had an able lieutenant in his second-in-command, Truschel, who was known as 'The Killer' and appears to have been worse than his Commandant.

One prisoner, a Pole, was found asleep in the boiler house on a cold night; Ebsen beat him severely with a length of cable. A Latvian prisoner was denounced by one of his comrades as being engaged in making daggers. He was reported to Truschel, who killed him with a revolver shot in the head, saying, 'That will teach him to make arms and he won't make any more now.'

Wherever he went Truschel carried a whip, and all those under him went in perpetual fear. Another of the guards was a big man who in civil life had been a waiter and was described by one of the witnesses at his trial as being 'as fat as a pig'. Clearly he was on no starvation diet. This man beat the prisoners regularly on every occasion and upon any pretext, and for the purpose used a spade or a plank or whatever came handy. He also administered the punishment of twenty-five lashes which was awarded for minor breaches of discipline. He used to keep back part of the food which he was supposed to distribute to the prisoners.

In this camp, as in all other concentration and labour camps, the Kapo system was in force. A Kapo was generally a German criminal brought from one of the ordinary concentration camps and appointed the superior of other prisoners. He was put in charge of a block of huts and in return for the brutal discipline which he enforced on his subordinates was better treated, did no work, got more food, and was given something to smoke. One of the Kapos at Schandelah was a man named Grosse who was head of the Arbeitdienst of the camp, that is to say, he was responsible for allotting work. He had a pretty sense of humour and when he saw an unusually frail prisoner, and to be unusually frail in Schandelah one had to be a living skeleton, he would say to him, 'You will soon be going to the crematorium.' One of the inmates, who had been managing-director of a sugar factory in France, was given a running beating by Grosse over a distance of eighty metres. Each time the prisoner fell down he was picked up and beaten again. Four hours later he died.

Such was the daily round of the so-called prisoners in the camp, and it should be remembered that they were not criminals, though even that could not have justified their treatment. They were ordinary, peaceful, law-abiding citizens whose only crime was that they were inhabitants of countries which the German armies had invaded, and Germany needed them to work. So they were torn from their wives and families, often in the dead of night, loaded into trains and after a torturous journey, sometimes lasting five days, were dumped like so much ballast at the railway siding of a labour camp, there to enter upon a life of slavery.

None but the stoutest of heart can have dreamed that he would ever survive; many must have looked forward to their last journey to the crematorium as a happy release from a life of insupportable misery.

Early in 1943, a directive was issued by the Reich Government to the effect that pregnant foreign workers were not to be repatriated but that facilities for the delivery of infants were to be provided by local authorities 'in the most simple but proper hygienic form'. Provision was also to be made for the accommodation, feeding, and nursing of the infants immediately after birth so that the women who bore them could return to the factories to work for Germany.

A very large number of foreign workers were employed at the Volkswagenwerke near Hanover, and in February 1943, a 'Children's Home' was established at Wolfsburg in the factory area and managed by a Russian staff. Later the Home, which was under the supervision of the Factory Welfare Department, was put under the care and control of the works doctor, Dr Korbel, and a matron named Ella Schmidt.[1] Eventually it was moved some twelve kilometres away to Rühen where it was housed in huts.

It is known that between April 1943 and April 1945, 400 infants died there, sixty in the month of August 1944 alone. At first the

[1] Both Dr Korbel and the matron were tried and convicted by a British War Crimes Court. Korbel was sentenced to death.

babies were admitted with their mothers, but the Reich Minister for Labour later insisted that the mothers should return to work not more than fourteen days after their confinement. The mortality rate thenceforth rapidly increased.

The medical officer in charge was guilty of the most wilful and culpable neglect. Although in 1944 the death rate in the Home was 254 out of 310 admissions and increasd towards the end of the year, Dr Korbel's visit diminished in frequency to a weekly inspection. He took no steps to obtain the advice and assistance of a specialist in children's diseases. He never personally examined any of the sick infants. No autopsy was ever performed upon the body of any baby who died there, and he himself signed and accepted from others death certificates with the flippant diagnosis 'feebleness of life'.

The matron's conduct was little or no better. She was brutal and callous in her treatment of the infants. There was a complete absence of the flimsiest hygienic precautions at times when the outbreak of boils and the ubiquity of bugs aroused the disgust of every visitor to the Home. She admitted that she was never on duty at night and never paid a surprise visit.

When at last these wretched babies died, infested with lice, covered with sores, and weak from diarrhoea, they were left lying in a small room from which they were eventually collected in batches, packed in cardboard boxes, and transported to the local cemetery where they were interred without ceremony. Nor was any notice of impending death or burial ever given to the mothers.

But the 'Children's Home' at Rühen was not the only baby-farm set up by the Nazis. In 1944, owing to reverses in the field, there was an acute situation in Germany in regard to the production of food. It will be remembered that many foreigners were deported from Poland and Russia and brought to Germany for agricultural work. Many of these slaves were women, and it was not long before German farmers were complaining to their local Nazi Party Leader that Polish women employed as farm workers were losing time through child-bearing, ante-natal care, and subsequently while nursing their babies.

In the province of Helmstedt a Home was accordingly established for the reception of the infant children of such women. The infants were to be taken from their mothers, by force if necessary, very shortly after birth so that the latter could return to work in the fields.

This Home was situated at Velpke and consisted of two huts on one of the farms in the district. A woman named Billien was appointed by the Nazi Party Leader, one Gerike, as matron, and a man named Hessling was put in charge of its internal administration apart from the medical side. Frau Billien protested to Gerike about her appointment, informing him that she was only a school teacher and had no qualifications for the post.

From the outset there was gross neglect of the babies and high mortality. The local doctor, who was supposed to keep an eye on the Home, was completely callous and indifferent; the farm huts were quite unsuitable for the purpose; there was no skilled supervision; the diet was unscientific and harmful; sick babies received no proper medical attention; and were not segregated from the healthy. The huts had corrugated iron roofs and the heat on the Helmstedt plains in summer was such that the babies suffered terribly.

What Frau Billien lacked in skill and experience she could have made up with care and diligence. She gave little of her time to her duties, however, took all her meals out and slept out, and even during the day was frequently away for many hours at a time, leaving in charge four inexperienced Russian girls and one other Russian woman of doubtful experience in the proper rearing of children. The cots were soiled and louse-ridden and although the babies were healthy on admission they soon developed sores on their buttocks, sunken cheeks, spindly legs, and became a 'greeny-bluish colour'. Their garments were seldom changed and their diet was unregulated. The death rate was so high that between the months of May and December 1944, out of one hundred infants admitted, eighty-four died.

In this Home, also, when the babies died their bodies were not removed at once for burial, but were eventually placed in cardboard boxes and taken in handcarts to a field behind the cemetery where they were interred. So perfunctory was the burial that one day a dog was seen carrying in its mouth an infant's skull covered with hair.

These conditions were known to the responsible authorities but the knowledge did not produce any remedial action.

The manner in which these and similar institutions were organized and administered illustrates once more the utter disregard of the Nazis for the human rights of those inferior beings who had neither the good sense nor the good fortune to be born Germans. Hundreds of innocent children could perish of disease and starvation; thousands of harmless men and women could be worked to death, and millions of Jews could be exterminated. All this was of no consequence, so long as it helped to fulfil Hitler's prophecy that the Third Reich would last for a thousand years.

CHAPTER VI

CONCENTRATION CAMPS

LONG before the invasion of Poland in 1939 the concentration camp system was in full swing within the Reich, and under Himmler its organization had been perfected and its methods tried out and practised upon his fellow countrymen in time of peace.

By the Presidential Emergency Decree of 28th February 1933 (Hitler lost little time in such matters) 'Schutzhaft' or protective custody was introduced into the legal system of the Third Reich. Anyone who gave the slightest sign of potential active opposition to the new régime could thus be put out of harm's way and by these means, during the next six years, thousands of Germans were thrown into concentration camps for 'treatment', many of them never to regain their freedom.

To the Gestapo was entrusted the task of 'eliminating all enemies of the Party and National State' and it was the activities of that organization that supplied the concentration camps with their inmates, and the SS who staffed them.

How this weapon, forged and tested during the years immediately preceding the outbreak of war in 1939, was used during the war years as a means of terrorizing the inhabitants of occupied territories, and exterminating many millions of them is described in this chapter.

When war was declared there were six concentration camps in Germany holding in all about 20,000 prisoners. During the next two years more camps were built, some of them now household names: Auschwitz, Belsen, Buchenwald, Fossenberg, Mauthausen, Natzweiler, Neuengamme, Ravensbrück, and Sachsenhausen.

During the war, on the lowest computation, twelve million men, women and children from the invaded and occupied territories were done to death by the Germans. At a conservative estimate eight million of them perished in German concentration camps. Speaking of these Sir Hartley Shawcross, the chief prosecutor for the United Kingdom at the trial of major war criminals, said in his closing speech, 'Twelve million murders! Two-thirds of the Jews in

Europe exterminated, moreth an six million of them of the killers' own figures. Murder conducted like some mass production industry in the gas chambers and the ovens of Auschwitz, Dachau, Treblinka, Buchenwald, Mauthausen, Maidanek, and Oranienburg.'

To these camps were brought millions from the occupied territories; some because they were Jews, some had been deported as slave labour and were no longer considered fit for work, many were Russian prisoners of war, some were victims of the 'Bullet Decree', many were 'Nacht and Nebel' prisoners. There they were herded together in conditions of filth and degradation, bullied, beaten, tortured, and starved and finally exterminated through work or 'eliminated', as the Germans called it, by mass execution in the gas chambers.

The deterrent effect of the concentration camp upon the public was considerable, and had been carefully planned. Originally, in Germany itself the veil of secrecy and officially inspired rumours were both employed to deepen the mystery and heighten the dread. There were many who did not know what went on behind those barbed wire fences but few who could not guess.

It was not intended that this veil of secrecy should ever be wholly lifted. A privileged few were allowed an occasional peep and the many civilians who were employed in concentration and labour camps must have passed on to their relatives and friends outside some account of what they saw within. But Germany's enemies were never to have real evidence of the crimes which were committed there and plans had been made for the destruction of all these camp sites and the liquidation of their surviving inmates which only the rapid Allied advance and the sudden collapse of Germany circumvented.

The world has since learnt the full tragedy of the story. The survivors have told of their experiences, and the camps themselves have given testimony of the horrors of which their very walls were silent witnesses. Those who were the first to enter these camps will be forever haunted by the horror of what they saw.

In the pages which follow an attempt will be made to describe the conditions in some of these camps, and the life of degradation, filth, and torture experienced by all confined in them.

AUSCHWITZ

The little Polish town of Auschwitz (Oswiecien), population 12,000 and situated about 160 miles south-west of Warsaw, was before the war quite unknown outside Poland. Its geographical situation was most unfavourable. Lying in the bottom of a flat basin, it was surrounded by a series of stagnant ponds and was damp, smelly, and pestilential.

It is not surprising that in this misty bogland surrounding Auschwitz, there was no human habitation. As someone once said, 'it was avoided by life for a thousand years as death kept watch there'.

If death kept watch there for a thousand years, it was not in vain, for it was here that the Germans established 'Konzentrationlager Auschwitz' where at one time ten thousand were passing through the gas chamber daily and not less than three million people, according to the Commandant's own calculation, were killed in this and in other ways.

When the camp was first opened it consisted of six old barrack buildings and a derelict tobacco factory; but later it was greatly extended. On 1st May 1940 SS Hauptsturmführer Rudolf Franz Ferdinand Höss was promoted, and transferred to Auschwitz from Sachsenhausen where he had held the appointment of Adjutant to the Commandant since 1938. Auschwitz was to be an important camp, principally for the suppression of opposition to the Nazi occupation of Poland, to which the inhabitants of that unhappy country were not taking too kindly. So an efficient Commandant had to be found.

Höss possessed the necessary qualifications and must have had little difficulty in getting on the 'short list'. After service in the First World War he worked on farms in Silesia and Schleswig-Holstein until 1923 when he took part in a murder, for which he was sentenced to ten years' imprisonment. He was released five years later and pardoned, and in 1932 joined the NSDAP in Munich.

Whilst in command of a horse SS squadron on a farm in Pomerania in 1933, he was noticed during an inspection by Himmler, who thought that his experience and bearing fitted him for an administrative appointment in a concentration camp.

From then onwards his future was assured. He went in 1934 to Dachau where he started as a Blockführer in the Schutzhaftlager and remained there until posted to Sachsenhausen in 1938.

In 1941 Himmler inspected Auschwitz and gave instructions that it was to be enlarged and the surrounding swamps drained. At the same time a new camp was established nearby at Birkenau for 100,000 Russian prisoners. From this time the number of prisoners grew daily although the accommodation for them was quite unsatisfactory. Medical provisions were inadequate and epidemic diseases became common.

In 1941 the first intake of Jews arrived from Slovakia and Upper Silesia, and from the first those unfit for work were gassed in a room in the crematorium building.

Later the same year Höss was summoned to Berlin by Himmler and told that Hitler had ordered the 'final solution' of the Jewish question in Europe and as the other extermination camps in Poland were not considered very efficient, and could not be enlarged, Höss was instructed to make a visit to Treblinka and inspect the extermination arrangements there.

He visited Treblinka in the spring of 1942 and found the methods in use there somewhat primitive. Small chambers were used, equipped with pipes to induce the exhaust gas from internal combustion engines. This device was unreliable as the engines came out of old captured transport vehicles and tanks and frequently failed. The gassing programme had, therefore, not been carried out according to plan although according to the Commandant's returns 80,000 had been gassed in the previous six months. But this was not enough for Himmler who was in the process of cleaning up the Warsaw ghetto.

It was accordingly decided that Auschwitz was the most suitable camp for the purpose as it was a railway junction of four lines, and the surrounding country not being thickly populated, the camp area could be completely cut off.

Höss was given four weeks to prepare his plan, and told to get in touch with SS Obersturmbannführer Eichmann, an official of some importance in Amt IV of RSHA.[1] Eichmann would arrange with Höss what drafts would be sent him for extermination.

The numbers of convoys began to increase, and as the extra crematoriums would not be completed before the end of the year the new arrivals had to be gassed in temporarily erected gas chambers and then burned in pits.

Two old farm buildings which were situated in an out-of-the-way spot near Birkenau were made airtight and provided with strong wooden doors. The transports were unloaded at a siding at Birkenau and prisoners fit to work were taken off to the camps at Auschwitz and at Birkenau itself. The others, who were to be

---

[1] Amt IV was the department of RSHA which dealt with all Gestapo affairs. Obergruppenführer Müller was then its Chief.

gassed and could walk, were marched to the gas plant which was one kilometre from the siding. The sick and those who were unable to march were transported in lorries.

Outside the farmhouse all were made to undress behind a screen of hurdles. On the door was a notice, 'Desinfektionsraum' (Disinfecting Chamber), and the prisoners were given the impression that they were being taken into the building to be deloused.

When they were undressed they went into the room, according to the size of the convoy, about 250 at a time. The doors were locked and one or two tins of 'Cyclon B' were thrown in through specially constructed apertures in the walls. 'Cyclon B' gas was generally used for this purpose and contained a crude compound of prussic acid. The time it took to kill the victims varied according to the state of the weather but was seldom longer than ten minutes.

Half an hour later the doors were opened and the bodies were removed by the prisoners' Kommando, which was permanently employed there, and were burned in pits. Before the corpses were cremated gold teeth and rings were removed. Firewood was stacked between the bodies and when approximately 100 bodies were in the pit the wood was lighted with rags soaked in paraffin. When the flames had taken hold more bodies were piled on. The fat which collected in the bottom of the pits was put into the fire with buckets when it was raining to keep it alight. It took six to seven hours to cremate a pit full of bodies in these conditions and the smell of burning flesh was noticeable in the camp even when the wind was blowing away from it.

After the pits had been cleaned out, the bones were broken up. This was done by prisoners from the camp: the bones were placed on a cement floor and pulverized with heavy wooden hammers. What remained was then loaded on to lorries, taken to the River Vistula, and thrown in.

The above description has been taken from a statement which Höss himself made in March 1946 and refers to the methods used at the temporary gas chambers while waiting for the new chambers to be constructed. What follows is a description, from the same source, of the improved methods which came into force after two of the four large new crematoriums had been completed at the end of 1942.

Mass transports from Belgium, France, Holland, and Greece now began to arrive and the arrangements for their reception

149

were as follows. The train drew up alongside a specially-built ramp situated midway between the camp store and Birkenau camp. On this ramp the prisoners were sorted out and their baggage taken away. Prisoners fit for work were taken to one of the various camps; those who were unfit and were to be exterminated were taken to one of the new crematoriums.

The victims were first conducted to a large underground dressing-room adjoining the gas chamber. This room was fitted with benches and coat hooks, and the prisoners were told by interpreters that they were going to have a bath and be deloused, and to remember where they had hung their clothes. From there they proceeded to another room which was fitted with showers to give verisimilitude to the instructions which they had received from the interpreters. These precautions were intended to prevent panic and two Unterführers remained with the prisoners until the last moment to deal with any unrest.

Nevertheless, occasionally the prisoners knew what was going to happen, particularly if they had come from Belsen. There were no gas chambers in Belsen and when prisoners from Belsen, which is in Western Germany, found themselves travelling many miles eastward and reached Upper Silesia their suspicions became deeply aroused.

When a convoy arrived from Belsen, therefore, safety measures were strengthened and the prisoners were split up into smaller groups and sent to different crematoriums to prevent disturbances. SS men formed a strong cordon and forced resisting prisoners into the gas chamber. Disturbances were, however, infrequent and the measures taken to put new arrivals at their ease were usually successful.

One occasion on which there was serious trouble was thus described by Höss in his statement:

I remember one incident especially well. One transport from Belsen had arrived and two-thirds of it, mostly men, were in the gas chamber and one-third still in the dressing-room. When three or four armed SS Unterführers entered the dressing-room to make the prisoners hurry undressing, mutiny broke out. The light cables were torn down, the SS men overpowered and disarmed and one of them stabbed. As the room was in complete darkness wild shots were exchanged between the sentry at the exit and the prisoners inside. When I arrived I ordered the doors to be shut and I had the process of gassing the first party finished and then went into the room with the guard, carrying small torches, and we forced the prisoners into one corner from where they were taken out singly into another room in the crematorium and shot, by my order, with small calibre weapons.

Women often hid their children under their clothes as they hung them up on the pegs and did not take them into the gas chamber. The men of the Kommando used, therefore, to search the clothing, under supervision of the SS, and any children found hidden were then put into the gas chamber. In the new improved gas chambers, after half an hour had elapsed from the time the gas was turned on, the electric air-conditioner was started and the bodies taken up to the cremating ovens by lift. The cremation of approximately two thousand corpses in five cremating ovens took twelve hours.

All the clothing and other property of the prisoners was sorted out in the store by a Kommando of prisoners permanently billeted and employed there. Valuables were sent monthly to the Reichsbank in Berlin. Clothing, after being cleaned, was despatched to armament firms for the use of slave labour. Gold from teeth was melted down and sent once a month to the medical department of the Waffen-SS.

In December 1943 Höss left Auschwitz, but this inhuman destruction went on. Höss himself took up an SS administrative appointment in Munich under Obergruppenführer Pohl. In that appointment he made frequent inspections of the concentration camps and much of the information which we possess today about those institutions was given by him. It is from him that we know that not less than 3,000,000 people were put to death at Auschwitz, 2,500,000 of them by means of the gas chambers.

It is from him we know that, in pursuance of one instruction alone, during the time he was Commandant of Auschwitz 70,000 Russian prisoners of war were put to death there. And it was he who at one time in 1943 was putting 10,000 prisoners through the gas chambers every day.

Death transports arriving at Auschwitz included 90,000 from Slovakia; 65,000 from Greece; 11,000 from France; 20,000 from Belgium; 90,000 from Holland; 400,000 from Hungary; 250,000 from Poland and Upper Silesia; and 100,000 from Germany.

Thus did Auschwitz earn its name, 'The Camp of Death.' 'Arbeit macht frei' proclaimed the scroll over its main gate.

Dante s Inferno had a more suitable inscription: 'Abandon hope all ye who enter here.'

An SS man who was employed at Auschwitz has given this description of it:

The mere view of the tightly drawn high double barbed wire fences with sign-boards reading 'Attention! Danger!', the towers manned by sentries with machine-guns and machine carbines, and the lifeless bleak brick blocks, put every newcomer into a hopeless state of mind as he realized that from there he would never return to freedom. And there were indeed few who did not come to a tormented end there. Many committed suicide after a few days. When out on a working party they would run through the chain of sentries in order to be shot or they 'went into the wire', as it was termed in camp jargon. A high voltage shock, a burst from a machine-gun, and death spared them from the tortures to come. Whenever shots were heard during the night, everyone knew that once again despair had driven yet another human being into the wire and that he now lay there, dressed only in rags, a lifeless bundle within the so-called neutral zone. This was a strip of gravel two metres wide which ran along the inner wire obstacle and anyone entering this strip was fired on.

Others were found hanged by their belts at their bedsides in the morning. In such cases the prisoner responsible for order in the block would report the number of suicides to the Camp Commandant. The 'Identification Service' would then hurry to the scene and photograph the corpse from all angles and statements would be taken from the other occupants of the room to ascertain whether the wretched suicide had not perhaps been murdered by other camp inmates. The farcical hypocrisy displayed on these occasions was unsurpassed. As if the SS authorities of a camp in which thousands of people were systematically murdered daily were the least interested in the fate of one unfortunate man.

In all concentration camps the minor appointments were generally held by professional German criminals taken from the civil prisons and specially trained for their work by experienced SS concentration camp staff.

Auschwitz was no exception, and the first arrivals there were thirty criminals selected to form the nucleus of the junior staff. Camp seniors (Lagerälteste); Block seniors (Blockälteste); room orderlies (Stubendienst), and the Kapos or foremen.[1] These men were chosen from the worst type of criminal and were generally serving long sentences for crimes of violence. What better agents for the execution of Himmler's criminal plans?

A fortnight later the first transport of Poles arrived, and for some time only Poles were imprisoned there. During the period of the camp's existence there were prisoners of twenty-six different nationalities and towards the end of that time, when the camp was almost wholly used for extermination, the majority were Jews. Few of them had committed any offence; they were there simply because they were Poles, Jews, Gipsies, or Soviet prisoners of war.

Those who were not earmarked for immediate extermination were registered and given numbers. These numbers were sewn on the prisoners' clothing and from 1942 were tattooed on their forearms. There was also special badges for certain categories of prisoners, a red triangle for political prisoners, green for professional criminals, pink for homosexuals, black for prostitutes and female perverts, and violet for the clergy. The Jews bore the Star of David, and later a yellow stripe above the triangle.

From the moment they were registered they lost all trace of individuality and became mere cyphers. They had no personality and no property. All their belongings were confiscated and stored, except for certain items about which there were special instructions and the articles looted by the SS staff and guards for themselves or their families.

In this camp were thirty-five special buildings for sorting and storing these belongings, and it will convey some idea of the quantity of property confiscated if it is realized that although the Germans succeeded in burning, together with their contents, twenty-nine of these stores before they evacuated the camp, the following articles were found in the remaining buildings after the enemy had retreated—348,820 suits; 836,255 women's complete outfits; 5,525 pairs of women's shoes; thousands of tooth and shaving brushes and spectacles; all kinds of kitchen utensils, and even artificial limbs.

When life was normally so hard in Auschwitz Camp, punishment, to be made effective, had to be still more severe. In making it so, the camp staff do not appear to have encountered any difficulties. The following punishments were regularly awarded by

---

[1] The Kapos were in charge of individual huts and were brutal to their charges and greatly feared.

the Commandant. Flogging, transfer to a penal group, standing or kneeling for hours on end, and confinement in a dark narrow cell.[1] These cells were so small that the prisoners could not move and had to stand up the whole time. In Birkenau the entrances to them resembled the opening in front of a dog-kennel and there was only just room for a human being to crawl inside.

Stehzelle was accompanied and enlivened by sundry forms of torture such as the removal of finger nails, pouring water into the ears, deprivation of all food for days except for over-salted vegetables in order to produce greater thirst.

Flogging was administered in public during evening roll-call on a specially constructed whipping block. It was inflicted on the buttocks with a leather whip. Although the regulations stipulated that the buttocks should be clad, the prisoners were, in fact, whipped on the bare skin until the blood flowed. If the prisoner fainted he or she was revived and the punishment completed.

The standing punishment which was designed especially for women consisted of standing to attention for long periods during which time the women had nothing to eat. The kneeling punishment involved kneeling down with the hands outstretched, a heavy stone on each. If the prisoners lowered their hands or dropped the stones they were beaten.

In the famous Block XI lived the penal company. The following is a description of this block by a former member of the camp staff:

Outwardly, it hardly differed from the other twenty-eight buildings in which the prisoners lived or which were used as kitchens and hospitals. A few innocent-looking stone steps led to the entrance at the front. Unlike the other blocks, the door of Block XI was always shut. When the bell was rung an SS sentry would appear, his steps already echoing from afar in the apparently deserted building. He regarded every caller suspiciously through the little grill before admitting him. In the semi-darkness of the corridor one could now recognize a massive iron grid gate which seemed to seal off the main part of the building. Even from outside one was struck by the fact that the windows were almost completely walled-in, admitting light through a narrow slit only. Noticing that the windows of the adjacent block were covered by oblique wooden bars one was convinced that thereby hung a special tale.

[1] The name of this punishment was Stehzelle.

In this dark, forbidding-looking building lived the members of the penal company when they were not out on working parties. Their work was always in the open, in all weathers, and often in water to the waist. When they were not at work they lay all night in freezing rooms on bare floors. The sick rate in these conditions was very high and as the sick in Block XI were not allowed to be admitted to hospital many of them died.

A still greater number, however, died of violence. The block-leader, named Krankenmann, killed many with his own hands. Lining the prisoners up against a stone wall he would strike their jaws so hard that they fractured and the backs of their heads struck the wall and were smashed in.

As the inmates became unfit to work they were weeded out and murdered. The selection was made on special parades. The sick and the aged who knew the object of the parades tried to appear healthy and younger. They held themselves upright and threw out their chests. When selected, they were put into separate blocks which the prisoners called 'blocks of death'.

Gassing was not the only means by which the useless were put to death. A method of killing prisoners by injections of phenol[1] was devised by SS Obersturmführer Dr Endredd: he was assisted by others of the camp medical staff and between them they murdered not less than 25,000 prisoners in this way. These injections were administered thus:

> The condemned man was seated in a chair similar to a dentist's, and two prisoners seized his hands while a third blindfolded him with a towel and held his head. Then Dr Klehr approached him and drove a long needle into his chest. The prisoner did not die immediately but everything turned dark before his eyes. Then other prisoners who had assisted at the injection led the half conscious victim into an adjoining room, and laid him on the floor where he died in less than half a minute.[2]

The third method of extermination was by shooting, and such executions were carried out by the political department under SS Untersturmführer Grabner, a man personally responsible, per-

---

[1] Lethal injections were used elsewhere for the same purpose. On 6th July 1944 at the Natzweiler concentration camp in Alsace four women members of SOE (Special Operations Executive), who had been parachuted into France to maintain communications between HQ, SOE, and the French Resistance movement and had been captured by the Germans, were murdered by injections of evipan.

[2] *German Crimes in Poland*, Vol. I. (Central Commission for Investigation of Crimes in Poland.)

haps, for more murders than any other individual in the whole SS. The following is a description by someone who knew him.

In the office of the political department all the department officials and clerks are assembled. The boss, SS Untersturmführer Ernst Grabner, is having a talk with them on official business. Behind his massive writing desk, this man of medium height is 'talking big' in his Austrian accent with an assumed air of importance. His disjointed sentences and bad German make it obvious that one is confronted by a totally uneducated man in spite of his silver epaulettes. Those in the secret know that his civilian job was shepherding cows on some Alpine pasture. Now he proudly wears the lapels of the Sicherheitsdienst. . . . He is dissatisfied with the work done by his section. There are too few denunciations of prisoners, too few recommendations for execution. He reproaches his subordinates for leniency. His order to be more brutal in future is answered by a dumb clicking of heels. Grabner has become the first man in the camp on account of his unscrupulous ruthlessness, his ambition, and his craving for esteem. Even the Commandant Höss himself, hardly backward in any way as regards sadistic cruelty, and entirely free from scruples, carefully refrains from getting on bad terms with him.

Grabner initiated daily mass executions and also introduced the practice of shooting victims in the back of the head[1] so generally employed by the SS throughout Europe. His principal assistants were Fritsch, Palitsch, and Aumeier. Fritsch used to address new arrivals in the following words: 'I warn you that you have not come to a sanatorium but to a German concentration camp from which there is no way out save by the chimney![2] If you don't like it you had better throw yourself on the high tension wires.' Grabner and his assistants tortured inmates during interrogations which took place frequently on almost any pretext. If a man, they would prick his testicles with needles, if a woman they would introduce a burning suppository into her vagina.

Executions by shooting were carried out by the posts which were outside the camp fence. The prisoners were tied to these posts with their arms behind them, and then were shot in batches of ten, the last batch having witnessed the shooting of all the

[1] The German for this practice was Genickschuss.
[2] 'By the chimney'(Durch den Kamin) meant, of course, by way of the crematorium. The saying, 'You had better be careful what you say or you'll go up the chimney', was a species of threat in fairly common use in Germany during the war years.

others. Palitsch did the actual shooting but Grabner gave the order and 25,000 prisoners were shot by them at Auschwitz in this way.

The fourth and last method of extermination in general use was hanging. This was used principally in cases where prisoners had attempted to escape and had been recaptured. The executions took place in the presence of all the other prisoners so as to deter them from escaping. Before being hanged the victims were flogged. Their bodies were left hanging all night, and the following morning the whole camp was made to file past them.

Such was Auschwitz, the 'Camp of Death'; but it is only half the story. Were everything to be written it would not be read. If read, it would not be believed.

BELSEN

Near the village of Bergen on the road from Celle to Hamburg was Belsen concentration camp. Originally small, it was later enlarged and November 1944 Joseph Kramer, a concentration camp executive of great experience, was set there from Auschwitz to open it as a convalescent depot for sick persons from the concentration camps, factories, and farms, and for displaced persons from the whole of North-west Europe.

The camp was staffed like any other, the master and prefect system being used. That is to say, all appointments in which the word 'Führer' occurs were held by members of the SS—the masters—whereas the appointments in which the word 'Altester' occurs, such as Blockältester, were generally held by habitual criminals brought from the civil jails for that purpose—these were the prefects.

There were no gas chambers in Belsen but thousands were nevertheless exterminated by disease and starvation. During the last few months of the camp's existence the shortage of food was so acute that the prisoners (the camp staff were still well fed) resorted to cannibalism, and one former British internee gave evidence at the trial of the Commandant and some of his staff that when engaged in clearing away dead bodies as many as one in ten had a piece cut from the thigh or other part of the body which had been taken and eaten, and that he had seen people in the act of doing it. To such lengths had they been brought by the pangs of hunger.

This witness said:

157

I noticed on many occasions a very strange wound at the back of the thigh of many of the dead. First of all I dismissed it as a gunshot wound at close quarters, but after seeing a few more I asked a friend and he told me that many of the prisoners were cutting chunks out of the bodies to eat. On my very next visit to the mortuary I actually saw a prisoner whip out a knife, cut a portion out of the leg of a dead body and put it quickly into his mouth, naturally frightened of being seen in the act of doing so. I leave it to your imagination to realize to what state the prisoners were reduced, for men to risk eating bits of flesh cut from black corpses.

It is not proposed to describe existence in this camp; there was little variation in the rhythm of life in any concentration camp and Belsen was not much worse and certainly no better than most of them.

But a description of the sight which met the gaze of the first British officers to enter after its capitulation will convey a vivid picture of what existence, for one cannot call it life, was within those wire fences.

With the first troops to enter the camp went Captain Derek Sington, then in command of No. 14 Amplifying Unit, in order to make any announcements which were thought necessary or desirable and to act as interpreter to Lieut.-Colonel Taylor, the officer in command of the 63rd Anti-Tank Regiment, Royal Artillery, who moved in with one of his batteries to take over direction of the camp.

At the gate, Captain Sington was met by the Commandant, Joseph Kramer, who said that there were 40,000 in No. 1 Camp and a further 15,000 in No. 2 Camp, mostly habitual criminals, felons, and homosexuals but that there were also Schutzhäftlinge[1] —the political prisoners. These comprised, of course, ninety-nine per cent of the inmates and came from every country the Germans had invaded since 1939.

When Brigadier Glyn Hughes, the Deputy-Director of Medical Services, British Army of the Rhine, entered the camp a few hours after Lieut.-Colonel Taylor, the conditions he found were indescribable. 'No description nor photograph,' he said, 'could really bring home the horrors that were there outside the huts, and the frightful scenes inside were much worse.'

Piles of corpses were lying all over the camp, outside and inside

[1] Schutzhäftlinge—literally, those in protective custody.

the huts, some of them in the same bunks as the living. Near the crematorium were massed graves which had been filled in, and there was one open pit full of corpses.

The huts were filled to overflowing with prisoners in every stage of emaciation and disease; in some, which were only suitable to accommodate a hundred people, there were as many as a thousand.

There was no sanitation and the condition inside the huts was revolting because most of the prisoners were suffering from some form of gastro-enteritis and were too weak to go outside. In any event, the hut lavatories had long been out of use. In the women's compound there was a deep trench with a pole over it but no screening or form of privacy at all.

Those who were strong enough could get into the compound: others performed their natural activities where they lay. The compounds were covered with human excreta.

In one compound there were 8,000 male prisoners and typhus was rife. In one of the women's compounds there were 23,000 women and many corpses were still lying about. In one hut, which was close to a pile of corpses, there were dead women lying in the passage; in one room leading out of the passage there were so many bodies that it was impossible to squeeze in even one more.

Seventy per cent of the inmates required hospitalization and it was probable that 10,000 of these would die before they could be admitted.

Every form of disease was prevalent but those most responsible for the hopeless condition of the patients were typhus, tuberculosis, and starvation. The conditions in the camp must have been bad for several months to produce death in persons who were fit and well.

The morning after his inspection, Brigadier Glyn Hughes made a further tour of the camp with Kramer who took him to one of the open graves. The Commandant appeared quite callous and indifferent. 'I have been a doctor for thirty years,' said Brigadier Glyn Hughes, 'and have seen all the horrors of war, but I have never seen anything to touch it.' He also stated that there appeared to have been no attempt made at all to preserve the lives and health of the inmates.

Within a short time of the arrival of the British Army at the camp a film was taken and this was shown at the Belsen trial. Speaking of this film the chief British prosecutor at the trial, Colonel T. M. Backhouse, said:

This film will give you some idea of the conditions and the degradation to which the human mind can descend. You will see thousands of corpses lying about and the condition of, the bodies. You will also see the well-fed condition of the SS who were stationed there. You will see people fishing for water with tins in a small tank. What you will not see is that the water was foul and there were dead bodies in it. That was all the water that was available to drink. You will see the dead; you will see the living, and you will actually see the dying. What the film cannot give you is the abominable smell, the filth and squalor of the whole place which stank to high heaven.

This same film was also shown to an audience of Germans in Lüneberg, where the trial took place. It appeared to cause some of them no little amusement, and many of them thought it was propaganda.

BUCHENWALD

On a wooded hill six miles from Weimar, one of the shrines of German culture and freedom, a new concentration camp was established in the summer of 1937. Dachau and Sachsenhausen were doing flourishing business and Hitler wanted another 'dungeon of democracy' in central Germany.

For nearly eight years this camp was the scene of daily barbarism and brutality. The inmates were experimented upon like human guinea pigs; thousands were shot to death, many inmates, driven mad by the misery and horror which was life, rushed through the cordon of guards when out on working parties eagerly courting death, for them the only release from an agony of body and mind.

At Buchenwald they were crushed with rocks, drowned in manure, whipped, starved, castrated, and mutilated. But that was not all. Every tattooed inmate was ordered to report to the dispensary. At first no one knew why, but the mystery was soon explained. Those who carried on their skin the most decorative specimens of the tattooer's art were detained and then killed by injections administered by Karl Beigs, one of the Kapos.

The corpse was then handed over to the pathological department where the skin was removed and treated. The finished products were given to the Commandant's wife, Ilse Koch, who had them made into lampshades, book-covers, and gloves.

Another discovery made at Buchenwald when the American

160

Army reached it in April 1945 were the preserved skulls of many of the victims. Someone in the camp had decapitated two Poles who had been hanged for having sexual relations with German girls. The skull bones were removed and the heads shrunken, stuffed and preserved. The heads were the size of a fist, and the hair and the marks of the rope were still there.[1]

In April 1947 SS Obergruppenführer and Waffen-SS General Josias Prince zu Waldeck, and thirty members of the camp staff, including Frau Koch, were brought to trial before a United States Military Tribunal. The venue of the trial was the concentration camp at Dachau, near Munich, which many of the accused had previously visited in very different circumstances. The charge against them alleged *inter alia*, that they had subjected many thousands of prisoners, from at least twelve different nations to 'killings, beatings, tortures, starvation, abuses, and indignities'.

In this camp for about eight years every type of horror known to man was practised with sadistic pleasure. Whether simple extermination as in the earlier years, or extermination by 'working to death', as later on, the pattern followed was always the same. 'Break the body: break the spirit: break the heart.'[2]

And what did the German people know of these things? It has often been suggested that they knew nothing. That probability is as unlikely as its converse, that they knew everything.

It has been said, 'You can fool all the people some of the time, and some of the people all the time, but you cannot fool all the people all the time', and there is an abundance of evidence that a large number of the Germans knew a great deal about what went on in concentration camps. There were still more who had grave suspicions and perhaps even misgivings but who preferred to lull their consciences by remaining in ignorance.

As the shortage of labour grew more acute it became the policy to free German women criminals and asocial elements from the concentration camps to work in German factories. It is difficult to believe that such women told no one of their experiences. In these factories the forewomen were German civilians in contact with the internees and able to speak to them. Forewomen from Auschwitz who subsequently went to the Siemens sub-factory at Ravensbrück had formerly been workers at Siemens in Berlin. They met women they had known in Berlin and told them what

[1] The author has himself seen these shrunken heads.
[2] Extract from the introduction to the official information pamphlet issued at the trial.

they had seen in Auschwitz. Is it reasonable to suppose that these stories were never repeated? Germans who during the war indulged in careless talk used to be told—'You had better be careful or you'll go up the chimney'. To what could that refer but the concentration camp crematoriums?

The concentration camp system had been in existence in Germany for several years before the war and many Germans had had friends and relatives confined in the camps, some of whom were subsequently released.

From Buchenwald, prisoners went out daily to work in Weimar, Erfurt, and Jena. They left in the morning and came back at night. During the day they mixed with the civilian population while at work. Did they never converse, and if they did, was the subject of concentration camps always studiously avoided?

In many factories where parties from concentration camps worked, the technicians were not members of the armed forces and the foremen were not SS men. They went home every night after supervising the work of the prisoners all day. Did they never discuss with their relatives or friends when they got home what they had seen and heard during the day?

And what of the SS executive staff and guards. It is true that they had all signed statements binding themselves never to reveal to anyone outside the concentration camp service anything which they had seen inside their camp.

But is it reasonable to believe that one of them was human enough to break that undertaking? The bully is ever a braggart.

In August 1941 the Bishop of Limburg wrote to the Reich Ministries of the Interior, of Justice, and of Church Affairs as follows:

About 8 kilometres from Limburg in the little town of Hadamar ... is an institute where euthanasia has been systematically practised for months. Several times a week buses arrive in Hadamar with a considerable number of such victims. The local school children know the vehicle and say, 'There comes the murder box again.' The children call each other names and say, 'You are crazy, you will be sent to the baking ovens in Hadamar.' Those who do not want to marry say 'Marry? Never! Bring children into the world so that they can be put into the pressure steamer?' You hear the old folks say, 'Do not send me to a state hospital. After the feeble minded have been finished off, the next useless eaters whose turn it will be are the old people. . . .'

If the local inhabitants knew so much in Hadamar is there any doubt that the inhabitants of Bergen, Dachau, Struthof, and Birkenau knew something of what was happening at their very doors in the Belsen, Dachau, Natzweiler, and Auschwitz concentration camps?

Höss himself said of Auschwitz, 'the foul and nauseating stench from the continuous burning of bodies permeated the entire area and all the people living in the surrounding communities knew that exterminations were going on at the concentration camp'.

Day after day trainloads of victims travelled in cattle trucks over the whole railway system of the Reich on their way to extermination centres. They were seen by hundreds of railway workers who knew whence they had come and whither they were going.

Whatever horrors have remained hidden behind the camp walls, such things as these went on in broad daylight and all those Germans who had eyes to see and ears to hear can have been in little doubt of what crimes were being committed in their name throughout the land.

DACHAU

Dachau, one of the earlier concentration camps, was situated near the village of its name and about twelve miles from Munich. At the side of the main road was a signpost showing the way. It was here that so-called medical experiments were carried out on hundreds of inmates who became human guinea pigs.

Between 1941 and 1942 some five hundred operations were performed on healthy persons. The object was to instruct SS doctors and medical students. Many of the operations were of a serious nature, for example, removal of the gall bladder, and were performed by students of only two years' standing. Such operations should not normally be performed except by doctors with at least four years' practice of surgery. Many of these patients either died while the operation was in progress or from post-operative complications.

Malaria experiments were also carried out on some 1,200 inmates, none of whom volunteered. These experiments were carried out by a Dr Schilling, on the personal instructions of Himmler. The victims were either bitten by mosquitoes or given injections of malaria sporozoites taken from mosquitoes. The object of the experiment was to test out certain drugs as specific for malarial fever. Thirty to forty of these 'patients' died from the malaria itself and several hundreds later died from other diseases as a result of their constitution having been undermined by the disease. A number were also poisoned by overdoses of neosalvarsan and pyramidon, two of the experimental drugs.

Other experiments were carried out in Dachau by Dr Sigmund Rascher, a major in the Luftwaffe. Twenty-five men were put into a specially constructed van in which air pressure could be increased or decreased. The object of the experiment was to watch the effects on the victims of high altitude or a rapid descent by parachute.

Many of the inmates who were subjected to this experiment, which must have been pure torture, died from haemorrhage of lung or brain. Those who survived were coughing blood when removed from the van. The internal organs of those who had died were sent to Munich for examination; the survivors were generally put to death.

Other tests conducted by Dr Rascher were to observe the effect of immersion for long periods in very cold water. These were described[1] by Dr Franz Blaha from Czechoslovakia who was arrested by the Germans in 1939 and became an inmate of Dachau. He was present at a number of these experiments.

> The subject was placed in ice cold water and kept there until he became unconscious. Blood was taken from his neck and tested each time his body temperature dropped one degree. . . . The lowest body temperature reached was 19° centigrade but most men died at 25° or 26°. When the men were removed from the icy water attempts were made to revive them with artificial sunshine, hot water, electro-therapy, or by animal warmth. For the last experiment prostitutes were used and the body of the unconscious man was placed between the bodies of two such women.

This was considered most entertaining and Himmler on occasions brought parties of his friends to see it. He even took sufficient interest in the experiment to write to SS General Pohl to tell him of its progress and that he had given orders that suitable women—*but not Germans*—should be earmarked at Dachau for the purpose of reviving those who had been so exposed. 'Four girls were set aside,' he wrote, 'who were in the concentration camp for loose

[1] Dr Blaha's affidavit made on 9th January 1946 and sworn at Nuremberg.

morals and because, as prostitutes, they were a potential source of infection.'[1]

Further experiments were conducted there by a Dr Schutz and others on large numbers of Polish, Czech, and Dutch priests. A group of these were selected and given intravenous injections of pus. No after-treatment was allowed so that inflammation or general blood poisoning set in. Various drugs were then used to attempt to deal with this condition. Great pain was suffered during this experiment and most of those who did not die of septicaemia became permanent invalids.

A large number of Hungarians and Gipsies were, in 1944, subjected to salt water experiments which consisted of being given nothing to eat or drink except salt water, during which time their blood, urine, and excrement were analysed.

Provided certain basic requirements are observed medical experiments upon human beings are in accordance with the ethics of the medical profession. To satisfy these requirements the experiments must first and foremost be conducted upon volunteers, persons who are entirely free to give their consent, not under duress; who are in a position to withdraw from the experiment at any stage; and who fully realize the implications and possible hazards. The experiment must also be calculated to produce results which will be beneficial to society and could not be obtained by other means. Finally, the experiment must be conducted by highly competent, qualified doctors and the highest degree of skill and care must be exercised during and after the operation.

The experiments carried out by doctors in the concentration camps were not of this kind. The subjects were not volunteers; compulsion was always brought to bear on them and often physical violence was used. The operations were sometimes performed by unqualified persons and generally in unhygienic conditions.

No steps were taken to prevent or minimize suffering and whether the patients lived or died mattered not. The experiments generally resulted in death and the survivors were often disfigured or mutilated, or became permanent invalids. Finally, many of the experiments were of no medical or scientific importance.

NEUENGAMME

The camp at Neuengamme was founded in 1938 and its popula-

[1] Extract from a letter written by Reichsführer SS Himmler to SS General Pohl on 16th November 1944.

tion grew so in numbers that by 1942 there were three times as many inmates as the camp could properly accommodate, despite the fact that no less than 55 satellites had been added to the 'Neuengamme Ring', satellite camps which included such well-known names as Banterweg, Bullenhausendamm, Hannover-Ahlem, and Schandelah.

It was in that year, 1942, that a change in concentration camp policy came about owing to German reverses and losses in Russia. Until then the policy laid down by Himmler was one of death by extermination of the unwanted inmates of these camps. Subsequently this was radically altered due to the rising shortage of labour, and it became one of the preservation of life at the barest subsistence level possible so as to extract from the inmates the maximum amount of labour at the minimum expense while they remained alive.

At Neuengamme after 1942 only the ailing who were unfit were actively encouraged to die. The remainder during that brief period they remained fit for work, were suffered to live.

In all, over 90,000 people passed through Neuengamme, of whom some 40,000 died; 3,000 from bona fide natural causes and 37,000 from natural causes brought about by unnatural conditions and unparalled callousness. Of the total number of inmates in the Neuengamme Ring during the last twelve months of the war ninety per cent were Allied nationals imported into Germany as slave labour, and ten per cent Germans of whom half were habitual criminals in minor positions of authority in the camp.

The main camp at Neuengamme was a depot from which the fitter people were selected to be sent to satellite camps, where they endured physical and mental hardships even more barbarous than in the main camp, and where a fair estimate of life was two months.

The Commandant, Max Pauly, a man of ruthless and domineering temperament, was feared by all. Like all his subordinates, he was a member of the SS; like all, save the two doctors, he was plebeian in origin. Anton Thumann, his Deputy, was in charge of all the prisoners' compounds and consequently of the welfare, if such a word can be used, of all the inmates. He was a conspicuously brutal scoundrel and directly responsible for many murders. Willy Dreimann, Thumann's second-in-command, a lesser figure but not a lesser scoundrel, often acted as camp executioner. Under these men were the various Compound Commanders each of whom had drastic plenary powers over a thousand inmates.

Finally there were the two doctors, Alfred Trzebinski and his assistant Bruno Kitt. The former arrived at the camp in the autumn of 1943, the latter in January 1945. Kitt was in every sense a lesser man than Trzebinski; less intelligent, less clear sighted, less aware of evil done though not a lesser evil-doer, less honest and less refined. He, unlike his senior, descended to striking his patients.

These two men were alone responsible for the health of some 14,000 inmates. They were expected to salvage those patients from whom more work might be obtained; to take 'appropriate measures' in respect of those too ill to be fit for future work. Trzebinski and Kitt fulfilled all expectations.

In the autumn of 1942, Bahr, the medical orderly, on the instructions of Trzebinski's predecessor, herded 197 Russian prisoners of war into a cell, assisted by Dreimann, and pumped 'Cyclon B' gas into it. All the Russians died, and were then dragged out, placed in trucks and taken away. The inmates were all paraded to witness this macabre scene and made to sing a song of which the first line was: 'Welcome sweet troubadour, let us be gay and joyful.'

Early in 1945 eighty Dutchmen were admitted to the main camp. Twenty soon died of general debility. The remaining sixty were hanged secretly without trial. Half these were sick men at the time of their execution. Thumann and Dreimann were the hangmen and they received an extra liquor ration for their labours.

In February the same year, twenty French and Russian Jewish children, between the ages of five and twelve confined in the main camp at Neuengamme, were selected by the infamous Dr Heissmeyer of Berlin as experimental material in the so-called interests of medical research. Heissmeyer made frequent visits to the camp and injected these poor children with TB bacteria. During the period in which these experiments were being carried out the children were given sweets and toys. Many of them became gravely ill.

In April the Allies were rapidly approaching Neuengamme and orders were issued by SS General Pohl, at the request of Dr Heissmeyer, that the children should be taken to Bullenhausendamm satellite camp to be executed so that all evidence of the experiments would be destroyed.

The children were duly moved to Bullenhausendamm by Dr Trzebinski together with four 'nurses' (in fact two French and two Dutch doctors, themselves to be executed) and six Russians. Later the same evening twenty-four other Russians arrived. A man named Jauch who was in charge of Bullenhausendamm Camp met

167

the party at the gate. He appeared to know the purport of Dr Trzebinski's visit and accompanied him to the cellar with the prisoners. The adults were taken away and hanged in another room.

In the cellar, waiting for them to arrive, was Johann Frahm. The children were at once undressed and Trzebinski, moved by a sudden humane impulse, injected them, happily never aware of their fate, with morphia so that they should be unconscious when they were hanged. Frahm then placed ropes round their necks and, in his own words, 'like pictures they were hanged on hooks on the walls'.

RAVENSBRUCK

In Mecklenburg, some fifty miles north of Berlin is a group of lakes surrounded by swamply land. Near one of these, Lake Fürstenburg, a new concentration camp was established shortly after the outbreak of war in 1939. It was known as Ravensbrück concentration camp and consisted of a main and auxiliary camps. The main camp contained only women and from the time of its inception until it was overrun by the Red Army in its advance westward, over 123,000 women were interned there. A large number were French nationals and it is from them that it derived the name which it so richly deserved and by which it is generally known, 'L'Enfer des Femmes'.[1]

Some of these women were prisoners of war, Russian Red Cross nurses captured on the field of battle, but the majority were civilians, either members of a resistance movement, or slave workers who had been deported from their homes to work in Germany and whose productive output had proved insufficient. All these were interned without previous trial and ninety per cent were Allied nationals.

The main camp was designed to accommodate 6,000. From 1944 onwards there were never less than 12,000 interned there and in January 1945 there were 36,000. At least 50,000 perished there and many thousands more doubtless met their death elsewhere on transfer to other camps. Apart from those who were murdered, the main reasons for this terrible death rate was undernourishment, overwork, exposure, overcrowding, complete lack of sanitation, and systematic brutal ill-treatment by the camp staff.

The whole treatment of the inmates by the members of the camp

[1] The Women's Hell.

staff from the Commandant down to the SS guards aimed at deteriorating the prisoners' condition, both physically and mentally. It was thus poignantly described by one of the prisoners herself:

The whole system in this camp had but one purpose and that was to destroy our humanity and our human conscience; the weaker individuals fell into the very bottom of moral and physical existence; all the lower bestial instincts developed while the better instincts were stifled and had no chance to show themselves. Even the stronger ones who have come out of the camp alive are marked with unnatural characteristics which will never be erased: they have lost all faith in goodness and justice.

One of the inmates was a Norwegian, very well known in her own country. Her presence in the camp was solely due to the fact of her being one of the King of Norway's friends. The British had made a raid on the coast of Norway taking back with them not only about two hundred young Norwegian volunteers but some Nazi prisoners and Quislings. A few days later an announcement was made over the radio that the Germans were to take as hostages twenty of the King's best friends. Sylvia Salvesen was one of them. She was arrested, then released, and eight months later was re-arrested, kept in prison in Norway for eleven months, and taken from there to the prison in Alexanderplatz in Berlin whence after five days she was removed to Ravensbrück.

When she arrived at the camp she was received in the usual way and taken after a few hours to a large room which she learned later was called the bathroom. There were no baths in it, merely holes in the ceiling through which water flowed. This is her description of what then took place:

We had to wait naked for two hours before the water came. Remember, we had been eighteen days on the road and were longing for a wash, but there were four to each shower and the water only flowed for about four minutes. We had a tiny piece of soap and what they called a towel, but it was little bigger than a handkerchief. . . . Then something happened which gave us the biggest shock, the first big shock in Ravensbrück. There entered two men dressed in uniform. We later heard that one was a doctor and the other a dentist. We were then lined up in

169

rows and still naked had to walk past them, but they merely examined our teeth and our hands. I am afraid we felt ashamed because we had not yet learned that the shame was not ours but theirs.

The food was scarcely enough to keep the prisoners alive and certainly insufficient to keep them in a fit state for work. The quantity varied; being particularly inadequate from 1942 onwards. The prisoners were so starved that they ate raw potato peelings and bits of cabbage which they found lying on the ground near the cookhouse and this is understandable when the daily menu was a bowl of ersatz coffee in the morning, a soup made of potatoes or cabbage at midday, and the same in the evening with a little bread.

This was, of course, known to the Commandant but nothing was ever done to improve the conditions. Indeed, the camp staff stole for themselves and their families large quantities of food belonging to the prisoners and when their guards also robbed them of the Red Cross parcels that arrived from time to time, they made the prisoners sign receipts for the parcels under threat of death.

Nor was this all. The camp staff delighted in tormenting the half-starved prisoners by throwing them pieces of bread which had gone mouldy in the stores. To watch these living skeletons fighting like wild beasts for such morsels was an entertainment which never failed to amuse the SS. It was upon a diet such as this that the inmates were expected not merely to exist, but to work ten or eleven hours a day. Work went on day and night with a double shift of about eleven hours each. Reveille was at 5.30 a.m. and roll call at 7 a.m. This generally lasted about two hours during which all the inmates had to stand to attention in the open and in all weathers both winter and summer. The working parties were then formed and marched away. When the shift was over, another roll-call took place.

The work was hard and the workers driven on relentlessly with blows and kicks. Spinning, weaving, loading and unloading, digging, road mending; at such work were these women kept, and threatened and beaten every time they stopped for breath.

The lack of sanitation was in itself enough to cause a heavy death rate. In the words of one of the inmates herself:

Vermin were very much in evidence; the huts were so lousy that sometimes lice could be found in the soup. The sewer and water systems had both broken down and the camp looked like a huge farmyard consisting of one big dungheap.

Underwear and clothing were seldom if ever changed, and if we got a change of underclothes they were always lousy and not infrequently still stained with blood and discharge. We had no socks and wore only wooden shoes. We slept on dirty palliasses covered with excrement and we had one blanket between three to cover us. There were insufficient soup bowls and we used to eat out of tins which we found on the rubbish heap.

It was upon such people that Sylvia Salvesen gazed as she left the 'bathhouse' and got her first glimpse of the camp itself; and when she gave evidence at the Ravensbrück trial in Hamburg in 1946 she thus described her impressions:

This for me was like looking at a picture of Hell—not because I saw anything terrible happen but because I then saw, for the first time in my life, human beings whom I could not distinguish whether they were men or women. Their hair was shaved and they looked thin, filthy, and unhappy. But that was not what struck me most; it was the expression of their eyes. They had what I can only describe as 'dead eyes'.

When the inmates became so ill that they could not be beaten to work they were admitted to the camp hospital which was known as the 'Revier'. It was a hospital in name only; otherwise it differed little from the ordinary huts in which the inmates lived—and died. There were the same rows of beds in tiers, and more often than not, two patients to one bed. The doctor in charge was named Treite, the matron was Oberschwester Marschall, and one of the nurses was Carmen Mory, herself a prisoner, and Swiss by birth.

Treite, who was half British, went to Ravensbrück, which he described as 'the best-class of concentration camp', in September 1943, and remained there until the end of the war. He was the second senior doctor in the camp. At his trial he endeavoured to create the impression that he alone of the entire medical staff adhered to the high standards of an honourable profession; that he was disgusted with all he saw and did what he could to improve the well-being of the inmates. He was, he said, merely 'a simple camp doctor' and what could he do against 'the Commandant, the whole staff, and all those SS officers'?

Undoubtedly the most skilful doctor in the camp, Treite seems to have shrunk from some of the more unpleasant tasks which fell to him. Nevertheless, the evidence given at his trial clearly showed that he was quite ruthless when it suited him, that he was an important cog in the machinery of extermination in operation in the camp, and that many of the inmates died through his actions.

In one of the camp blocks was a special room in which lived the women who were supposed to be mad. It was a very small room about five yards by six and at times as many as sixty or seventy women were confined in it. They were half naked, having only chemises, no dresses. The room was so overcrowded that there was hardly room to sit, let alone lie down. There was one window, without a pane, and in winter it was icy cold. The women had no blankets nor anything else with which to cover themselves. The sole sanitary arrangements consisted of a bucket in the centre of the floor, which always got upset during the night and by the morning the occupants were smeared with their own excreta.

Many of this room's occupants were not even mad. But they were shut in day and night and were unable to go outside for any purpose. They only left it to die.

Fighting often broke out among them and one morning four were found to have been strangled during the night. The following day, Treite, at the request of Carmen Mory, gave orders that the 'ten maddest women' should be killed to make room for more.

He also gave instructions to the nurses that old women who had been admitted to hospital suffering from bad or incurable ulcers should receive no treatment as they were 'unproductive', being unable to work. He gave orders that bandages must never be changed more than twice a week. Sick women who were still physically capable of work he would discharge from hospital whatever their clinical condition.

He ended the lives of some of his patients by administering lethal injections. All positive TB patients were sent to the gas chambers. He personally took part in selecting about 800 women to be transferred to Lublin. The selection took place in the extermination room, and Oberschwester Marschall was also present. The poor women passed by them stark naked and were put down haphazardly for the convoy to Lublin irrespective of their age or physical condition. Many, of course, died on the journey.

One of Treite's duties as medical officer was to attend the beating of prisoners who had been sentenced by the Commandant for petty crimes. The maximum sentence was three beatings of twenty-five strokes carried out at intervals of four weeks. Present at the beatings were the Commandant or his deputy, the head doctor or his deputy, the head wardress, and the two prisoners who did the actual beating. The victim was strapped on to a block. Treite's duty was to see that no blood was drawn and that the victim was fit to receive the punishment. Whether the prisoners screamed or not made no difference to the sentence being carried out.

Treite was also present when inmates were shot. These executions were done near the crematorium. Prisoners were usually killed in batches of fifty and the doctor's presence was necessary because the victims were not always killed immediately. Describing these 'executions' when giving evidence at his trial Treite said, 'I must make it quite clear that it was not only sick people who were involved, but as a result of the haphazard method of selection young women fit for work were also shot.'

Each day fifty prisoners were disposed of by being shot through the back of the neck and then cremated. This procedure began towards the end of 1944 after Himmler had paid one of his routine visits to the camp. The Commandant received orders from the Reichsführer that all inmates who were ill or incapable of marching were to be killed, for the Germans anticipated having to evacuate these camps in face of the ever-approaching Russian armies and they had made plans to remove all evidence of their iniquity by destroying the camp sites and taking the inmates along with them as they retreated westward.

About this time, the Auschwitz concentration camp in Poland, having been evacuated for a like reason, two experts in extermination arrived at Ravensbrück; Schwartzhuber, who became Assistant Commandant, and a Dr Winkelmann.

With their arrival began the organized mass slaughter of all those whom it was considered impracticable to evacuate. Such women were selected on special parades and given pink identity cards. These cards, which had previously signified that the holders were exempted from hard labour, now became veritable passports to death. After being selected, the women were transferred to the adjoining Jugendlager[1] for extermination. Many of these were shown in the camp records, with macabre deception, as having been evacuated to Mittelwerde, a convalescent home in Silesia.

When the women were paraded for selection they were inspected by one of the camp officials accompanied by a doctor, who

[1] Lit., youth camp.

used to look at their hair to see whether it was grey, at their legs to see whether they were swollen, and then made them walk past to see whether they had a steady gait.

In order to avoid selection the older women tried to blacken their hair to make them appear younger. All they could get for this was the soot which they scraped from the kitchen chimneys. It must have been heartbreaking to see these aged skeletons on selection parade trying to march past with the light springy step of a young girl so that they should not be sent off to their death.

At first the extermination of those unable to be evacuated was carried out by shooting, and a specialist in shooting people in the nape of the neck was posted to the camp from Berlin. After several hundred had been shot in this manner the Commandant decided that progress was too slow and had a gas chamber built. This was hastily erected in the Jugendlager and in the few weeks which followed prior to the arrival of the Russians, about seven thousand women are estimated to have been gassed.

The Assistant Commandant, Schwartzhuber, has described the operation of the gas chamber in these words:

> I attended one gassing. 150 women at a time were forced into the gas chamber. Hauptscharführer Moll ordered the women to undress, as they were to be deloused. They were then taken into the gas chamber and the door was locked. A male inmate climbed on to the roof and threw a gas container into the room through a window which he again closed immediately. I could hear groaning and whimpering inside. After two or three minutes all was quiet. Whether the women were dead or just unconscious I could not say as I was not present when the chamber was cleared out.

Few who reached the Jugendlager ever left it alive. One of those who did was Mary O'Shaughnessy, who described the conditions there when giving evidence at the trial of members of the camp staff at the War Crimes Tribunal in Hamburg.

It was, according to her evidence, a small camp consisting of about ten huts, smaller than those in the main camp. On arrival the women were made to stand about for three or four hours before they were allocated to their 'rooms'. These 'rooms' were just partitioned areas in each hut. There were no beds but the floor was littered with bags filled with straw. Each 'room' was so overcrowded that it was impossible for all to lie down at the same time. It was not even possible for all to sit down in comfort. No food was handed out until 5 p.m. on the day following arrival, nor was there anything for the inmates to drink during the first twenty-four hours of their stay there.

Miss O'Shaughnessy spent nearly five weeks in the Jugendlager during which time the diet diminished, the number of 'Appells' increased and hundreds of women were picked out for gassing. Selection parades during this period were held almost daily. On one of these parades were two French girls who were sisters; only one of them was picked out for the gas chamber but her sister refused to leave her and eventually they went to their death hand-in-hand.

There was also a crematorium. This was latterly not only used for disposing of dead bodies and there is evidence that some internees were thrown into the ovens whilst still alive.

One of the inmates of the camp in April 1945 was Odette Sansom[1] and she could see the building from the window of her cell. The ovens were working day and night from the latter part of 1944 and Mrs Sansom could hear the doors being opened and shut and people screaming. A full description of this was given in evidence by her at the Ravensbrück trial in answer to questions by the Judge Advocate.

Q. Will you describe as clearly as you can any incident that you saw in which you say some human being was put alive into that crematorium?

A. The last few days of the war I saw people being driven to the crematorium, I could hear them screaming and struggling and I could hear the doors being opened and shut.

Q. I wanted to know whether you were prepared to swear that you had seen somebody being forcibly pushed inside the crematorium so that they were burned to death.

A. I can certainly swear that I have seen people dragged but I cannot swear that I have seen them in the crematorium.

Q. When they were dragged to the crematorium what did you see then? How did it end when they were dragged there?

A. I did not see them any more.

Q. Did they vanish out of your sight?

A. Yes.

[1] Odette Sansom was dropped in France by SOE and when arrested was tortured by the Gestapo in an effort to get information out of her. The Gestapo were unsuccessful and she was then sent to Ravensbrück. Odette Sansom was awarded the George Cross for her services.

Q. Where did they go, so you could not see them?
A. I do not know; probably into the crematorium.
Q. Did they go inside the building?
A. Yes.
Q. Did you see them come out again?
A. Never.
Q. And after they disappeared you heard something, is that it?
A. Yes.
Q. And the sound you heard you thought was the noise of the crematorium being opened and shut?
A. Of that I am sure.

Ravensbrück concentration camp was staffed on the same pattern as all other concentration camps. The Commandant and the other officers on the camp establishment all belonged to the SS, with the exception of some of the medical staff who were only attached. So did the camp guards.

The Commandant was Fritz Suhren, the Assistant Commandant Schwartzhuber, and the head of the Labour Department was Pflaum. These three men formed the executive staff. But under them were a number of men and women in subordinate positions who were in day-to-day contact with the inmates and it was they who by their brutality and devilry made the camp a living hell.

Ramdohr, the head of the so-called Political Department; Binder, the foreman in the tailoring workshop; Dorothea Binz, the head wardress; Skene, an under wardress; Greta Bösel, another wardress and leading assistant to Pflaum in the camp labour office; Margarete Mewes, in charge of the punishment block; Carmen Mory, a former prisoner turned Blockälteste; Vera Salvequart, originally a prisoner, later in charge of the Jugendlager hospital; and Elisabeth Marschall, a nurse by profession, and the camp matron.

The medical staff were Schidlausky, for some time the senior medical officer; Treite, senior assistant to Schidlausky's successor Trommer; Rosenthal, and the dentist Hellinger.

Each and every one of these was a working part of the machine of brutality, oppression, terror, and extermination which was Ravensbrück. Each and every one had their allotted duty; each contributed in some small way to the total sum of misery which made up the day-to-day existence of those under their control and in their power.

It is only by learning of some of their crimes that it is possible to appreciate the magnitude and enormity of the concentration camp system or to realize how, while it lasted and as long as its power went unchallenged, virile peoples could be kept in subjection and brave spirits could be broken.

Schwartzhuber was a pastmaster in brutality, for he joined the SS in 1933 and could therefore claim twelve years' service in that criminal organization. Trained at Dachau before the war, he must have been a promising pupil, as between the years 1935 and 1944 he received systematic promotion. Graduating from Dachau he acquired further professional knowledge and experience at other seats of sadistic learning, Sachsenhausen and Auschwitz, from which latter place he arrived at Ravensbrück on 12th January 1945 where he remained, in the appointment of camp leader and second-in-command, until the end. When he took up these appointments the women prisoners numbered about 25,000; when the camp dissolved three and a half months later there were only 12,000 left.

The mass murder started as soon as he arrived. He went through all the records and parties were sent regularly to the Jugendlager where many executions took place. There was no question of any trial; the victims were either selected by reference to the office files or picked out on parade.

The order to kill these women came from the SIPO and was countersigned by the commandant Suhren. They were shot in the back of the neck by the expert, Corporal Schultz, outside the crematorium, then taken inside and burned. It is significant that their clothes were burned with them. These women faced death with such fortitude that even Schwartzhuber confessed to having been 'deeply moved' when he attended one of the executions.

Shortly after his arrival at Ravensbrück with the remainder of his prisoners from Auschwitz, the selections for Mittelwerde began, and 3,500 inmates were shown in the camp books as having been 'transferred to Mittelwerde Convalescent Camp' during March/April 1945. A glance at the map will show that Mittelwerde was then in a part of Germany already occupied by the Red Army.

Ramdohr, who was chief of the camp 'political department', was a criminal police officer by profession and responsible for all interrogations. He was not a member of the SS, but evil communications corrupt good manners, and during the time he held that appointment, which he took up in 1942, he was second to none in brutality.

A clerk who worked in a room next door to his office frequently heard women's screams during interrogation. If he did not get the information he wanted he was known to have kept a woman for a week without bed or food in a cold dark cell from which she emerged half mad.

A Polish woman named Szeweczkova was interrogated by Ramdohr and, as she refused to give her friends away, was sent to the punishment block where she spent twelve days without blankets and without food. On the twelfth day she was taken in front of Ramdohr but as she still refused to talk she was ordered 'six water douches'.

This treatment, which had been devised by Ramdohr, consisted of special high-pressure showers of icy cold water from a fire hydrant. These were continued twice a week for three weeks after which Szeweczkova was again interviewed by Ramdohr, but without success. She was then sent again to the punishment block for six weeks, receiving a little coffee and bread each day and cooked food every fourth day. At the end of that time she was brought before the Commandant and as she still refused to speak was dismissed and sent to hospital. By some freak of chance she escaped the Jugendlager and is alive to this day.

Ramdohr carried out the cruellest physical and mental torture. One woman was so badly beaten that she afterwards tried to commit suicide by opening a vein in her neck and was treated by Treite. He admitted depriving prisoners of food, beating them, giving them narcotic injections, and questioning them under the influence of such drugs. He also used to tie prisoners' hands behind their backs and make them lie on their stomachs on a table in such a way that their heads protruded over the end of the table where he had placed a chair on which there was a bowl of water: he then gripped the women by the hair and pushed their faces into the water.

Thus did Ramdohr carry out his interrogations. Such methods were not those of the KRIPO, to which he belonged, but of the Gestapo, of which he was an apt disciple.

This man, like so many others who have strutted across the stage of German history like frenzied marionettes, was a strange study in psychology. A curious mixture, like so many of his fellows, of sadism and sentimentality, of tenderness and tyranny.

When he was convicted by a War Crimes Tribunal at Hamburg in 1947 and sentenced to death by hanging, many of his relatives and friends wrote to say that 'dear kind Ludwig could never do harm to any animal'; that he was a comrade 'who had delight in nature'; that he was a 'protector of the poor and oppressed'; that when 'walking in the country he sometimes gave queer little jumps to avoid crushing a snail or a lizard under his foot', and that when burying his mother-in-law's canary he 'tenderly put the birdie in a small box, covered it with a rose and buried in under a rose bush',

It is not easy to reconcile the brutal Ramdohr of Ravensbrück. the terror of the camp, with the 'dear kind Ludwig' remembered by his family and his friends.

Binder was in charge of one of the workshops and a man of great brutality. A tailor by trade, he entered the SS in 1933 as a volunteer and, like Schwartzhuber, graduated at Dachau. His early training and experiences of SS methods must have stood him in good stead whilst employed as foreman in the notorious tailors' shop in the factory colony at Ravensbrück.

He beat and kicked the women in his workshop and persecuted them at every turn. He always carried a whip and it was a common sight to see women sitting there still sewing but bleeding from the blows he had dealt them.

This is what a Dutch inmate who used to have to work under him has said:

Binder was very rough and brutal to the women in his workshop. He used to beat us every day and seemed only to calm down when he saw blood. Once I saw him beating a Polish woman in such a way that she had to be taken straight off to hospital. I never saw her again and was told that she had died. If we did not work hard enough to please him he would take away the small pieces of bread we had for the eleven hours' shift and make us work standing up for hours.

Sometimes he hit women with a stool, and I have seen him drag them along by the hair and beat them up. Undernourished and tired as we were, when he noticed a woman with her head bent down he used to come and take her head and push it against the work-table. He also used to make us take all our clothes off and stand naked; his excuse for that was to ensure that we had not hidden pieces of cloth in our clothing because at that time we had so little to wear.

Another young Polish girl who was sent to work in Binder's workroom had an open sore on her arm from lack of vitamins.

Binder objected to her complaining and reporting to hospital. He tore off the bandages saying, 'You are not sick at all.'

The girl then fell down and when she had risen he hit her in the face with his fist with all his strength. The blow felled her and he then proceeded to kick her all over.

Many women had wounds caused by having scissors thrown at them by Binder, and others through being hit in the face with tunics which had metal buttons on them. He was responsible for the deaths of many women by forcing them to work when no longer fit to do so, and making them stand outside in the rain stark naked, often for more than an hour at a time.

Dorothea Binz was head wardress with the rank of Aufseherin (Supervisor) and was feared by all.

This young girl was born in 1920 and just before the war had been in service as a kitchen maid. By 1939 she was already tired of household drudgery and through the good offices of a friend was accepted by the SS as a volunteer, on 1st September 1939, when only nineteen-and-a-half, and was immediately sent to the newly-opened concentration camp at Ravensbrück. Much to her disgust she was posted to the camp kitchen, doubtless because of her previous experience.

But she soon convinced her superiors that she was destined for higher things. Within a few months she had been appointed Aufseherin and it must have been a proud day for Thea Binz when she first donned her field-grey uniform and strutted round the camp in her black top boots, whip in hand.

A brutal and sadistic creature, from that day she became an integral part of the camp system which crushed the life out of thousands of innocent women; and the female of the species was more brutal than the male.

She beat, she kicked, she hit all and sundry, day in and day out, sometimes as punishment for petty disciplinary offences, sometimes for no reason at all—merely for 'Schadenfreude.'[1] Sometimes she used a stick, sometimes a whip, sometimes a belt, sometimes the blotter on the desk in her office—anything handy. The whole camp was in terror when she appeared.

Once, Binz beat a woman until she fell down, and then trampled on her: once, outside the camp when she was visiting a working party in the forest, she felled a woman with a pickaxe and con-

[1] A German word, with no equivalent in the English language, signifying a feeling of enjoyment at another's misfortune.

tinued hitting her with it until, covered with blood, the woman moved no more. Binz then mounted her bicycle and pedalled back to camp.

She had authority to send people to the punishment block for a minor breach of discipline when she chose not to deal with it by a summary beating. She also carried out the Commandant's summary awards of twenty-five, fifty, or seventy-five strokes.

Anyone who was late for 'Appell'[1] she beat, or made them stand to attention for hours, slapping their faces while they stood, and a slap from Binz was no light matter, as one of her victims has testified; 'It was the same as if a big man had hit me, for they have studied that kind of thing: if she slapped your face it was so hard that it could be heard two rows farther down.'

Binz also carried out the 'water-douche punishment'. Stanislawa Szeweczkova who had been ordered six douches by Ramdohr because of her lack of co-operation at an interrogation, described it thus:

Binz took me into the douche room. In a corner stood a douche and the water was already turned on; it ran from pipes at various heights and was pumped out at great pressure. After about twelve minutes I fell over and Binz threw a bucket of water in my face. As I tried to hold my hands over my face she opened a door and whistled for her two dogs. One of them bit me in the hand. I then fainted. I assume that I was dragged into my cell as my back was covered with bruises when I came to, and my clothes were lying beside me . . . from then on I received a douche twice a week from Binz, on Tuesdays and Fridays. Each time I fainted.

One of Binz's favourite sports was to ride her bicycle into a group of women who were standing nearby. As they were so weak they were generally knocked down and she then rode over them, laughing as she did so. She also delighted in setting her dogs on the inmates. One day she set her dog on a Russian woman, exciting him and urging him on so that he bit the woman continually. One of the woman's emaciated arms was literally torn off.

Another entertainment which she found highly diverting was to visit Block 10 and inspect the mad women who were under the care of Carmen Mory. These women were exhibited as an attraction—like the freaks at a circus sideshow—and Binz enjoyed taunting them and making fun of them.

[1] The name for the daily early morning roll-call.

181

It is impossible to give more than a rough sketch of this girl's activities at Ravensbrück. She came to the camp on the first day of the war and remained there until the end. She had been trained in her duties by the notorious Irma Grese of Belsen and had proved a ready pupil. For over five years she struck terror into the hearts of thousands of wretches in her power, and when she was hanged in Hamelin prison in 1947 it was a better fate than she deserved.

In charge of the 'mad women' was Carmen Mory. This woman, though herself a Swiss subject, became a willing tool of the Germans and whilst a prisoner at Ravensbrück accepted the position of Blockälteste and, working under the Commandant, was responsible for great cruelties and persistent ill-treatment of other prisoners over whom she was placed in authority.

Mory was, unlike the German members of the female camp staff, a woman of education. Born in Berne in 1905 she was educated in Switzerland, France, Holland, and England. Later she attended a course in journalism at Munich University and became a free-lance journalist in Switzerland and England. Born of Protestant parents, she was later converted to Roman Catholicism.

In November 1939 she was arrested in France and tried in 1940 for espionage in connection with the Maginot Line. The Military Tribunal which tried her sentenced her to death, but she received a pardon three months later.

On 7th June, as the Germans were approaching Paris, she was set free but was captured by the Germans near Tours on 24th June and taken back to Paris. Her case was referred to RSHA in Berlin from whom instructions were received for her arrest. After being confined in the French prisons of Cherche-Midi and Fresnes, she was taken to Germany in August 1940 and whilst in custody in the Alexanderplatz prison was interrogated by the Gestapo. Eventually, on the instructions of Heydrich, she was released, but subsequently re-arrested on suspicion of espionage against Germany and sent to Ravensbrück in February 1941.

This third-rate Mata Hari soon ingratiated herself with her captors and became Blockälteste, in which appointment, as one of the witnesses at her trial said, 'she behaved like a real SS'. She even had opportunity to practise her old trade as she was, during part of the time she was in her camp, one of Ramdohr's stool-pigeons.

For some months she was in charge of Block 10 where was

situated the room in which the 'mad women' were confined. Also in Block 10 was a room occupied by TB patients. Mory appointed a German criminal as prisoner in charge of those patients and he used to beat them and steal from them. Mory herself habitually beat her charges. One such, a Polish woman, was beaten by Mory, who also threw buckets of cold water in her face and over her body when she was stark naked. This woman was charming and generally liked. She also sang well and it was for this reason and no other that Mory ill-treated her. She died the following day.

The Belgian women in the camp called Mory 'The Monster'. She used to drag sick women, half-dead, out of their beds in Block 10, have them pulled into the wash-house, dumped on the cold stones, and have buckets of cold water poured over them, saying, 'Now you will be clean.'

Violette Le Coq was a lieutenant in La France Combattante, one of the organizations in the French resistance movement. Before the war she had been a hospital nurse. She was arrested on 20th August 1942, and in October 1943 arrived at Ravensbrück as a Nacht und Nebel prisoner. A few months after her arrival Mlle Le Coq was taken by Mory to help in Block 10.

At the Ravensbrück Trial Mlle Le Coq described in her evidence an incident which occurred one night in Block 10.

One night we were awakened by shouting which came from the room where the insane prisoners were housed. Carmen Mory, a student of medicine, a French nurse, and myself got up and went to the room to see what was happening. We opened the door and we saw two women fighting with each other. One of these was apparently a Russian. Mory took one of the leather belts which were always hanging there and started belabouring both the women. She sent the medical student to get some ampoules, and then gave both the women injections. The following morning I returned to the room where I saw five women lying dead, including the two whom Mory had injected the night before.

Mory remained at Ravensbrück until the end of the war, when she was released with many others and eventually made her way to the British Zone where she found employment with a British Army Field Security unit near Hamburg where she was finally arrested as a war criminal on 5th October 1945.

One of the most sinister figures in this camp was a young woman

183

named Vera Salvequart. She also had a curious history and first came to the camp as a prisoner.

At the date of her trial she was only twenty-seven years of age. Born in Czechoslovakia, her mother was a Czech and her father a Sudeten German, and she had trained as a professional nurse in Leipzig.

During the war she was arrested no less than four times. In 1941 she had been arrested, interrogated, and sent to a Jewish camp in Flossenberg. The reason for her arrest on that occasion was that she had become engaged to a Jew who was wanted by the Gestapo and could not be found. As she refused to tell the Gestapo his whereabouts she was kept in Flossenberg for ten months and then released.

She was arrested again in May 1942, charged with breaches of the Nuremberg Laws, including 'relationship' with Jews, and was sentenced to two years' imprisonment, being released in April 1944.

She was re-arrested on the 8th of August 1944 and charged with espionage and aiding the enemy, and was tried together with her fiancé and his sister at Dresden. Her fiancé took all the blame and was condemned to death. Salvequart and her prospective sister-in-law were sent temporarily to the concentration camp at Theresienstadt, whence they arrived after a long and devious journey at Ravensbrück on 6th December 1944.

This young woman, for whom otherwise some sympathy might well be felt, during the few months she remained at Ravensbrück was personally responsible for the death of a large number of her fellow prisoners by poisoning them, though the exact figure is not known. But she has given us a great deal of information about the extermination programme which was carried out at Ravensbrück and in which she later became an active participator.

When she arrived she was taken to the notorious 'Tent for the Jews'. There were two thousand women in it, all Jews from Hungary or Czechoslovakia who had previously been interned at Auschwitz and were passed on to Ravensbrück as the Russians advanced through Poland.

There were no beds, no palliasses, no straw, no floor boards, just the bare earth. On the right of the entrance to the tent a corner was roped off and there were ten old four-gallon drums which were used as lavatories. There were no washing facilities. Dr Treite called it 'The Tent for Pigs'.

In this tent were inmates who were suffering from typhus and two or three of them died every night. It was, so she said, the first time Salvequart had ever had to sleep with corpses.

For a few days Salvequart was kept in quarantine but after that she was put to work with the Jewish squad in what they called the corn cellar. For those who have read some of the earlier chapters of this book the conditions in which the Jewish squad worked will come as no surprise. Their very race was enough to subject them to the hardest and most cruel conditions in the whole camp.

The women who worked in this corn cellar had to carry to it sacks weighing a hundredweight each from the River Havel. The distance from the river to the corn cellar was 800 metres, all up-hill, and only two women were allowed to carry each sack. For the first two or three sacks it was possible, but after that fingers became numb with the cold. The frost got under their nails and they could not get a grip. Consequently they dropped the sacks and each time that happened they were beaten by an Aufseherin.

Salvequart worked for some time with this squad until it was discovered that she was a trained nurse. She was then told that she would be sent to another camp nearby and would find enough work there. It was in this way that at the beginning of February 1945 she found herself in the Jugendlager.

This small camp, which was only a few kilometres away from the main camp, had to be seen to be believed. When Salvequart arrived there it was already overcrowded. There were only five blocks of living huts although there were three thousand inmates. In the so-called hospital there were sixty women suffering from TB and there were practically no drugs because the two SS orderlies, Rapp and Kohler, sold all the medical stores on the black market.

The day after Salvequart arrived, three hundred women were admitted to the camp together with a nominal roll headed 'Transfer to Mittelwerde Convalescent Camp'. The nominal roll was checked by Rapp and Salvequart, who was instructed to write down the name of some disease against the name of each woman on the roll. The women were then undressed and their prison number written on their left forearm with an indelible pencil. They were then re-dressed and waited in the corridor until dusk, when they were taken away in lorries. They were told that they were going to be disinfected; in fact they went to the Ravensbrück gas chamber, which had recently been erected and was by then in full swing.

It was not long, however, before Salvequart began to carry out a little extermination on her own. She started giving injections to Polish women who were later seen lying incapable on the floor of the washroom writhing and groaning and calling out for water.

She also administered a 'white powder' to large numbers of women in the camp. How these women used to die has been told by a woman named Ottelard who was in the Jugendlager at that time.

> After they got this white powder the patients went to sleep. Some of them, who I suppose were younger and still had some resistance in their bodies, tried to get up but they were incapable of standing on their feet. The next morning the great majority of those who had taken the powder were still asleep and snoring. They slept until about 4 o'clock in the afternoon when the snoring stopped and they were dead.

Salvequart denied giving any lethal injections and maintained that she saved hundreds from dying by falsifying the lists of dead and sending in names of certain persons three or four times as having been exterminated.

There was, indeed, some evidence that she did use her discrimination regarding whom she poisoned and her particular cronies appear to have been spared the fatal dose. She was very friendly with the two SS orderlies and all her friends were housed in one part of the Revier which was reputedly more comfortable than the rest. But two swallows do not make a summer, and for every woman Salvequart refrained from killing there were scores who died by her hand.

But the last nail in Vera's coffin was driven in by a Viennese woman, Lotte Sontag, whom Salvequart called to testify in her defence and whom her counsel put into the witness-box without any previous consultation. The result was disastrous for Salvequart. The witness Sontag was being questioned in order to bring before the Court evidence that Salvequart had been kind and considerate to the patients of the Jugendlager hospital in general and to Lotte Sontag in particular, and that she lost no opportunity by virtue of the responsible position which she held in the Revier to further the interests of the women in her charge and circumvent the evil intentions of the camp staff.

'Do you remember,' asked her counsel, 'that Salvequart obtained boots for you at any time?' 'Yes,' answered Lotte, 'I remember she got boots for us but at the same time I must say they came from the sick that were poisoned by Vera.' 'Is that really

what the witness said?' asked the Judge Advocate. 'Yes,' answered
the interpreter.

'Did you not feel any scruples about wearing those shoes that
had belonged to other people?' asked Salvequart's counsel with
some indignation.

'We felt terribly sorry for them,' answered Fräulein Sontag,
'but there the shoes were and we had none to wear, so we wore
them.'

Fräulein Sontag then went on to tell the Court that Vera
Salvequart had told her that she administered the white powder
because the prisoners refused to accept it from the SS because
they did not trust them, but that as she was herself a prisoner with
a kind voice and apparently friendly to them they took the powder
thinking they were taking medicine.

That Salvequart, for what reason it is difficult to say, co-
operated with the camp staff in the extermination of the inmates
of the Jugendlager is without question.

Nor was her conduct after her capture by the Allies in April
1945 consistent with her contention that she worked against the
SS and on behalf of the prisoners. Although she had been an eye-
witness of mass murders and other criminal acts about which she
could have made a report to her captors she did not do so, but
preferred to cover up her identity by changing her name to Anna
Markova, under which pseudonym she was arrested.

The matron, or Oberschwester, in the women's camp at
Ravensbrück from April 1943 until its liberation in 1945 was
Elisabeth Marschall, of whom it was truly said that 'she had her
finger in every filthy pie in the camp'.

Marschall, though a professional nurse, was a Nazi Party
member of fifteen years' standing and, according to her own
story, was posted to Ravensbrück as a punishment for a breach of
SS regulations at the hospital of the Hermann Göring works in
Brunswick, where she gave food to two French slave workers.

This woman was a disgrace to her high calling. Whilst matron
she was brutal to the patients, refused treatment to the sick,
starved little babies, and stole Red Cross parcels.

In 1944 when disinfection of some of the blocks was being
carried out Marschall was in charge of the operation. It took place
during the night and the women were made to undress and stand
naked during the process. Some sort of chemical was poured over
their heads and they were given ointment to use on infected parts

of the body. When Marschall saw a woman not using the ointment in the proper way she would hit her brutally. According to one woman, 'We were then led into another block where we stood all night without getting any sleep at all. The following day we were led to the washhouse but before we were allowed to enter we were made to stand outside in the rain for three hours.'

A few days later the hospital was full of pneumonia and inflammation of the lung cases and owing to the weak condition of the patients and the absence of any effective treatment many died.

Marschall also took an active part in the selection parades for the Mittelwerde Convalescent Camp convoys, a euphemism for gassing parties, and she also helped with the selection of the 800 women who were sent away to Lublin in November 1944. She, in collaboration with Dr Treite, decided to whom the pink cards should be issued. Marschall had the final say because on one occasion the Norwegian prisoner, who has already been referred to in this chapter as Fru Salvesen, approached Dr Treite to get two Norwegian women struck off the list of one of the 'death' transports. Dr Treite told her that he could not decide and she must go and ask the matron. When she was asked to delete the names matron asked, 'What is their work?' 'They are knitting,' answered Fru Salvesen. 'The knitters all have to go,' said Marschall. The knitters were, of course, not worth keeping alive. They were old women too weak to do heavy work.

The conditions in the camp hospital were the responsibility of the matron. They could scarcely have been worse and Marschall did not merely acquiesce in them, she appeared to approve of them. Certainly nothing was done by her to improve them.

Let Fru Salvesen, who worked in the Revier, describe one of the hospital rooms where most of the patients had deep incised wounds.

The smell was dreadful because bandages had not been changed for a week. The bandages were only made of paper and most of them came off at the end of one day. As all the wounds were open and festering you can imagine what the bedclothes were like. How often they were changed I cannot remember but they were always dirty. In the isolation block it was ten times worse. I remember once I went in there without permission. The occupants were lying on the floor which was crowded with sick and dying, so much so that I had to step over them to reach my Norwegian friend for whom I had brought some food.

She was in despair and said, 'This is worse than hell.' If you arrived in the Revier with typhus and you survived and were discharged, you very soon came back with some other disease. Often one only changed rooms because one had changed illnesses.

Mlle Le Coq who, it will be remembered, was a trained nurse, and was also employed for a time in the camp hospital, passed through the hospital courtyard one day on her way to the laboratory for anaesthetics when she saw five wheelbarrows each containing pieces of human flesh and a human body. On a closer inspection the bodies turned out to be five Jewesses—the triangle on their dresses indicated that—and each was lying in the barrow on her back, her legs dangling over the side. Mlle Le Coq went to the barrows and touched the bodies to see whether they were still alive and whether anything could be done for them. Three were alive. At that moment Marschall came on to the scene and, shouting across the yard, forbade the French girl to do anything to help the women. She returned to her block and brought back two friends to see whether they could not do something for the Jewesses but Marschall reappeared and drove her away. The barrows remained there all night, and by the morning the three survivors were dead.

During the time she was matron of this camp, Marschall contravened every known canon of humanity and decency. Trained as a nurse, she had risen to a high place in her honourable profession which she so degraded and debased. Disregarding the strict code of her humane calling, she preferred to follow the nauseating principles of her Party and her Führer and did all in her power to further their evil ends.

Let Fru Salvesen pronounce the final verdict on Elisabeth Marschall.

As she was a trained nurse I am afraid we all had the picture of Florence Nightingale in our minds: we thought that a nurse was bound to help, sworn to help people irrespective of nationality at any time. What I think hurt my prisoner friends and myself most was to see doctors, sisters, and nurses sink so low and forget their duty.

The scores of doctors who were employed in concentration camps during the war left a stain upon the honour of the medical profession in Germany which will not be erased for many decades.

Utterly unmindful of their Hippocratic oath, these men, generally without the faintest protest, became active participators in the concentration camp system of extermination and collaborated fully with the SS staff to make the camps a living hell.

For a considerable period, the senior medical officer at Ravensbrück was Dr Schidlausky. He first joined the SS in 1933, two years after becoming qualified. Arriving at Ravensbrück in December 1941 he remained there until December 1943 when he was posted to Buchenwald concentration camp. Buchenwald was a larger and more important camp than Ravensbrück and his posting was in the nature of a promotion. He went there with all the experience of two years' bestiality behind him; and proved himself in his new appointment so worthy of the promotion he had received that had he not been sentenced to death by a British Court for his crimes at Ravensbrück he would later have faced trial upon similar charges, together with Ilse Koch and his other colleagues, before the American Tribunal which tried the Buchenwald case in Dachau in April 1947.

When a convoy of new arrivals was inspected in the bathhouse, as previously described in this chapter by Fru Salvesen, Schidlausky was generally one of the inspecting officers. The women were always made to strip naked but no medical examination was ever made. Schidlausky's only contribution to the parade was to walk down the ranks indulging in obscene abuse.

He, like Thea Binz, found it amusing to ride his bicycle into the queues of women when they were waiting for sick parade. When taking sick parades he rarely gave any treatment but pushed the patients away and told the orderlies to remove them. As the inmates knew that the chances of being given any treatment by the medical officers were negligible, they never attended sick parades unless they were so seriously ill that they could not even crawl to work. When Schidlausky refused them treatment, therefore, it often happened that within a day or two they were dead.

In September 1943, a few months before he went to Buchenwald, Schidlausky selected ten women in perfect health for experimental operations. Two of these, who were sisters, were operated on by another doctor with the assistance of Schidlausky, who attended to them after the operation. He had incisions made in both the legs of one, and the other had a piece of bone removed and an incision made in each leg. Artificial gangrene was then induced in the wounds.

Schidlausky himself admitted that he had assisted in operations connected with research into gas gangrene. At one such operation he assisted Doctors Oberhauser and Rosenthal and supervised the administering of the anaesthetic. He also admitted that with his knowledge and approval lethal injections were given to patients who were seriously ill though not incurable, and that he carried out bone transplantation tests in the camp upon perfectly healthy young women, small pieces being taken from the shin bone and put in a different place in the same patient, many of whom were permanently disfigured.

This murderous medico was described by those who knew him in his home circle 'as unable to have an evil idea, much less do an evil thing'. Such a description ill fits the Schidlausky of Ravensbrück where he did so much evil and no good.

The part played by Percy Treite, the second doctor in the camp, has already been described. His was a complex character. He was completely ruthless when it suited him and many prisoners died directly through his actions, yet he appears to have shrunk from some of the more unpleasant tasks which fell to him, and it was not surprising, therefore, that some of those over whom he once exercised powers of life and death were still prepared after their liberation to say something in his favour.

Some of these have stated that Treite did the best he could for the inmates making full allowance for all the circumstances. Some asked for clemency on his behalf on the grounds that there were extenuating circumstances; others called for 'just punishment according to the strictest standards'.

Some, while admitting that they knew little about the case, took the view that it was 'a little hard to judge Germans according to the standards of civilized nations'.

One distinguished lady even expressed doubt as to the fairness of his trial. His counsel, Dr von Metzler, in his final address, speaking for himself and all the other counsel, said:

I feel it to be my duty, as spokesman for the defence, to express our most respectful appreciation of the fair and just manner in which this trial has been conducted. You will no doubt realize, Mr President, that the position of the defence in a trial of this nature, when public feeling is running high, is rather difficult, but in spite of all this may I be permitted to say that the just and fair manner in which this trial has been conducted will always be outstanding in our memory as a fine example of justice and fairness.

In some ways inexplicable, a mixture of refinement and inhumanity, Percy Treite was perhaps more morally guilty than any of his colleagues, for he was a young man of good birth and education, not a low brutal moron like Binder, not a trained SS thug like Schwartzhuber, not a sadistic slut like Binz, and in so far as he sinned, he sinned against the light.

Another of the camp doctors, Rolf Rosenthal, had been well educated for a medical appointment in a concentration camp, for he joined the Hitler Youth as early as 1928 and the Party in 1929. He had even been a member of the SA (Hitler's thug army) in 1932 when it was still an illegal organization. He was posted to Ravensbrück ten years later.

This disgusting creature had been himself in trouble during the war in his own country and had been sentenced by an SS court to eight years' imprisonment for having illicit relations with one of the female prisoners on whom he had carried out several abortions.

According to many of the prisoners, Rosenthal surpassed all the other doctors in his brutality to the sick. On one sick parade some of the patients were so weak that they had to lean against a wall. Rosenthal kicked them and hit them and sent them away without seeing them.

One patient reported sick, being ill with suspected typhus and a temperature of 106°. Rosenthal never even examined her; her diagnosis was 'get out'. He was present when Schidlausky selected a large number of healthy young women for experiment at which he assisted. In July 1942 seventy-five women were so selected, eight of whom died as a result of the operations.

There is ample evidence that this doctor had no regard whatsoever for the sanctity of human life. He has admitted giving lethal doses of morphia to sick prisoners; it was easier than to try to cure them. He described such conduct as 'affording facilities to people who were seriously ill to die by administering injections of morphine'; he has admitted hitting patients 'in order to maintain discipline, and as an example to them'; he has admitted assisting in experimental operations of bone transplantation and to discover an effective drug against gas gangrene, on unwilling inmates.

In September 1942 he assisted at an operation performed by a Dr Oberhauser on a young Polish woman named Zofia Sokulska.

192

Dr Oberhauser, a woman, was subsequently tried by a United States Military Tribunal in Nuremberg, together with a number of other German members of her profession for performing operations on non-consenting human guinea pigs.

One day in September 1942 Zofia Sokulska was told to report to the camp hospital. She was undressed, examined, and informed that she would have to undergo an operation. At that time she was in good health. When she recovered from the anaesthetic she found that her left leg was in plaster from the thigh down to the foot. Present at the operation were Dr Oberhauser, Dr Schidlausky, and Dr Rosenthal, and also some SS Sisters. Sokulska describes the post-operative care thus:

> After eleven days the plaster was removed in the presence of the same three doctors and I was employed in the hospital for the next three weeks on making bandages. . . . On 2nd December I was told that I was to be operated on a second time. I protested, but in vain. The old wound was reopened and I remained in hospital for another two weeks. During this time I received no medical treatment and my bandages were not even changed.

In the spring of the following year Sokulska was threatened with another operation but none took place.

During this period seventy-three other Polish women were operated on experimentally. None of these consented. Five of them died as a result of the operations and nearly all were seriously disfigured.

In March 1943 a third attempt was made to operate on Sokulska. She obtained advance information about this, however, escaped from the hospital, and hid in one of the blocks. For some reason she was not submitted to a third operation but was sent instead to the punishment block. Here she was under the tender care of Margarete Mewes, a little shrew of a woman, who consoled herself for the rather unhappy life she had led before coming to Ravensbrück by making the lives of her prisoners as wretched as she could.

For over four years Margarete Mewes remained in charge of the 'Strafblock' to which the prisoners were sent upon the flimsiest of pretexts and there they were systematically ill-treated. It is reasonable to assume, therefore, that during this period she retained the confidence of her superiors, and there is little doubt that she deserved it.

The conditions in the 'Bunker', as the punishment block was called, were grim. Prisoners were confined in tiny, dark, damp cells for long periods.

Mrs Odette Sansom was confined in the Bunker for many weeks. She had arrived at Ravensbrück in July 1944, and after the usual reception in the bathhouse where she was made to spend the night, was brought before the Commandant the following morning. She had arrived at Ravensbrück under the name of Mrs Churchill and this was not without interest to Fritz Suhren, who asked her if she was a niece of the British Prime Minister.

Mrs Sansom obtained the impression that the Commandant had received orders from RSHA to give her exceptionally bad treatment, but that he did not much relish his instructions and was more interested in keeping her as a hostage. The circumstances of her final departure so graphically described in Jerrard Tickell's book *Odette* fully confirmed her impression.

She was, nevertheless, as a result of her interview in the camp orderly-room sent to the Bunker. There she spent nearly three and a half months in a small cell ten by six feet, her daily diet consisting of ersatz coffee and a small piece of bread in the morning, some cold soup at eleven, and some more coffee or tea at three.

After having been in confinement for five weeks, Mrs Sansom was then kept a whole week without any food at all. This, Mewes said, was in accordance with orders she had received. The other prisoners in the Strafblock were similarly treated.

In August, central heating was put on at full strength for three days as a punishment. This was not an uncommon form of German 'frightfulness' and was used at the German Air Force Interrogation Centre near Frankfurt in order to induce Allied airmen to be more co-operative during their interrogation by German Intelligence officers.

Such was the Strafblock and such was its chief jailer. Had it not been for the severity of the punishment régime and the callousness and cruelty of Mewes, some of the prisoners might have appreciated its privacy after so many months of the overcrowded filth and squalor which they had experienced in their living quarters.

Last but not least in this gallery of rogues was the camp dentist, Hellinger.

He, too, was an early member of the SS, having joined it in 1933, and by 1944 he had been promoted to Hauptsturmführer. He arrived at Ravensbrück in the spring of 1943 and remained there until the end.

The dental treatment which the inmates received was negligible and occupied but little of Hellinger's time. He was, however, an executive SS officer and assisted the other official members of the camp staff in their general duties. He was present at the illegal execution without previous trial of fifty women in one evening and made no attempt to stop it.

His most important professional duties, however, were performed as scavenger to Reichsbank President Walther Funk. As a result of an agreement between Himmler and Funk, the SS sent to the Reichsbank the personal belongings, including gold teeth and gold fillings, taken from the victims who had been exterminated in concentration camps.

To collect gold from the mouths of corpses at Ravensbrück was the personal responsibility of the camp dentist. In a deposition which he made while he was in arrest pending trial he admitted carrying out this grim duty. When he could not do it himself he delegated the task to one of his 'collaborators'. When the prisoners had died from what in the camp were known as 'natural causes', that is to say from neglect, starvation, and other ill-treatment, no time was lost. Hellinger soon arrived, forceps in hand. He was present at all executions and when the officiating medical officer had ascertained death, Hellinger immediately looked for gold teeth or fillings and removed them before any 'unauthorized' withdrawals could take place.

In this capacity he was present at the execution of two young English women who were captured after being dropped in France in 1944.[1]

At his trial, Hellinger was closely questioned about these incidents. He admitted that he had on one occasion stood in the crematorium for an hour and a half with Dr Treite whilst women were being pulled in 'like carcasses of meat', still bleeding, having just been executed by being shot in the back of the head; and that he, a qualified dentist, then examined 'those shattered heads' to see whether he could get a small quantity of gold out of their mouths.

Nevertheless, he resented the suggestion that by so doing he had

[1] Both were members of the Women's Transport Service who were dropped in France by SOE (Special Operations Executive) as W/T operators and arrested by the Germans. After being interrogated and tortured by the Gestapo, they were sent to Ravensbrück and eventually executed in the usual manner, by Genickschuss.

abandoned the professional standards of his calling and adopted those of the SS concentration camp hierarchy. He even argued that the extraction of gold fillings in such circumstances, 'though it hurt one's feelings of reverence' did not constitute an indictable offence and that the practice had historical precedent. Such an argument is not attractive to cultured peoples and throughout the civilized world it has long been a criminal offence to rob the dead.

Such was the Hell they called Ravensbrück—L'Enfer des Femmes—and such were the men and women who ran it.

The concentration camps were the final link in the chain of terror with which Nazi Germany bound Occupied Europe from 1940 to 1945.

Every road of misery led to the concentration camp and death. The Jew, the Russian prisoner of war, the partisan, the slave no longer fit for work, the Allied Commando, the Nacht und Nebel prisoner, and a host of other innocent men and women who had been dragged from their homes by the Gestapo because they refused to collaborate with the aggressor, or showed some spark of resistance to the conquering Master Race.

Thousands of these eventually found themselves at Belsen, at Buchenwald, at Dachau, at Mauthausen, at Ravensbrück, there to die or perhaps emerge years later, broken in body and warped in mind.

CHAPTER VII

THE 'FINAL SOLUTION' OF THE
JEWISH QUESTION

HANS FRANK, who for many years of the German occupation of Poland was Governor-General, gave evidence in his own defence at the trial of German major war criminals at Nuremberg in 1946.

'We have fought against Jewry for years,' he said, 'and have indulged in the most horrible utterances—my own diary bears witness against me . . . a thousand years will pass and still this guilt of Germany will not have been erased.'

The persecution of the Jews in the countries which the Nazis invaded and occupied between 1939 and 1945 was indeed on a stupendous scale, but it cannot have taken by surprise anyone who had followed the rise of the Nazis to power in 1933 or their Party programme.

Point Four of that programme declared: 'Only a member of the race can be a citizen. A member of the race can only be one who is of German blood, without consideration of creed. Consequently, no Jew can be a member of the race.'

This masterpiece of German logic was preached throughout the length and breadth of Germany from the moment of Hitler's accession to power. The Jews were to be regarded as foreigners and have no rights of German citizenship. It was used by the Nazis as one of the means of implementing their master-race policy.

The first organized act was the boycott of Jewish enterprises in April 1933, and thereafter a series of laws was passed which in effect removed Jews from every department of public life, from the civil service, from the professions, from education, and from the services.

The spearhead of this anti-Semitic attack was 'Jew-baiter Number One', as Julius Streicher styled himself, whose duty it was to fan the Germans' post-war dislike of Jews into a burning hatred and to incite them to the persecution and extermination of the Jewish race. Having due regard to the statistics available Streicher may truthfully be said to have aided and abetted more than 5,000,000 murders.

He was an obvious choice for the post, for he had been Jew-baiting since before 1922 when he first published *Der Stürmer*,[1] a weekly anti-Semitic journal. In 1933 he founded a daily paper, with the same policy, the *Fränkische Tageszeitung*. In those early days he had said: 'We know that Germany will be free when the Jew has been excluded from the life of the German people.'

The lengths to which Streicher went to put this propaganda over must be seen to be believed and here are a few specimens.

'The Chosen People of the Criminals', was an article in his own paper.

> The history book of the Jews, which is usually called the Holy Scriptures, impresses us as a horrible criminal romance which makes the shilling shockers of the British Jew, Edgar Wallace, grow pale with envy. The 'holy' book abounds in murder, incest, fraud, theft and indecency.

In June 1937 when the airship *Hindenburg* caught fire, Streicher published a photograph of the burning hull with the following caption:

> The first radio picture from the United States of America shows quite clearly that a Jew stands behind the explosion of our airship *Hindenburg*. Nature has depicted quite clearly and correctly that devil in human guise.[2]

There was also that fantastic nonsense about what the Germans called 'race pollution'.

> It is established for all time: 'alien albumen' is the sperm of a man of alien race. The male sperm in cohabitation is partially or completely absorbed by the female and thus enters her blood-stream. One single cohabitation of a Jew with an Aryan woman is sufficient to poison her blood for ever. Together with the 'alien albumen' she has absorbed the alien soul. Never again will she be able to bear purely Aryan children. . . . They will all be bastards. . . . Now we know why the Jew uses every artifice of seduction in order to ravish German girls at as early an age as possible, why the Jewish doctor rapes his female patients while they are under anaesthetics.

It is hard to credit the fact that the above appeared in a semi-

---

[1] A pornographic and anti-Semitic newspaper edited by Streicher.
[2] This 'Jew' was a cloud of smoke which had been touched up in the photograph to resemble the face of a Jew.

medical journal called *German People's Health*, but less difficult when it is known that Streicher was its editor.

Contemporaneously there appeared in *Der Stürmer* a picture depicting the upper part of a girl's body being strangled by the arms of a man, with his hands around her neck, and the shadow of the man's face is shown against the background with obviously Jewish features. The caption of the picture was: 'Castration for Race Polluters. Only heavy penalties will preserve our womenfolk from a tighter grip from loathsome Jewish claws.'

Even the young were fed with these dangerous doctrines. These are extracts from a short story which appeared in a book for children called 'Poisonous Fingers';

> Inge sits in the reception room of the Jewish doctor. She has to wait a long time . . . she glances through the papers on the table but is too nervous to read: she remembers what her mother has told her and again and again her mind reflects on the warnings of her leader of the League of German Girls. A German girl must not consult a Jew doctor. Many a girl who went to a Jewish doctor to be cured has met with disease and disgrace. Inge has now been waiting for over an hour. Again she picks up the papers in an endeavour to read. Then the door opens. The Jew appears. She screams. In terror she drops the paper. Horrified she jumps up. Her eyes stare into the face of the doctor, and his face is the face of the Devil. In the middle of the Devil's face is a huge crooked nose. Behind the spectacles gleam two criminal eyes. Around the thick lips plays a grin that means, 'Now I have you at last, you little German girl!'
>
> And then the Jew approaches her. His fat fingers clutch at her. But now Inge has got hold of herself. Before the Jew can grab her she smacks his fat face with her hand. One jump to the door. Breathlessly she runs down the stairs and escapes from the Jew's house.

Poisonous fingers? Poisonous fiddlesticks! It may indeed be wondered how anyone could even read such absurdities, but they did: and the poison spread, as it was meant to, throughout the whole nation until they were willing and ready to support their leaders in the policy of mass extermination upon which they had embarked.

By 1938 pogroms were commonplace, synagogues were burned down, Jewish shops looted. Collective fines were levied, Jewish assets seized by the State and even the movement of Jews subjected to regulations. Ghettos were re-established and Jews forced to wear the yellow star on their clothing.

And a few months before the outbreak of war this menacing German Foreign Office circular must have clearly pointed out the course of future events to all but those who did not wish to see it.

It is certainly no coincidence that the fateful year of 1938 has brought nearer the solution of the Jewish question simultaneously with the realization of the idea of Greater Germany. ... The advance made by Jewish influence and the destructive Jewish spirit in politics, economy and culture, paralysed the power and the will of the German people to rise again. The healing of this sickness among the people was therefore certainly one of the most important requirements for exerting the force which, in the year 1938, resulted in the joining together of Greater Germany in defiance of the world.

The persecution of Jews in the countries invaded by Germany far transcended anything that had come before, for the Nazi plan of Jewish extermination was not to be confined to the Reich. Its only boundary was the limit of opportunity, and as the flood of German conquest rushed ever forward into other lands, so more and more Jews became engulfed in its cruel waters.

The persecution and murder of Jews throughout the conquered territories of Europe from 1939 onwards clearly violated Article 46 of the Regulations of the Hague Convention of 1907 to which Germany was a signatory: 'Family honour and rights, the lives of persons, private property, as well as religious convictions and practices must be respected.'

Steps were taken immediately the Germans had successfully completed the invasion of a foreign country, or had occupied a considerable part of it, to put into force the requirements and restrictions which were already applicable to Jews in the Reich. By January 1941 the registration of Jews had been enforced by decree in Poland, France, and Holland.

The next manoeuvre was to segregate all Jews into ghettos. Rosenberg's suggestion for handling the Jewish question in the Eastern territories stated that all rights of freedom for Jews would be withdrawn and they would be placed in ghettos and separated according to sexes. Every care was also taken to ensure that there should be no further intermingling of the blood of Jews with that of other people.

The official organ of the SS which was called *Das Schwarze*

Korps[1] wrote in 1940: 'Just as the Jewish question will be solved in Germany only when the last Jew has gone: so the rest of Europe must realize that the German peace which awaits it must be a peace without Jews.'

The question brooked no delay and was regarded by all Gauleiters as of the utmost priority. Indeed Hans Frank, then Governor-General of Poland, made this apologetic note in his diary: 'I could not, of course, eliminate all lice nor all Jews in only a year, but in the course of time this end will be attained.'

One of the largest ghettos was in Warsaw. It was inhabited by 400,000 Jews. An idea of the condition in which these Jews lived can be gathered from the fact that at least six lived in every room.

In April 1943 the liquidation of this ghetto was begun and SS Major-General Stroop was able to report to his superiors on 16th May that the Warsaw ghetto was no more. On the title page of his report of this 'Grossaktion', or major operation, was inscribed in decorative Gothic lettering, the words, 'There are no more Jewish dwellings in Warsaw.'

Stroop's report was a fine example of the bookbinders' art, ornately bound in leather and typed on superior superfine paper. Was not its theme worthy of so luxurious a presentation: the extermination of several thousand defenceless Jewish men, women, and children, and the destruction of their homes?

Some seventy-five pages in length, the report gives a day-to-day account of the action. The following are extracts from it:

The resistance put up by the Jews could be broken only by the relentless and energetic use of our shock troops by day and night. . . . I therefore decided to destroy the entire Jewish residential area by setting every block on fire. . . . The Jews then emerged from their hiding places and dugouts. Not infrequently the Jews stayed in the burning buildings until finally, through the heat and fear of being burned alive, they preferred to jump down from the upper stories after having thrown mattresses and other upholstered articles into the street. With their bones broken they still tried to crawl across the street into buildings which were not yet alight. . . . They even took to the sewers, but after the first week their stay there ceased to be pleasant. Men of the Waffen-SS or the Wehrmacht Engineers courageously climbed down the manholes to bring out the Jews . . . it was always necessary to use smoke candles to drive them out. A

[1] The Black Corps—named after their black uniforms.

great number of Jews who could not be counted were exterminated by blowing up sewers and dugouts.

The longer the resistance lasted the tougher the Waffen-SS, Police, and Wehrmacht became. They fulfilled their duty indefatigably in faithful comradeship and stood together as models and examples of soldiers . . . only through the continuous and untiring efforts of all involved did we succeed in catching a total of 56,065 Jews whose extermination can be proved. To these should be added those who lost their lives in explosions or fires but whose numbers cannot be ascertained.

Summing up the results of the operation on page 45 of the report, Stroop writes: 'Of the 56,065 caught, about 7,000 were destroyed in the former Jewish residential area during large-scale operations; 6,929 Jews were destroyed by transporting them to T.II.[1] The sum total of Jews destroyed is therefore 13,929. An estimated number of 6,000 Jews were destroyed by being blown up or by perishing in the flames.'

SS Brigadeführer, Major-General Stroop appears to have been well satisfied with the result of his 'Grossaktion'. In order that there should be a permanent record of his gallantry on that occasion which he could show to his relatives and friends and pass round the table after the annual dinner of the 'Stahlhelm', he inserted in his photograph album a number of snapshots taken in Warsaw during the great 'battle'. These were found in his possession when he was arrested by the United States Military Police.

A different method of getting rid of the Jews was adopted in the Baltic States where they were not placed in ghettos before being eliminated. A document found in Himmler's private files after the war contains a report of 'Action Group A', in which over 130,000 Jews were murdered in 1941 in Lithuania and Latvia. A series of pogroms was initiated by a partisan leader at the instigation of the Germans in such a way that they did not appear openly in any way to be connected with it. During the first pogrom more than 1,500 Jews were killed, several synagogues destroyed and many homes burned in one night, and on the following two nights, 2,300 more Jews were murdered.

Sometimes, but not often, and certainly not often enough, higher authority did not approve of the methods used by their subordinates. Such scruples might well cause surprise were it not for the fact that the criticisms were generally made upon the grounds of expediency and not for humanitarian reasons.

The following extract is from a letter to the Reich Minister for the Occupied Eastern Territories:

> The fact that Jews receive special treatment requires no further discussion. Nevertheless it appears hardly credible that this was done in the way described by the General Commissioner in his report of 1st June 1943. What is Katyn against that? What if such occurrences should become known to the other side and be exploited by them? To lock men and women and children into barns and to set fire to them does not appear to be a *suitable* method for combating bands, even if it is desired to exterminate the population. This method is not worthy of the German cause and hurts our reputation severely.

It will be remembered that when at Oradour-sur-Glâne the SS Reich Panzer Division about a year later locked the male inhabitants into barns and the women and children into the church and burned them all, no German protest was heard. Nor should it be forgotten that this same 'German cause' involved amongst other things the 'final solution' of the Jewish question.

Between September 1941 and February 1943 the Special Action Group (Einsatzgruppe D) which consisted of SS, SD, Gestapo, and other police units and was attached to forces under the command of von Manstein in Russia, was responsible for the mass extermination of many thousands of Jews by shooting, hanging, gassing, and drowning. The units of which this Einsatzgruppe was composed were under the command of Otto Ohlendorf. This young man, who in 1941 was only thirty-three years old, joined the SA at the age of eighteen and the SD a year later.

Some months before the invasion of Russia began, arrangements were made for the separate use of SIPO units in the operational areas. These were called Einsatzgruppe and were sub-divided into Einsatzkommandos. The arrangement was between OKH and OKW on the one hand and RSHA on the other. A representative of the Chief of SIPO and the SD was to be assigned to each Army Group and Army and he would have at his disposal mobile troops of the SIPO and SD. This agreement created a new situation, because formerly an Army had on its own responsibility and with its own resources performed the duties which would in future be the sole responsibility of SIPO.

Henceforward the Einsatzgruppe would be attached to a

specific Army Group and move with it. Its operational area would therefore be that of the Army Group. The Army Group representative of the SIPO and SD was entitled to issue instructions to units with regard to their duties but the Army Group could also issue orders if the operational situation made it necessary.

Four Einsatzgruppen were formed and Einsatzgruppe D under Ohlendorf was directly attached to the Eleventh Army then under command of von Manstein and operating in the Ukraine. It was given orders that in its operational area the Jews were to be 'liquidated'. These orders were repeated personally by Himmler when he visited the Einsatzgruppe at Nicolaiev in September 1941. He assembled the leaders and men of the Einsatzkommandos and told them that they bore no personal responsibility for executing this order which was Hitler's.

The existence of these orders and their execution were known to the Army Commander. An order was issued by the Eleventh Army that no liquidation must take place within 200 kilometres of headquarters.

Furthermore, at Simferopol, where 10,000 Jews were killed in a mass execution, the Army command asked Ohlendorf to push on with the liquidations because of the threat of famine and the acute shortage of houses. The following description of a mass execution was given by Ohlendorf himself who was present at a number of them.

The local Einsatzkommando attempted to collect all the Jews in its area by registering. The registration was performed by the Jews themselves. This was made possible by telling them that its object was that they were to be resettled.

After the registration they were collected and transported to the place of execution which was usually an anti-tank ditch. The shooting was carried out in a military manner by firing squads.

On Ohlendorf's suggestion, only as many Jews as could be executed immediately were taken at one time to the place of execution. This was done in order to reduce to a minimum the length of time between the moment the victims knew of their fate to their actual execution.

The victims were shot standing or kneeling along the edge of the trench in which they then fell. Before their bodies were finally buried the firing squad commanders had orders to make sure that all were dead and themselves to finish off any who were not.

All the victims' valuables had been confiscated when the Jews were rounded up and these were forwarded to the Finance Ministry. Occasional exceptions were made to this rule.

Until the spring of 1942 all Jewish exterminations in the Ukraine were carried out in this manner. Orders were then received, however, that in future women and children were not to be shot, but must be put to death in gas vans. Previously they had been killed in the same way as the men—by shooting. The gas vans, a new instrument of murder, were so constructed that their real purpose was not visible from the exterior. They looked like plain vans but were so contrived that at the start of a motor, gas was inducted into the van, causing death in ten to fifteen minutes. The ingenious inventor was a Dr Becker who also held the rank of SS Untersturmführer, and he was in charge of those on the vehicle establishment of Ohlendorf's Einsatzgruppe.

The Nazis were experts in the use of euphemism and when it came to killing never called a spade a spade. Special treatment, extermination, liquidation, elimination, resettlement, and final solution were all synonyms for murder, and it would not be without interest to speculate by what innocent description these vans were listed in the SS vocabulary of stores.

A full description of them and their operation is contained in a top-secret document which the inventor sent to SS Obersturmbannführer Rauff, a senior SS staff officer at RSHA, reporting their final tests and overhaul.

Becker reported that the tests of both types of vans 'Series I' and 'Series II' had been completed and adjustments and modifications made. Series I could be operated in most weathers. Series II were useless after even a little rain and could only be used in absolutely dry weather. It was a matter for consideration whether the vans should only be used when stationary at the place of execution. Many difficulties were experienced. First of all the vans had to be driven there and the place usually selected for the execution was some ten miles off the main road and inaccessible in wet weather. If the victims were marched all that way they at once became suspicious and restless. This was 'undesirable'. The only solution recommended by Becker was to 'load' them on to the vehicles (he wrote as though they were goods) and drive them to the spot.

Becker gave instructions that 'D' Group's vans should be camouflaged as trailer caravans by putting a set of window shutters on each side of the small trucks and two sets on the larger type. Nevertheless they became so well known that they were very soon called the 'death vans' not only by the troops, but by civilians as well, and in Becker's opinion it was impossible to keep their purpose secret even by camouflage. The rough ground and bad roads over which the vans had to be driven rapidly made them rattle, and the rivets and caulking became loosened. This, of course, meant a leakage of gas and it became necessary to have this seen to frequently in the unit workshops. The drivers and operators were also ordered to keep well away when the gassing operation was in progress to avoid any ill-effects from the escaping fumes.

Becker's report continued:

I should like to take this opportunity to bring the following to your attention: several commands, after the gassing is completed, have had the bodies unloaded by their own men. There is great danger that this will lead to their health being affected, if not immediately, at least later on. The commanders do not want to countermand these orders as they fear that if prisoners were employed they would find some opportunity to escape.

The application of gas is not always carried out in the correct manner. In order to get the job finished as quickly as possible, the driver presses the accelerator down to the fullest extent. Thereby the victims suffer death by suffocation and not by dozing off as was intended. By correct adjustment of the levers death comes faster and the prisoners fall asleep peacefully. Previously the victims' faces and other signs showed that they died in agony.

In 1941, during the month of September alone, 35,000 Soviet citizens, mostly Jews, were killed by Ohlendorf's Kommandos in the neighbourhood of Nicolaiev. All these massacres were duly reported to headquarters in detail: 'The Kommandos continued clearing the area of Jew and Communist elements. In the period covered by this report, i.e. 16th-30th September 1941, the towns of Nicolaiev and Cherson in particular were cleared of Jews and the officials still left there were treated accordingly . . . total number 35,782.'[1]

Another 2,000 Jews were killed by SD units attached to von Manstein's forces on 13th October 1941. This was the subject of a routine report by the Town Major of Melitopol to Rear Army HQ. The report described the arrival of the advance party of the HQ in the town where 40,000 inhabitants remained. All the Jews,

---

[1] Report from RSHA to the Führer, dated 2nd October 1942.

numbering 2,000, were executed by the SD. The report ended: 'The population shows confidence in the German Armed Forces and in particular the Ukrainians were grateful for their liberation.'

Only a fortnight later a further 8,000 Jews met their death in Mariopol. When the German troops entered this town all the Jews were executed by the SD and their vacant homes taken over by the Army. All the victims' clothing, after being cleaned, was handed over to a military hospital. A new Mayor was then appointed by the Kommandantur as the wife of the existent Mayor was, until her death, a Jewess.

When the Germans entered the Crimea they began to experience some difficulty as the following report from Einsatzgruppe shows:

Jews: Simferopol, Jewpatoria, Aluschta, Karasabarsar and Feodosia and other districts of the Western Crimea have been cleared of Jews; between 16 November and 15 December 1941, 17,645 Jews have been executed. Rumours about executions in other areas rendered the situation at Simferopol very difficult. Reports about action against Jews gradually filter through from fleeing Jews or from the careless talk of German soldiers.

In the Western Crimea, the Jewish population was estimated by the Germans at the end of 1942, to be about 40,000, of whom approximately one quarter still lived in Simferopol itself.

At the beginning of December 1941, Einsatzgruppe D HQ had moved from Odessa to the Crimea and was stationed at Simferopol. The preparatory registration and segregation of Jews had already been carried out by one of the Kommandos and Ohlendorf was informed by the SS liaison officer at Army HQ that the Army required the shooting of all the Jews in Simferopol to be completed before Christmas.

The task was entrusted to Kommando II B whose commanding officer, Karl Rudolph Braune, being unable to carry out the mission with unit resources, visited the 'Q' Branch at Army HQ to obtain assistance. Lorries, cars, motor-cycles, drivers, and guards were placed at his disposal upon the understanding that the soldiers were not to take any part in the actual shooting but used for transport and security purposes only.

The execution then began. The Jews were assembled, men, women, and children, at collecting points, put on to the lorries, and transported in convoys at suitable intervals to the scene of the execution, an anti-tank ditch a short distance outside the city.

There they were shot. By the end of the third day they had all been disposed of in this way.

The usual arrangements were in force with regard to the disposal of the victims' property except that on this occasion about 120 watches were sent by special request to the Eleventh Army.

Thus the carnage proceeded—a senseless remorseless annihilation of innocent citizens—merely because they were Jews.

There were some German officials, however, who were not afraid to criticize the wholesale nature of the persecution in the Ukraine, albeit not from the highest motives.

The local representative of the Industrial Armament Department in Berlin reported the industrial situation in the 'Reichskommissariat Ukraine' to his chief, General Thomas.

The report was not sent through official channels and was headed, 'For the personal information of the Chief of the Industrial Armament Department.' Its contents leave no doubt as to the reasons which led the writer to by-pass the usual channels. This is what he says:

The attitude of the Jewish population was obliging from the beginning. They tried to avoid everything that might displease the German administration. That they hated it and the army inwardly goes without saying and cannot be surprising. There is, however, no proof that Jewry was in any great degree implicated in acts of sabotage, though there were some saboteurs among them as among other Ukrainians. It cannot be said that the Jews represented a danger to the German Armed Forces. The Jewish output production which was the result of nothing but a feeling of fear was satisfactory to the troops and the German administration.

The Jewish population remained unmolested for a short while after the fighting. But later specially detached formations of police executed and planned mass shootings. It was done entirely in public and unfortunately in many instances members of the Armed Forces voluntarily took part. The way these 'operations', which included the killing of old men, women, and children of all ages, were carried out was horrible. So far, about 150,000 to 200,000 Jews have been executed in this part of the Ukraine: no consideration has been given to the interests of the economic situation.

Summarizing, it can be said that this kind of solution of the Jewish problem as applied to the Ukraine, and which was obviously based on ideological theories has had the following results:

(a) Elimination of a number of superfluous eaters in the cities.
(b) Elimination of a part of the population which undoubtedly hated us.
(c) Elimination of badly needed tradesmen who were, in many instances, indispensable even in the interests of the Armed Forces.
(d) Consequences in relation to foreign policy propaganda which are obvious.
(e) Bad effects on the troops who, in any event, are indirectly concerned with the executions.
(f) Brutalizing effect on the formations which carry out the executions.

The report of that zealous official, who appears to have been not without the bowels of human compassion, is revealing.

It has frequently been contended by German defendants in War Crime Trials that as the purpose of war is the overpowering of the enemy, the achievement of that purpose justifies any means including, in case of military necessity, the violation of the laws of war if such violation will afford either the means to escape from imminent danger or to overpower the enemy.

This theory dates very far back in the history of warfare and originated in those times when warfare was not regulated by the laws of war but by usages. It is not without significance that it is of German origin though by no means all German writers on International Law endorse it. One of them, Strupp, disposes of it in these words, 'If this opinion were justified no laws of warfare would exist, for every rule might be declared impracticable on the ground that it was contrary to military necessity.'

Furthermore, in the preamble of Hague Convention IV it is expressly stated that the rules of warfare were framed with regard to military necessity, the provisions of the Convention 'having been inspired by the desire to diminish the evils of wars *as far as military requirements permit*'.[1]

When an Occupying Power is administering a territory in which its armed forces are engaged in military operations or stationed as garrison troops it is entitled to take all proper measures necessary to ensure the safety of its forces and to secure the provision of their needs.

[1] Vol. II, Oppenheim's *International Law*, 6th Edition. Ed. by Lauterpacht.

It is evident that in the Ukraine, the Jews as such did not constitute a menace to the security of the German Armed Forces and were more disposed to co-operate with them than to rise against them.

It could not, therefore, even be argued by those responsible for it, that this wholesale murder of Jews was a military necessity; and to do the Nazis justice they made no such pretence. These Jews were killed because of their race. The final solution of the Jewish question had begun.

As one of the German witnesses at the Nuremberg Trial himself said, 'If for years a doctrine is preached to the effect that the Slav race is an inferior race and the Jews not even human beings, an explosion of this sort is inevitable.'[1]

But it was not only the Russian Jews who were to be exterminated. Wherever the German forces marched under the 'Crooked Cross'[2] the 'resettlement of the Jews'[3] went with them.

In Poland, the Treblinka extermination camps A and B were set up during the spring and summer of 1942. These camps were part and parcel of the machinery used for the total annihilation of the Jewish community in Poland.

In these two camps hundreds of thousands of Jews were murdered. The first railway transports of victims arrived in July 1942 and from then until the end of 1943 these convoys arrived with unfailing regularity.

The massacres were carried out by two methods, steam and gassing. The first building to be erected contained three gas chambers, but by the autumn of 1942, a new building containing ten others had been completed. The arrangements for burning the corpses were primitive in comparison with the more up-to-date methods in some of the concentration camps. There were no ovens in the crematorium, only large gridirons made out of railway lines mounted on concrete supports across which the corpses were laid, 2,500 at a time.

In the camp there was a building known as the 'Lazarett' or hospital, but no sick were ever tended there. It was enclosed by a high fence and was entered through a small hut on which flew the Red Cross flag. The hut led into a waiting-room with plush coloured sofas, and here the unsuspecting victims waited. Beyond this was a pit, at the edge of which an SS man shot each victim, as he was ushered in from the waiting-room, through the back of

---

[1] The evidence of von Dem Bach—Zelewski, 7th January 1946.
[2] The Swastika—called by the French 'La Croix Gammée'.
[3] Another euphemism for extermination.

the neck with a revolver. In this way were killed invalids, old people, and small children who were too weak or too young to enter the gas chambers themselves.

When the Jews arrived at Treblinka station, as there was no time to lose, the waggons were opened and those still alive were driven out and on into the special enclosures where the men were separated from the women and children. Meanwhile Jewish workers removed the corpses from the trucks which they cleaned out. As many as 200 Jews were crammed into each van and many died on the journey.

What happened to the new arrivals is described in an official report made by a Polish Government Commission which investigated German crimes in Poland.

> After unloading at the siding, all the victims were assembled in one place . . . where they had to take off their clothes and shoes. The men did this in the courtyard, the women and children in a hut nearby. The women then had all their hair cut off and the whole convoy, men, women and children, now naked and shorn, were driven along the road to the gas chambers, having been told they were going to the bathhouse.
>
> When they reached the lethal chambers they were driven in with their hands above their heads so that as many might be squeezed in as possible. The children were piled on top. Sometimes the infants were first killed. . . . One SS specialized in this, seizing them by their legs and killing them with one blow on the head against a wall. . . . The actual gassing in the chamber lasted about fifteen minutes and when it was thought that they were all dead the doors were opened and the Jewish working party removed them and prepared the chamber for the next batch.

The belongings of the victims were collected and sorted before being despatched to the Reich. The human hair was steamed, packed in bales, sent to Germany, and used in the manufacture of mattresses.

But camps at Treblinka were unable to meet all demands and another extermination camp had to be established at Chelmno. There 300,000 Jews from the provinces of Poznania and Lodz were put to death.

The procedure was the same as at Treblinka and Jews were employed to do the 'dirty jobs'. From time to time these Jewish working parties were themselves done away with and a fresh supply obtained. When the time came to liquidate a batch of these workers the SS men had great sport, sometimes using them 'as living targets, shooting them like hares'.

As far as can be ascertained, for the last pre-war census in Poland was in 1931, there were more than 3,300,000 Jews living there when the Germans began their invasion. The final solution of the Jewish question in Poland was, therefore, no light task.

The Governor-General, Hans Frank, had said in 1941, 'What are we to do with the Jews? Do you think that we shall settle them in the Ostland? Why all this prattle? In short liquidate them by your own means. We must take steps to extirpate them. The Government General must be as free from Jews as is the Reich.'

The Nazis began to put their plan for the extermination of the Jews into operation from the first day of the invasion of Poland.

Jews were first subjected to discriminating leglislation; their right to own property was extinguished and they had to wear special markings on their clothing. Ghettos were instituted, valuables confiscated, and even the Jews' scale of rations was less than that of other inhabitants. They performed forced labour and were habitually terrorized and severely punished for minor offences.

The persecution continued and increased in intensity. Hostages were taken and the Jews were consistently derided and humiliated. Their women could be violated with impunity, their places of worship were desecrated and set on fire. Their shops were looted, and executions began. Jew hunts were organized and when Rabbis were caught their beards were cut or torn off. The Jews were made to perform the filthiest and most degrading tasks: to clean out latrines with their hands; to collect horse droppings in the streets and fill their caps and pockets with them.

Then followed the final solution—the mass murders in extermination camps which have already been described. From the statistics available it would appear that the total annihilation ordered by Himmler in 1942 was almost accomplished. Of the 3,000,000 or more Jews living in Poland in September 1939 not more than 50,000 could be traced in 1946 and not less than 2,600,000 perished.

In France, all books by Jewish authors as well as those in which Jews had collaborated were withdrawn from sale by German occupation authorities save works of a scientific nature in respect of which special exceptions were made. Even biographies of Jews which were written by Aryans were on the prohibited 'Otto' list.[1]

---

[1] So named after Otto Abetz.

The biography of Offenbach had to be withdrawn from sale for this reason.

Later came the economic measures, bullying and petty irritations, the yellow star and other indignities. A large number of anti-semitic decrees were proclaimed lowering the civic status of French Jews.

There was always an intention eventually to deport all Jews from France for the purpose of extermination and it was only the pace of the programme which differed from that elsewhere.

It might have been supposed that in order to get rid of the Jews the solution of emigration would have commended itself to the Germans. It clearly did not as the following correspondence shows.

From Civil Administration HQ in Bordeaux to Paris head office, 22 July 1941.

It has just been established that about one hundred and fifty Jews are still in the territory of the District Command of St Jean de Luz. At the time of our conversation with the District Commander, Major Henkel, the latter asked that these Jews should leave his District as soon as possible. At the same time he pointed out that in his opinion it would be far better were they allowed to emigrate rather than they be sent to concentration camps.

A reply was received to the effect that Major Henkel's suggestion was not approved, as RSHA had decreed that the emigration of Jews living in the occupied territories of the West and in Unoccupied France was, if possible, to be prevented.

This decree had been received by the Military Command in Paris and transmitted in the following terms: 'The Reichsführer SS has given orders that the emigration of Jews from Germany and the occupied territories has to be prevented on principle.'

In charge of Jewish affairs in Occupied France was SS Obersturmführer Dannecker. In 1941 he drew up a voluminous report entitled, 'The Jewish Question in France and its Treatment.' This gave a preliminary survey of the problem in that country and categorically stated that the final solution of the Jewish question was the objective of the SD and SIPO services who were handling the matter.

Further sections dealt with the history of the Jews in France and their organization and then the report went on to deal with the importance of a campaign against 'leading Jewish personages'.
'From a study of the records collected in Germany, Austria

213

Czechoslovakia, and Poland,' states the report, 'it was possible to conclude that the centre of Judaism in Europe, and the chief lines of communication to overseas, must be sought in France. Realizing this, the offices of great Jewish organizations such as the World Jewish Congress have been searched and sealed.'

A great bond is stated by Dannecker to exist in France between Catholicism and Judaism and as evidence of this he produced the results of searches made in the homes of the Rothschild family, Georges Mandel former Minister for the Colonies, the Press Attaché to the British Embassy, and Maîtres Moro-Giafferi and Torres of the French Bar.

Seven months later Dannecker issued a further report which shows that there had been a marked speed-up in dealing with the Jewish problem since the first report had been issued.

The headings of various sections of the second report bear witness to the quickening rhythm. 'Task of the SIPO and SD in France'—'Card Index of Jews'—'French Commission for Jewish Questions'—'The French Anti-Jewish Police'.

These titles show that the Gestapo net was closing round French Jewry, that all Jews now had police dossiers, that there was co-ordination on this subject between the Occupying Power and Vichy and that the hated Milice had a special branch to deal with Jews.

In the spring of that year the first deportations of Jews began and all were deprived of their French nationality before leaving. By June, over 10,000 had been deported. In order to conceal their real purpose, which was forced labour until no longer fit for work and then the gas chamber, these deportations were called 'Jewish resettlement'. Following a further conference between Dannecker and RSHA, new directives for the deportation of Jews from France were issued. In these they were merely referred to as 'Jewish livestock'.

By the end of October 1942 over 50,000 had been deported from the Occupied Zone, but the pace did not satisfy the authorities who were also anxious to include Jews from the Unoccupied Zone.

At further conferences Vichy was told that most of the other European countries were much nearer to a final solution of the Jewish problem than France was, and that she must make up the leeway. The German authorities at the same time expressed their dissatisfaction at the attitude of Italians towards the deportation of Jews from the part of France which was under Italian Occupation. The Italians had indeed strongly opposed this policy and Ribbentrop was instructed to discuss the situation with the Duce.

Large numbers of the Jews who were being deported had been sent to Auschwitz. For a time deportation to the Government General had been suspended, but it was meanwhile decided that as soon as these convoys could be resumed, trainloads of children could also be despatched.

The Nazis tried by every means to conceal this practice and to create the impression that entire families were sent out of France together. To further this deception they arranged that adults and children should both be included in the convoys in fixed proportions.

This was one of their deportation instructions: 'The Jews arriving from the Unoccupied Zone will be mingled at Drancy with Jewish children now at Pithiviers and Beaune-la-Rolande, so that out of a total of 700 at least 300 will be children. According to instructions from RSHA no trains containing Jewish children only are to leave.'

The treatment of Jews in the Netherlands was no less severe and Seyss-Inquart as Reich Commissioner for Holland was relentless in his attitude towards them. In a speech made in Amsterdam early in 1941 he said: 'The Jews for us are not Dutch. They are those enemies with whom we can come to neither an armistice nor a peace. . . . We will beat the Jews wherever we meet them and those who join them must bear the consequences. The Führer has declared that the Jews have played their final act in Europe and they *have*, therefore, played their final act.'

A series of anti-semitic decrees was then promulgated subjecting all Jews to the usual humiliating disabilities. They were deprived of their property rights and of their civic liberties. They were forced to register their businesses, including any firm or partnership which had a predominant Jewish interest, and the occupation authorities could arbitrarily terminate the employment contract of any Jew.

All the above were merely the preliminary measures which later enabled the German occupation authorities to put their programme of wholesale deportation into operation.

Of a total of 140,000 Jews residing in Holland at the time of the Nazi invasion over 115,000 were deported to Poland where the ultimate fate of the majority was never in doubt. Two thousand others were sent to Buchenwald and Mauthausen camps whence, after cremation, their ashes were despatched to their families against payment of 75 guilders.

The Jews of Hungary suffered a similar fate. In 1944 more than 200,000 Jews were rounded up and many of them loaded into railway trucks and sent to extermination camps.

Accompanying the German occupying troops on their arrival in Budapest was another Einsatzkommando of the SIPO whose task, as in the other countries in which they operated, was to liquidate Hungarian Jews. In command was SS Obersturmbannführer Adolf Aichmann, a senior official from RSHA. The Unit arrested all the leaders of Jewish political and business circles in Hungary, together with journalists and all democratic and 'anti-fascist' politicians.

Of the Hungarian Jews who were sent to Auschwitz, children up to the age of fourteen, people over fifty years of age, the sick and those with criminal records, were transported in specially marked waggons. All were sent to the gas chamber immediately after their arrival in the camp. The Commandant of Auschwitz, Rudolf Höss, admitted putting to death about 40,000 Hungarian Jews during the summer of 1944.

The Jews of Denmark would have suffered a similar fate but for the action of Danish patriots who hid them until they could be got away to Sweden by boat. Hundreds of Danish patriots risked their lives in order to carry Jewish men, women and children to safety in this way, and of 8,000 Jews living in Denmark, only 800 fell into German hands.

This dreary catalogue of murders could be continued but it would always be the same old story. Registration, segregation, humiliation, degradation, deportation, exploitation, and extermination. These were the milestones on the road of suffering along which these luckless Jews made their last journey.

To those who have never heard the tramp of the jackboot along the village street or the Gestapo knocking at their door; who have not seen fifty of their friends and neighbours shot in the market place as a reprisal for the ambush of a single German despatch rider; whose sons and daughters have not been taken away from their homes in the dead of night and never seen again, to such people all this cannot but seem incredible and unreal.

216

The murder by the Germans of over five million[1] European Jews constitutes the greatest crime in world history. That the total Jewish population of Europe was not exterminated is due solely to the fact that the Nazis lost the war before they could bring their 'final solution of the Jewish question' to its conclusion.

[1] The estimated number given by the Prosecution at the Nuremberg Trials of Major War Criminals was six million. Of subsequent estimates, one was as low as 4,372,000. The real number will never be known.

EPILOGUE

THERE was one concentration camp which in 1945, when it had been swept clean of its deathly garbage, could be visited by the general public. This was at Dachau, not far from Munich, and a visitor to it came away with a memory he could never forget.

The only prisoners he saw there were Germans accused of committing war crimes and awaiting trial or discharge. Each one of these lived in comfort in a light airy cell, had electric lighting, and in winter central heating, a bed, a table, a chair, and books. Well fed and sleek they looked, and on their faces was a look of slight astonishment. They must indeed have wondered where they were.

Leaving the living quarters now so clean and tidy, the visitor crossed to the other side of the camp where the crematorium compound was situated. There, in good preservation, was the whole machinery of death which for so long had been used to get rid of those who had dared to cross the Führer's path.

Gone were the corpses which once lay in the annexe waiting their turn to be burnt when the gas chamber killed more than the ovens could hold: gone too were the queues of hapless humans waiting outside in the changing room for their turn to enter the lethal chamber. Gone they were for ever; but their ghosts remained and their memories filled the air.

But there, clean and swept, still for all to see was the room where the victims undressed, the gas chamber itself with the peep-hole through which the operator watched for the last death agony so that he could switch on the electric fan to clear the air of its deadly fumes, the adjacent crematorium, and the iron-wheeled stretchers by which the corpses were brought to the oven's mouth, the little room where bodies lay piled up ceiling-high and where the marks of their feet could still be seen on the plaster walls, the machine for grinding bones to make them into fertilizer for the adjoining farm-lands, and the room where the ashes were stored.

As the visitor passed through these rooms and surveyed the scene of so much suffering and tragedy, the stench of rotting

218

bodies and the smell of burning flesh seemed to rise to his nostrils, and as he came out into the clean fresh air and raised his eyes towards the heavens to clear away this haunting vision of evil, what did he see? Nailed to a pole on the crematorium room, a little rustic nesting box for wild birds, placed there by some schizophrenic SS man.

Then and then only was it possible to understand why the nation which gave the world Goethe and Beethoven, Schiller and Schumann, gave it also Auschwitz and Belsen, Ravensbrück and Dachau.

APPENDIX I

The German Soldier's Ten Commandments
[Printed in every German soldier's paybook].

1. While fighting for victory the German soldier will observe the rules of chivalrous warfare. Cruelties and senseless destruction are below his standard.
2. Combatants will be in uniform or will wear specially introduced and clearly distinguishable badges. Fighting in plain clothes or without such badges is prohibited.
3. No enemy who has surrendered will be killed, including partisans and spies. They will be duly punished by courts.
4. P.O.W. will not be ill-treated or insulted. While arms, maps, and records are to be taken away from them, their personal belongings will not be touched.
5. Dum-Dum bullets are prohibited, also no other bullets may be transformed into Dum-Dum.
6. Red Cross Institutions are sacrosanct. Injured enemies are to be treated in a humane way. Medical personnel and Army chaplains may not be hindered in the execution of their medical, or clerical activities.
7. The civilian population is sacrosanct. No looting nor wanton destruction is permitted to the soldier. Landmarks of historical value or buildings serving religious purposes, art, science, or charity are to be especially respected. Deliveries in kind made as well as services rendered by the population may only be claimed if ordered by the superiors and only against compensation.
8. Neutral territory will neither be entered nor passed over by planes, nor shot at; it will not be the object of warlike activities of any kind.
9. If a German soldier is made a prisoner of war he will tell his name and rank if he is asked for it. Under no circumstances will he reveal to which unit he belongs, nor will he give any information about German military, political, and economical conditions. Neither promises nor threats may induce him to do so.

10. Offences against the a/m matters of duty will be punished. Enemy offences against the principles under 1 to 8 are to be reported. Reprisals are only permissible on order of higher Commands.

APPENDIX II

In December 1914 a distinguished Committee, under the chairmanship of Viscount Bryce, OM, was appointed by the Prime Minister, Mr Asquith, to inquire into alleged German outrages in Belgium and France during the opening months of the war.

The Committee issued its Report in 1915. The members stated that they had come to the definite conclusion, upon the evidence, that in many parts of Belgium deliberate and systematically organized massacres of the civil population had taken place, and that in the conduct of the war generally, both in Belgium and France, 'innocent civilians, both men and women, were murdered in large numbers, women violated, and children murdered'.

They found that looting, house burning, and wanton destruction of property were ordered and countenanced by the officers of the German Army, where no military necessity could be alleged, as part of a system of terrorization.

There had also been frequent breaches of the rules and usages of war, such as the use of civilians, including women and children, as a shield for German troops exposed to fire, the killing of the wounded and prisoners, and the frequent abuse of the Red Cross and White Flag.

Finally the Committee stated that despite the gravity of their conclusions, they would be doing less than their duty if they failed to record them as fully established by the evidence. 'Murder, lust, and pillage prevailed over many parts of Belgium on a scale unparalleled in any war between civilized nations during the last three centuries.'

THE END

THE KNIGHTS OF BUSHIDO by LORD RUSSEL OF
LIVERPOOL

War books may come and War books may go, but this is one with a
difference. As with his other study, THE SCOURGE OF THE
SWASTIKA, Lord Russell has written a book that will perpetrate
the most violent of controversies, evoke the most bitter memories,
yet remain with its salutary lesson for years to come . . .
(Books and Bookmen)

Lord Russell has performed a service of the greatest importance
. . . it is important that it should be clearly understood in this
so-called enlightened age to what depths great nations are willing
to descend . . . *(The Daily Telegraph)*

0 552 10301 2 – 85p

THE YELLOW STAR by GERHARD SCHOENBERNER

The Yellow Star is a shattering book of pictures about the persecution of the Jews in Europe during the Nazi regime from 1933 to
1945. The book contains approximately 200 photographs – many
of them published here for the first time – which the author has
selected from more than 10,000 pictures in all the accessible
archives between Washington, Moscow and Jerusalem. The
pictorial sections are supplemented with an informative text,
together with numerous documents and testimonials.

THE YELLOW STAR shows the Way of Sorrow for millions
of people: through defamation, terror and rape to organised
genocide. The individual chapters document the gradual develop-
ment of the measures taken by the Nazi regime. Original photographs in the book show the terror in Hitler's pre-war Germany,
the misery of the Polish ghettos, the wholesale shooting in the
Soviet Union and deportations from all countries of occupied
Europe, the general massacre in the extermination camps, the
rebellion and destruction of the Warsaw ghetto, and the liberation
of the concentration camps by the Allied troops in the Spring of
1945.

Gerhard Schoenberner, the author of the book, is a German
journalist of the post-war generation, who has particularly
devoted himself to the study of contemporary history and has
won a considerable reputation with his books, exhibitions and
television documentaries.

0 552 98080 3 – £2.95

HOLOCAUST by GERALD GREEN

Two families – the Dorfs and the family Weiss – one swept up in a frenzy of murderous rage, the other, anguished victims ... victims of the most monstrous crime the world has ever witnessed, victims of the HOLOCAUST.

Erik Dorf ...
His diary reveals a charming, brilliant young German lawyer; the SS officer so consumed with love for his country and Führer – and so aflame with ambition – that he can justify plans for the mass murder of Jews.

Rudi Weiss ...
His story exposes a spectacularly fearless young Jew; a man so tough, so brave, he rushes into love and defies death in a world ablaze with passion and hatred.

Two men, two families, all tossed into a maelstrom of terror, where simply to survive was to succeed. HOLOCAUST is a story of heroism and survival ... a story beyond tears of a time without compassion.

0 552 10889 8 – £1.25

ASSIGNMENT GESTAPO by SVEN HASSEL

Their more unorthodox weapons were lengths of steel wire and knives with double-edged blades, and some of their most prized possessions were gold teeth snatched from corpses. . . .
  The 'Disciplinary Regiment', a tank company in Hitler's army – without a tank to its name – was fighting a brutal war against the Russians. A bunch of hardened killers in filthy rags, stinking to high heaven, this company was worth an entire regiment of freshly laundered troops from Breslau. Guerilla warfare on the Eastern front was for them a prelude to the bloody massacre of Russian troops who'd attacked the German reserves and occupied their headquarters. Then the 'Disciplinary Regiment' was sent to Hamburg, where their next assignment was guard duty for the bestial Gestapo. . . .

0 552 08779 3 – £1.00

A SELECTED LIST OF WAR BOOKS
PUBLISHED BY CORGI

WHILE EVERY EFFORT IS MADE TO KEEP PRICES LOW, IT IS SOMETIMES NECESSARY TO INCREASE PRICES AT SHORT NOTICE. CORGI BOOKS RESERVE THE RIGHT TO SHOW AND CHARGE NEW RETAIL PRICES ON COVERS WHICH MAY DIFFER FROM THOSE ADVERTISED IN THE TEXT OR ELSEWHERE.

THE PRICES SHOWN BELOW WERE CORRECT AT THE TIME OF GOING TO PRESS (MAY '79).

☐ 10869 3	THE WILD CEESE		*Daniel Carney*	95p
☐ 10889 8	HOLOCAUST		*Gerald Green*	£1.25
☐ 10400 0	THE BLOODY ROAD TO DEATH		*Sven Hassel*	£1.00
☐ 09761 6	BLITZFREEZE		*Sven Hassel*	£1.00
☐ 09178 2	REIGN OF HELL		*Sven Hassel*	95p
☐ 08874 9	SS GENERAL		*Sven Hassel*	95p
☐ 08779 3	ASSIGNMENT GESTAPO		*Sven Hassel*	£1.00
☐ 08603 7	LIQUIDATE PARIS		*Sven Hassel*	95p
☐ 08528 6	MARCH BATTALION		*Sven Hassel*	85p
☐ 08168 X	MONTE CASSINO		*Sven Hassel*	85p
☐ 07871 9	COMRADES OF WAR		*Sven Hassel*	£1.00
☐ 07242 7	WHEELS OF TERROR		*Sven Hassel*	95p
☐ 07241 9	LEGION OF THE DAMNED		*Sven Hassel*	95p
☐ 10343 8	CROSS OF IRON		*Willi Heinrich*	75p
☐ 09485 4	THE SAVAGE MOUNTAIN		*Willi Heinrich*	65p
☐ 10393 4	THE BLUE MAX		*Jack D. Hunter*	75p
☐ 08371 2	THE DIRTY DOZEN		*E. M. Nathanson*	£1.50
☐ 10954 1	THE FIVE FINGERS	*Gayle Rivers & James Hudson*		95p
☐ 10301 2	THE KNIGHTS OF BUSHIDO		*Lord Russel of Liverpool*	85p
☐ 10741 7	633 SQUADRON: OPERATION CRUCIBLE			
			Frederick E. Smith	80p
☐ 10155 9	633 SQUADRON: OPERATION RHINE MAIDEN			
			Frederick E. Smith	85p
☐ 08169 8	633 SQUADRON		*Frederick E. Smith*	75p

All these books are available at your bookshop or newsagent; or can be ordered direct from the publisher. Just tick the titles you want and fill in the form below.

CORGI BOOKS, Cash Sales Department, P.O. Box 11, Falmouth, Cornwall.

Please send cheque or postal order, no currency.

U.K. send 22p for first book plus 10p per copy for each additional book ordered to a maximum charge of 82p to cover the cost of postage and packing.

B.F.P.O. and Eire allow 22p for the first book plus 10p per copy for the next 6 books, thereafter 4p per book.

Overseas Customers please allow 30p for the first book and 10p per copy for each additional book.

NAME (block letters)..

ADDRESS ....

(MAY 1979) ....